KU-731-191

WITHDRAWN
SOCIAL STUDIES CENTRE, GEORGE ST
OXFORD. OX1 2RL

SOCIAL STUDIES
LIBRARY.
WITHDRAWN
OXFORD.

STUDIES IN INTERNATIONAL SECURITY

*

STUDIES IN INTERNATIONAL SECURITY: 7

STRATEGIC MOBILITY

Neville Brown

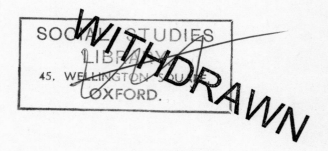

SOCIALIST STUDIES LIBRARY
45. WELLINGTON SQUARE
OXFORD.

WITHDRAWN

40669

SOCIAL STUDIES
LIBRARY,
SOCIAL STUDIES CENTRE GEORGE ST
OXFORD.

WITHDRAWN

CHATTO & WINDUS, LONDON
for
THE INSTITUTE
FOR STRATEGIC STUDIES

Published by
Chatto and Windus Ltd
42 William IV Street
London W.C.2
*
Clarke, Irwin and Co Ltd
Toronto

© The Institute for Strategic Studies 1963
Printed in England
by W. and J. Mackay and Co Ltd, Chatham

CONTENTS

Foreword

As the nature of the strategic balance between East and West has altered, and as the relationship of the Western powers to the new countries of Asia, the Middle East and Africa has developed, strategic mobility has become an increasingly important aspect of Western policy. This is especially true of Britain and the United States.

This study represents an attempt to draw together a number of threads, political, geographic, and technological, so that the student of war and politics may assess for himself the potentialities and the limitations of mobile forces and operations. This is not a subject to which any general theories or principles of war can be rigidly applied.

If I have imposed a great many detailed considerations on the reader, it is because the feasibility of reinforcing deterrence by mobility can only be assessed by a close study of topography, political developments, technological trends and military doctrines.

In the course of conducting the study I have received assistance from so many people on both sides of the Atlantic that I shrink from the responsibility of thanking individuals by name. I would like, however, to express especial gratitude to the members of the advisory group that met periodically at the Institute for Strategic Studies under the chairmanship of the Director, Mr. Alastair Buchan. They included Rear-Admiral Sir Anthony Buzzard, Mr. David Divine, Mr. Philip Goodhart, M.P., Major-General J. L. Moulton, Brigadier W. F. K. Thompson, Mr. Anthony Verrier and Brigadier Peter Young. All of them willingly gave me the benefit of their knowledge and experience; I must stress, however, that the opinions stated herein are entirely my own. In conclusion, I would like to convey my thanks also to all members of the Institute staff and in particular to the librarian, Miss Eve Streatfeild, for her many constructive suggestions about source material.

April, 1963.   NEVILLE BROWN.

Chapter 1

The Strategic Environment

OVER the past decade innumerable warnings have been issued to the effect that the days of American thermonuclear supremacy are numbered. Time and time again we have been told that the Russians have already constructed or will soon construct a vast strategic umbrella to shield themselves and their allies and that this will upset the balance that has existed between United States long-range nuclear delivery systems and the huge armies, navies, and tactical air forces of the Sino-Soviet Bloc. Therefore, the argument has run, one of the chief restraints on the use of Communist non-nuclear power is about to be removed.

These predictions are now little heeded, largely because on so many occasions they have turned out to be premature. However, they are of such a kind that they must prove right eventually and it is hard to believe that their moment of triumph is very far away. Although the United States still has more strategic weapons than the Soviet Union and has them in greater variety, there is already a stalemate for most practical purposes. This stalemate will inevitably deepen and it is very likely that by 1970 at the latest there will be a state of parity between the two super-powers in terms of their ability to wage or deter a thermonuclear war. Therefore, Western thinking about deterrence must be increasingly concerned with meeting a local challenge with a local response—that is to say, with confronting an aggressor at the time and place of his choosing.

Furthermore the arguments against using nuclear weapons tactically in any local conflict are getting stronger as both the major blocs acquire them in great numbers and many different varieties. The risks of widespread escalation of any nuclear conflict have increased in recent years and the probable consequences of escalation have become more terrifying. There is, however, no justification for saying that it would be unavoidable. The dangers would obviously be less if nuclear explosions were used merely to destroy communications or to create contaminated ground ahead of an enemy advance or if they were used against small, isolated, and purely military targets. In all cases some hope for containment would lie in using nuclear warheads only after very specific decisions had been taken at high political or military levels and after an aggressor had been given very explicit warnings. We are, in fact, in the paradoxical position that whilst there is a strong premium on being able to deter or defeat local aggression by the use of purely conventional firepower the deployment and application of such firepower has to take place against the background threat of the introduction of nuclear weapons.

One of the most significant lessons of the 1962 Cuban crisis lay in the explicit acknowledgement by both the super-powers that, during any vital clash of interest between them, diversionary or retaliatory military pressure on points remote from the area of initial tension was conceivable. President Kennedy gave a special assurance to the people of Berlin and at one stage Mr. Khrushchev implied that he had the moral right to invade Turkey. A pattern of conflict in which there was Soviet aggression against, say, West Berlin, in reply to some Western action in the Caribbean or elsewhere, can be spoken of as world-wide limited war. Such a war would be dangerously unstable right from the start, but would become acutely so as soon as either side introduced nuclear or even thermonuclear weapons, especially if they did so in secondary areas of fighting far removed from the original focus. Furthermore, if one accepts the classic view that the rational justification of military action is that of persuading an opponent to change his mind, it is hard to imagine even a very short-lived version of such a conflict leading to any very desirable results. It might deprive the opposition of the dividends that could have accrued from one particular aggressive act, but in so doing could generate so much mistrust, hate, and demoralization as to render a lasting *rapprochement* infinitely more improbable. It would be far preferable to contain or deter diversionary or retaliatory probes at their inception with the appropriate amount of non-nuclear power. The desirability of being able to do this, if the need arises, strengthens the case for having strong, strategically mobile, conventional forces.

The reason for Mr. Khrushchev's implicit offer not to attack Turkey if the United States did not use force against Cuba was clearly that the Soviet Union was incapable of challenging American sea-power within the Caribbean. This inability highlighted the supreme fact about the geography of Russia, which is its isolation. It is a huge continental block surrounded by an almost unbroken rim of polar ice, landlocked sea, folded mountain, high plateaux, and desert. At times this structure has served as an almost impregnable natural fortress able to keep hostile armies out or else let them part of the way in only to wear them down with its sheer size. More generally it has functioned as something of a prison, preventing its inhabitants from playing as big a part on the world stage as might otherwise have been expected of them. Both these aspects are of decreasing significance as technical advances reduce the importance of geographical factors, but they still count for quite a lot. The fear of diplomatic and strategic isolation is something that is still likely to inhibit the Soviet Union from exploiting her interior lines for purposes of military conquest, whatever the state of the overall strategic balance. Such a policy would lead either to the expulsion of the Soviet Union from the United Nations or to the break-up of that organization in circumstances in which Russia would be clearly identifiable as the guilty party. Either event would be a disaster for her. The great hopes she has of spreading the Communist ideology in various countries far removed from her borders would be dashed if she came to be universally regarded as an uncompromising enemy of world peace, and if the processes of international economic, cultural, and diplomatic exchange did not continue in approximately their present way and on at least their present scale. For these reasons such Soviet expansionist urges as are not canalized into the space race or other kinds of 'competitive coexistence' are more likely to take the form of the support of 'tough' policies on the part of China and certain neutrals rather than that of direct aggression. This is always provided, of course, that, as a result of a series of mishandled crises, there is not a general deterioration in great power behaviour.

Of course, most armed conflicts since 1945 have had their origins in local tensions rather than in the rivalry between the

Soviet bloc and NATO and this no doubt will remain true. In particular we may see a widespread application of the doctrine that force may be used to eradicate such 'remnants of colonialism' as the sheikdoms of the Persian Gulf, the Portuguese Empire, and Formosa. A more general root cause of strife will probably be the increasing gap between the actual living standards of most Afro-Asians and their material expectations. The next ten years may witness frequent domestic political upheavals with civil wars and acts of intervention as occasional concomitants. Several kinds of intervention intended to affect the outcome of a domestic dispute have occurred during the post-war period, but a strong tradition survives that such interference is illegal, immoral, and generally unwise. There is also the fear in the West that initiatives in such matters on their part will remove Russian inhibitions about doing likewise in Eastern Europe, thereby crystallizing the existing power pattern and perpetuating the Cold War. All the same, an *a priori* case for intervening exists when to do so might result in the speedy conclusion of a civil war. This is because an armed rebel minority, even if only moderately successful from the military standpoint, can inflict damage on an incumbent régime out of all proportion to its popular following. It could also be argued that action might be taken against military *élites* intent on blocking, say, land reform schemes or any diversion of budgetary resources from an arms programme. In any case, the leading Western powers may need to intervene in certain situations to protect the lives, and perhaps the property, of their fellow countrymen. If a crisis had been precipitated by, say, an uprising preceded by a military *coup*, such action might be required at very few hours' notice.

As far as Europe is concerned the threat most likely to materialize is that of a renewal of the Berlin Blockade. Although the city would be able to hold out unaided for at least six months, and although Mr. Khrushchev once said he would not tolerate a repetition of the 1948 to 1949 airlift, the possible need to repeat that performance has to be borne in mind. Over the last two or three years there has been much talk about the threat of a Communist descent on North Norway or Greece— the most exposed flanks of NATO. However, a pounce on Arctic Norway would only be a rational policy in the context of a world-wide limited war or if it was intended to humiliate the West during a period of 'cold war' much more bitter and uncompromising than anything we have endured as yet. Similarly it is hard to believe in aggression against Greece in the world climate prevailing today. It could surely only occur, under present conditions, through Bulgaria providing base facilities for Greek Communist guerillas. The success of such a guerilla movement depends on its receiving widespread popular support, and it is difficult to imagine this being forthcoming, particularly in view of the grim memories of the civil war of the late 1940s. In fact, potential trouble spots are much more numerous outside Europe than within it. Furthermore, the problems they present must be evaluated against the background of a steady expansion of military strength, and especially of the power to interdict against sea and air communications, on the part of many secondary powers.

Between 1900 and 1934 the United States sent troops into Central American republics about thirty times, leaving them in some places for years on end. The tradition was broken by President Roosevelt and is not likely to be renewed. A precedent seems to have recently been established in the case of Cuba for the principle that in this area nothing except offensive arms build-ups or physical support of armed subversion elsewhere can be held to justify military action. In any case, such forces as do intervene in any conflicts within or between Latin American republics in the years ahead will probably operate under the auspices of the Organization of American States, and the United States is more likely to be asked to provide lift capability than combat units unless very large-scale operations are required.

The emergence of a large number of new states in Northern and Equatorial Africa with insecure frontiers and inadequate domestic cohesion may well be productive of strife. Here again the leading Western nations, apart from France, who has special responsibilities within the Community area, are not likely to be involved in collective security operations except as sources of strategic transport. The proposed Africa High Command or the United Nations, drawing very largely on ground forces from the Afro-Asian bloc, will most probably assume the responsibility. All the same, some sort of Western great power 'presence', actual or potential, may at times be useful as a deterrent to sudden large-scale attacks on, say, United Nations security forces. As far as Southern Africa is concerned, Britain still has absolute authority to move troops into Northern Rhodesia and Nyasaland, but is unlikely to use any reserve powers she may still be felt to have in Southern Rhodesia without the consent of the government in Salisbury. Britain also has commitments in the Bechuanaland, Swaziland, and Basutoland protectorates, as has the United Nations in South West Africa. Though internal politics as such are still not the concern of the United Nations, developments in Portuguese Africa, the Federation, and the Union will become a United Nations concern in so far as any resort to force by African nationalists is given external assistance. In these circumstances the fears of local European authorities and communities would only be relieved by white contingents making up a good proportion of United Nations expeditionary forces.

The possibility of a Communist government in Iraq cannot be excluded as a cause of added tension in the Middle East and neither can that of a civil war in Iran with Soviet Russia supporting the Tudeh Party and also, perhaps, Azerbaijani and Turkmenistani separatist movements. Under the 1927 Treaty Russia is entitled to intervene physically in a Persian crisis if she feels it threatens her own security. Afghanistan is split in two down a north east-south west topographical axis with which a religious cleavage and the boundary between Russian and American spheres of influence closely coincide. It seems potentially liable to either a civil war or a pro-Soviet *coup*. Pakistan has border disputes with Afghanistan and India and would become strategically vulnerable if a break occurred between its east and west provinces. Meanwhile the Arab-Israeli armistice line has still to be guaranteed.

All along the Himalayan axis the Indian position is being challenged by the Chinese. Where they share a common frontier there is dispute about the precise demarcation of the boundary line. Where they do not they compete for power and influence with the respective buffer states. The largest of these states is Nepal, and Britain shares with India an explicit obligation to defend the Nepalese northern border. Meanwhile, social, economic, and physical geography combine to make the monsoon lands of South East Asia ideal loci for guerilla movements.

Although the Soviet Union has indicated that she regards such campaigns as that currently being waged in South Vietnam as national liberation struggles, which she intends to help towards 'inevitable' victory, her policy to date has been a very cautious one. However, if China eventually displaces Soviet influence in Vietnam and Laos this may produce much more rigorous policies of sponsored subversion. An expansionist China might also try to help Singapore in any conflict between that island and other parts of the Federation of Malaysia. She might wish to intervene, too, in an Indonesian civil war waged, perhaps, between a Communist Java and more traditionalist outer islands. We can assume that if Western forces become actively involved anywhere in Asia, except perhaps Kashmir, they will do so through treaty arrangements rather than under United Nations auspices.

Much use has been made in recent years of the sovereign right of states to ban foreign military flights through their airspace. The United States refused to permit Dutch troop movements to New Guinea via California in 1962, and Britain refused an intended Portuguese reinforcement of Goa via her Middle Eastern air bases. That same year Canada temporarily banned Soviet overflights to Cuba. The leading Western powers themselves have frequently disregarded similar vetoes on their own operations, but such cavalier behaviour is becoming less and less desirable. For one thing other countries are becoming more capable of enforcing their wishes in this matter, and this trend will presumably be accelerated in the Middle East in particular now that the informal agreements not to supply Israel and the Arab states with guided missiles are breaking down. Additionally there is the more fundamental point that the West has a strong vested interest in preserving what exists of the rule of law in international conduct, and especially in avoiding precedents that would leave the Soviet Union free to deploy its long-range transport fleet, which now includes planes like the 182-seat *Ilyushin 62*, across the 'rimlands' of Eurasia.

By contrast movement by sea is almost free from impediments resulting from the exercise of territorial sovereignty. The only case during the last eighteen years of it being thus prevented is the illegal Egyptian refusal of passage through the

Suez Canal to Portuguese warships *en route* to aid the Goa garrison against the Indian attack. In theory Indonesia's claim to control over all sea areas within her island limits could constitute a limitation on the deployment of seaborne forces, but in practice it is most unlikely to do so for a very long time to come because of inadequate means of enforcement. It is, of course, true that sea transport is not bothered by national control of land areas merely because it has to travel round rather than across them, but its inherent cheapness and independence of fixed bases for long periods makes the task of circumnavigation far less irksome for the mariner than for the aviator. These same attributes give seaborne forces the capacity to hover for long periods of time ready to move ashore at short notice. On the other hand, despite its high cost and despite its continuing inability to move some of the heavier items of equipment, its sheer speed makes airlift generally the best means for the emergency transfer of forces across or between continents.

If and when the world starts disarming many of the problems and many of the techniques normally discussed under the omnibus heading of 'strategic mobility' will assume an added significance. Disarmament and the adoption of arms control schemes are gauntlets that no big power is going to be prepared to run unless it can feel confident that those of its forces that remain at each stage of a phased reduction will be at maximum effectiveness. Thus, the partial or total abolition of foreign bases, for which the Soviet Union continually presses, is only likely to take place freely if they do not seem essential to the fulfilment of remaining collective security agreements. The demilitarization of, or reduction of armaments in, particular zones will probably only prove acceptable if both sides know that they can rapidly move forces in again if agreements break down. 'Strategic mobility' may yet prove to be the latest and last of the so-called principles of war.

Chapter 2

A Forward Strategy?

THIS term has been used in three different senses during the Cold War. In debates about the disposition of NATO forces in Germany it has been taken to mean a strategy that involves the stationing of a higher proportion of our troops close to the Iron Curtain than would seem desirable in the light of most doctrine about modern mobile warfare. The purpose of this is the discouragement of minor Soviet sallies and the prevention of various kinds of accidental conflict. Meanwhile, some American writers—in particular Messrs. Kintner, Possony, and Strausz-Hupé—have used the phrase to embrace a set of proposals for the global containment of Communism by the adoption of much more 'dynamic' political policies. In the present context, it is used to denote the view that a large percentage of our forces should be stationed close to likely trouble spots around the world rather than held in strategic reserves in their metropolitan countries.

The stationing of combat formations in a particular area obviously implies an unqualified preparedness to defend it. One can reasonably suppose that the Korean War stemmed from the Communists assuming that the United States would not come to the aid of South Korea. Since 1953 a garrison of two divisions has removed uncertainty about American intentions. The hostage theory was well put by Marshal Foch before 1914 when he was asked how many British troops he wished to see in France: he answered that he only needed one provided it could be arranged that the man was killed in action on the first day of fighting. Today the consequences of general war would be so grave that no nation would engage in it to avenge one soldier's death; it probably requires at least a division to imply such a commitment. However, the general principle still holds good, as does its corollary that the absence of standing forces of one country on the territory of one of its allies often means that the first country will not guarantee the second armed support irrespective of the circumstances. On the other hand, except perhaps in the special case of Germany, the movement in of forces during a period of sustained or mounting tension may in itself be important as a symbol of determination. Conversely in other situations such movements might appear unduly provocative, particularly perhaps if they were global rather than regional.

The great practical advantages of troops being always 'on location' are that their response is rapid, that they are acclimatized, and also, presumably, that they know the country. Of course, it is easy to make too much of a cult of knowing the country. Germany presents a very different aspect to the soldier on peacetime manoeuvres from what it would in even a non-nuclear war, when towns would become rubble-laden strongpoints, refugees would jam the roads, and the rights of property would count for nothing. Nevertheless familiarity with the local geography must be of some value and acquaintance with the local language certainly is. It has been argued persuasively that if more of their officers had been able to speak modern Greek thousands of British soldiers would have evaded capture in the 1941 campaign.[1] Also, experience in one place is an invaluable preparation for service in others enjoying similar geographical régimes. Successful jungle operations in particular depend on thorough knowledge of the special tactics, health precautions, and fieldcraft required and also on mastery of the fear and depression that the vastness, noisiness, and humidity of a tropical rain forest can induce. The story of the British 53rd Infantry Brigade in Malaya in 1942 is a sad demonstration of what can happen to men who, in addition to being unacclimatized, are lacking in jungle 'know-how'. It went into action in Johore seven days after coming off its troopship and, before withdrawing to Singapore six days later, suffered 50 per cent casualties in a series of ambushes and repulses.

The distribution of the British regular army before 1939 would probably be regarded by most people as reflecting about the purest example of a global forward strategy yet seen, but, in fact, the percentage normally overseas was only 45 per cent

<hr>

[1] Anthony Heckstall-Smith and H. T. Baillie-Grohman, *Greek Tragedy* (London, Blond, 1961), p. 229

as against 52 per cent today.[1] Meanwhile, though only 36 per cent of American servicemen are stationed outside the continental United States many of those inside are posted far from their family hearths. One difficulty inherent in such dispositions is that of dependants. It is often felt that troops in married quarters cannot be battle-ready, and this is why, for example, very few of the troops in Korea are accompanied by families. On the other hand, there is a morale and re-enlistment problem if prolonged separation occurs. The British Grigg report on recruiting in 1958 implied that the upheavals caused by recurrent postings, especially those to overseas stations, was a disincentive against re-enlistment, especially for married men.[2] It is true that the report also noted that the hope of travel was a powerful motive for men joining up in the first place, but such hope can obviously be largely satisfied through membership of a strategic reserve that carries out occasional mobility exercises abroad.[3] The US Secretary of the Army has admitted that a prolongation of the 1961 ban on dependants could have a serious effect on morale.[4]

One way of getting round the problem is by leaving dependants at home and making tours of overseas duty short. This evades the children's education problem, lessens balance of payments problems, and utilizes surplus military airlift capacity. It also avoids minorities of lonely bachelors being left in their barracks in an alien land by married comrades enjoying the pleasures of family life. Unaccompanied men in Korea do fourteen-month tours of duty as compared with twenty-four-month ones for those who take their wives. Korea, as low delinquency rates reveal, is a station in which men settle down well; but experience has shown that unaccompanied troops in Europe need to be rotated faster. The United States army has started sending whole battle groups to Europe on six-month tours without dependants, whilst TAC with a view, it is said,

---

[1] Leonard Beaton, *The Guardian*, August 22, 1962

[2] Cmnd. 545; Report of the Advisory Committee on Recruiting, p. 34

[3] *Ibid.*, p. 19

[4] Department of Defence Appropriations: Fiscal 1963. Hearing before Subcommittee of House Committee on Appropriations. Pt. 2, p. 252

to keeping the divorce rate down runs four-month ones. Soldiers with dependants currently do three years in Europe.[1]

The presence of dependants aggravates the balance of payments problems created by fixed bases. Britain in 1958, for example, spent £180,000,000 abroad on military items very largely connected with such bases.[2] Since then certain commitments have been reduced or abolished, but, conversely, the Germans have stopped paying support costs to the British Army of the Rhine. This has increased the cost in foreign currency of that force from £12,000,000 in 1957 to about £45,000,000 in 1962. Furthermore, since sterling became fully convertible in 1958, payments to the rest of the sterling area have represented as serious a drain on reserves as expenditure in the world outside. The figures quoted may seem small compared with a total value of goods and services imported in 1958 of £4,389,000,000.[2] However, the average annual surplus on the British current account between 1953 and 1958 was only £220,000,000.[3] But for military expenditure this figure would have been nearly doubled, which is significant bearing in mind the facts that sterling is backed by reserves that are still low in proportion to the amount of world trade it finances, and that British economic expansion since 1950 has been made slower and more erratic since governments have felt obliged to pay great regard to even short runs on these reserves. It is not surprising that the 1962 Defence White Paper explicitly states that the proportion of the British Army stationed on the continent of Europe will have to be related to balance of payments pressures.[4]

An outflow of foreign exchange from the United States began during the early 1950s, but until five years or so ago it was generally felt to be a temporary aberration. Since then it has come to be treated more seriously and military expenditure overseas has therefore been subject to increased scrutiny. In 1961 the administration banned dependants from travelling to

[1] L. G. Richards, *Tactical Air Command* (New York, John Day, 1961), Chapter XII

[2] Cmd. 700, 1959

[3] London and Cambridge Economic Bulletin in *Times Review of Industry*, March 1959

[4] Cmd. 1639, *Statement on Defence*, 1962, p. 7

Europe. It has been argued that this was done to free logistic support to accelerate reinforcement of the VIIth Army in Germany, but it seemed to coincide significantly with an increased government concern with the balance of payments deficit.[1] In July 1962 the price differential that service authorities abroad are instructed to accept to obtain an American-made item was raised to 50 per cent.[2] But these economy measures can only be successful up to a certain point, beyond which a country may have to reconsider its strategic deployments. In 1958 and 1959 the United States had an annual average surplus on goods, transport, and investment income of $5,100,000,000. However, foreign economic and military aid cost $2,400,000,000 p.a. and outflows of gifts and private investment capital $3,100,000,000. Payments of $3,000,000,000 for military services were largely responsible for expanding the consequent deficit to $3,300,000,000 p.a.[3] About $800,000,000 of the military expenditure was in Germany, and as much again elsewhere in Western Europe.

Predictions in this field are notoriously hazardous, but it is reasonable to expect pressure on the dollar to increase rather than diminish over the next decade. This is partly because American demand for imports is likely to rise more rapidly than world demand for American exports. It is also because the need for economic aid will increase. Mr. Paul Hoffman has estimated that during the last decade *per capita* income rose by 1 per cent per annum in the underdeveloped two-thirds of the world. To double this rate one would need to boost the annual investment of the countries concerned by $3,000,000,000 p.a.[4] If a programme to achieve this were adopted the European NATO countries who today dispense about $2,000,000,000 of foreign aid would no doubt assume part of the extra burden.[5]

[1] Department of Defence Appropriations. Fiscal 1963. Hearing before Subcommittee of House Committee on Appropriations. Pt. 2, p. 252.

[2] *The Times*, July 18, 1962

[3] *The United Nations Statistical Yearbook 1961*

[4] Andrew Shonfield, *The Attack on World Poverty* (London, Chatto & Windus, 1960), p. 80; (New York, Random House, 1960), p. 87.

[5] *The Annual Register of World Events 1961* (London, Longmans, 1962), pp. 460–2

The Soviet Bloc would probably contribute something, either in co-operation or competition. Most of the rest would, however, have to be accepted by the Americans as an extra strain on their finances.

If the American payments position gets worse, she may have to cut down her forces overseas. Alternative solutions like dollar devaluation, recurrent deflation, import controls, or raising tariffs are most unlikely to be adopted. Of course, some substantial reductions of overseas bases will take place for purely military reasons, as the B-47 medium bombers and the land-based IRBMs are phased out in favour of more modern forms of strategic deterrence located predominantly within the continental United States or on the high seas. Drastic reductions involving general purpose forces may be inhibited by the thought that military expenditure in a foreign currency constitutes a kind of economic aid even if in a sporadic and lopsided form. Thus, the closure of the three Strategic Air Command bases in Morocco is being spread over four years because they originally contributed $40,000,000 per year to the local economy.[1]

Floating bases for ground troops and air squadrons have the great advantage that nearly all their costs are paid in the national currency of the state concerned, but, on the other hand, both their capital and their running costs are high. Thus, in a 1955 calculation it was 'proved' that carrier-borne airpower was cheaper than land-based airpower but the proof depended upon the assumption that six clusters of airfields were needed to cover a theatre of operations as effectively as one carrier task force.[2] However, if the intra-theatre mobility aspect is ignored and one cluster of airfields is regarded as equivalent to a task force of comparable plane-carrying capacity the results, taking the same hypothetical figures for construction costs, are very different. Forty-five bombers and 300 fighters were reckoned to cost $350,000,000 and a comparable seaborne force of 100 attack planes and 300 fighters $180,000,000. The cost for the four carriers required was put at $460,000,000 as against installations for the land force of $430,000,000. Furthermore,

[1] *Aviation Week*, November 11, 1959
[2] T. U. Sisson in *United States Naval Institute Proceedings*, March 1955

the escort forces required for the former were conceded to cost an extra $690,000,000. This calculation ignored the cost of fixed naval installations, and also the fact that to maintain, say, two warships on a given station a modern navy has to have at least three within the theatre in question as well as a considerable amount of logistic shipping.

A good index of comparative running costs for land- and sea-based forces is obtained by calculating the aggregate manning levels in each case. The comparison becomes more precise if one takes into account the fact that in, say, the United States 1962 defence budget the operating cost of the Air Force, including troops' pay, was $9,800 per head, and of the Navy $8,500. Published figures show that the average United States Air Force combat wing attached to each division within a theatre of operations is 7,000 strong and the corresponding slice within the continental United States about 2,500.[1] Therefore, the land-based force in this example would amount to 28,000 within the theatre and 38,000 altogether. The aggregate warship complement would be about 28,000 which becomes 42,000 allowing for rotation. Since a modern navy has a man ashore for everyone afloat the total manpower commitment would be 84,000. From this it seems that a balanced carrier task force would usually cost rather under twice as much both to build and to operate as a similar amount of land-based air striking power.

Likewise the commando ship or, to use American terminology, the amphibious assault ship, is an expensive item viewed simply as a floating barracks. Some British figures, which are not likely to be widely in conflict with American ones, give the cost of tropical cantonments for 1,500 infantrymen and 600 dependants as being about £3,000,000 ($8.4 million) and the cost of the men's fighting equipment at around £1,000,000 ($2.8 million). The construction of an assault ship able to lift such a body of soldiers is $40,000,000 and, to provide it with an escort screen of, say, one anti-aircraft and two anti-submarine frigates and a radar picket ship, some $200,000,000 more has to be budgeted for. Again all the naval construction cost figures should be multiplied by not less than 50 per cent to allow for rotation. The result is a sum that utterly dwarfs the

[1] See Chapter 8, Section II

expense of £4,000,000, or about $11,000,000, involved in establishing 1,500 infantrymen as a land base.

In the same way the number of men tied up in providing a seaborne battle group, 1,500 strong, is several times that figure. The assault ship would have a complement of 2,500 with its marines on board and the other ships if present 1,200 at war strength. When shore establishments and the need to relieve ships are allowed for the total becomes 11,100. The corresponding land force figure is indeterminate but certainly well below 5,000. The American 1962 budget tables quoted above imply that the Army incurs running costs of $7,700 per soldier per year, but the costs for a lightly equipped infantry unit of the kind now being considered would lie well above that average. Thus, as we might expect, ground formations are less expensive to maintain at sea than air groups of comparable numerical strength, but that the differentials in costs between fixed bases and floating ones are proportionately greater in the case of the former than in that of the latter. But this calculation is based on the assumption that the troops ashore are close to where they may have to fight and that therefore they do not need to have any long-distance air or sea transport available at short notice to lift them to trouble spots. This assumption is valid for some situations but for others it is completely unreal.

Obviously an inherent financial drawback of a strategic reserve is the desirability, if not necessity, of having enough transport aircraft readily available to ensure that the whole force and its combat equipment and essential supplies can be transported in a very few lifts. However, in comparative terms the capital and running costs are not unduly high. At the end of Fiscal Year 1962 the Strategic Reserve Army Corps in the United States numbered six regular divisions. It had an airlift attached that was capable of moving about a half of one division over 1,500 miles simultaneously, and rather less than that over 4,000 miles. Assuming that 30 per cent of the army budget was spent on STRAC during that period, its pay and other operating costs were, at $1,900,000,000, about six times those of the military airlift. On procurement, construction, research, and development for STRAC, $850,000,000 was spent, which was only 135 per cent of the sum invested in its airlift: however, the year in question was one in which the latter was being rapidly expanded. In any case a permanently available airlift makes possible long-range mobility exercises, which are perhaps the best of all ways of 'showing the flag', and which can meet the soldier's demand for travel and adventure in a way that places little strain on family ties. Also if one extends the economic analysis to include an assessment of how well the classic military requirement of 'economy of force' is met on a world-wide scale, the United States strategic reserve appears in a most favourable light. This is because it is poised to deploy West or East in very much the same way as the old British Indian Army lay in a position of 'balance' half-way along the lifeline of Empire. Unfortunately the same is not true of the metropolitan forces of Britain and France.

One argument in favour of overseas bases that can appeal to even the most fervent enthusiast for strategic reserves is that they are places where stockpiles can be established under national command. The case for stockpiles rests largely on the fact that on account of shape or density many military items are very awkward and costly to move by air. Thus an *Argosy* costing £600,000 could take at one time not more than three 3-ton trucks costing £1,000 each. For a one thousand mile hop it could manage alternatively five hundred *Vigilant* anti-tank missiles, but even this exceptionally high-value cargo would only be worth £250,000. Petroleum is an important class of consumable supplies that would always be uneconomic to move by air, since the general market price ranges from £5 a ton for marine fuel to £20 for motor spirit. The long-term storage of petroleum products is not easy, however, and it is advisable to maintain stocks in places where they can be 'turned over' through routine usage every three years or so.

Other commodities are vulnerable in varying degrees to deterioration under the action of heat, humidity, salt spray, and sand particles: and so, for example, ammunition is normally stored for a maximum of fifteen years under temperate conditions and ten under tropical. The need to check deterioration and to carry out frequent modifications of the more complex items makes it inevitable that some troops are permanently engaged on maintaining the stockpile, but the actual size of this contingent is usually governed by estimates of the speed at which material would have to be ready for use. It takes six man hours to take a 105 mm. howitzer out of a state of preservation and it then has to be recalibrated. Probably one or two hundred men could look after a division scale of vehicles, but they would need one or two weeks to get them all out of storage. Furthermore there are certain kinds of equipment that incoming troops would justifiably resent having issued to them just before going into action, such as delicate and complex electronic systems, or personal weapons, where user familiarity is a direct aid to efficiency.

There are certain even more fundamental objections to stockpiling. In the leading Western armies, it generally takes several years to get a complete inventory of a new weapons system and, since stockpiles must presumably be at the end of the priority queue, this means that they are usually filled with equipment that is a generation out of date. Other weaknesses are their vulnerability to pin-point interdiction and the fact that they will often be quite remote from the place where it is desired to apply force: the US VIIth Fleet has, however, anticipated these objections by creating a small 'floating stockpile' consisting of *Victory* ships loaded with various war materials including tanks. Mr. McNamara has indicated that this policy is to be extended to other theatres.[1] Certainly enough of the old wartime *Victory* and *Liberty* vessels are lying in reserve to make it an economic proposition, and where necessary their hulls could be reconditioned to give them a lease of life of another ten years or so. They would be unable to use many minor ports to offload directly but they would still be much more satisfactory than land-based stockpiles separated from potential areas of conflict by perhaps hundreds of miles of ocean. Land-based stockpiles are best suited for location within the countries that the troops that would draw on them would be required to defend. We therefore find the most conspicuous example of their employment in the 100,000 tons of stores, plus several thousand vehicles which, together with an advance party of one or two thousand men, were put into Europe in 1961 by the United States Army. This was done largely to make it possible for an armoured and an infantry division to be flown in as reinforcements from the United States with little more

[1] Testimony before a Sub-committee of the House of Representatives Committee on Merchant Marines and Fisheries, April 18, 1962

than their personal equipment. This example alone affords a striking demonstration of the extent to which the American authorities are prepared to apply the principle of stockpiling in situations where geography and politics both favour and require it.

One controversial question is the extent to which a navy can operate satisfactorily at great distances from any shore establishment. In the post-war period there has been a marked improvement in the capacity of larger ships to carry out their own repairs either at sea or in a friendly civilian port, but all ships have to spend some time in dry dock at least once a year to clean hulls, tanks, and boilers. Destroyers, submarines, and minesweepers are too small to possess machine shops, foundries, large power sources, and other repair facilities or to contain adequate recreation space; but these needs can be met by specialist depot ships which, anchored in sheltered waters, can each maintain a squadron of 'daughters' for several months without assistance from local installations on land. Of course, even if forward fixed bases are entirely absent the maintenance problems can be got round in peace by allowing more time for visits to home ports. Admittedly the casualties and battle damage of war present more basic problems, but examples of what can be done were provided by the heavily scarred escort vessels that steamed from Britain to American repair yards during the Battle of the Atlantic.

Since civilian relay stations might not give adequate service in time of war there is a strong case for naval long-distance radio transceivers located on land somewhere in each potential theatre of operations. The absence of space and weight restrictions gives them certain inherent advantages over shipborne systems. They can be well spread out to cut down the risks from bombing, and can have larger aerials and stronger power sources than sets on board ship. Another kind of naval installation that might be developed in the future is a very low-frequency sonar for the ultra-long-range detection of submarines. Such a system would require a very great deal of power and so would have to be shore based.

It is undoubtedly feasible for warships to draw all their supplies from groups of logistic ships serving as 'floating bases'. Furthermore the techniques for doing so are being substantially improved, as witness the new Fast Automatic Shuttle Transfer that can move dry cargo in extreme weather conditions, more safely and several times faster than the current range of equipment. What is less certain is whether the claims made, to the effect that the US VIth and VIIth Fleets could both be supported from the continental United States in time of war, are valid. The United States Navy as a whole is currently composed 45 per cent of warships, 27 per cent of logistic ships, and 28 per cent of combat-cum-logistic ships.[1] In 1945 the respective percentages were 29, 29, and 42.[2] The warships of today are on the average rather larger and much more demanding than was the case then, whereas the auxiliaries are still largely the residue of the 1945 armada. In any case, even in 1945 there was heavy dependence on forward fixed bases at Guam, Leyte-Samar, and elsewhere. It seems that the two fleets in question could not become independent of the many shore installations without a considerable increase in their supply trains. This increase could be effected by calling upon the resources of other parts of the United States Navy, the Military Sea Transportation Service, and the merchant marine, but this would always take time and time there might not be. An alternative answer could obviously be that of increasing the logistic task forces permanently available, but apart from the fact that such a policy would be in conflict with the traditional nautical preference in favour of fighting ships, it would involve undue expense. Of course, Admiral Eccles has long argued that 'floating bases' are cheaper than shore ones, because, he says, the potential economies of the latter are completely undermined by their tendency to expand continuously due to incompetence, over-insurance, empire-building, and other destructive behaviour patterns.[3] However, he draws the evidence for what he calls the 'logistic snowball' largely from the 1945 era and it is certain that with tighter budgetary control in peacetime and with increasing resort to cost analysis procedures that this tendency is not as marked now as it was then.

---

[1] *The Military Balance 1962–3* (London, The Institute for Strategic Studies, 1962), p. 20

[2] Admiral H. E. Eccles, *Logistics in the National Defence* (Harrisburg [Pa], Stackpole Co., 1959), pp. 136–40

[3] *Ibid.*, Chapter VII

The value of air staging posts is examined later in this study, but it must be noted now that if long-range strategic airlifts are contemplated, there are certain advantages in using military air force stations rather than such civilian facilities as may be made available.[1]

The word 'base' is sometimes loosely used to describe any geographical region mobilized to provide support for a nearby theatre of operations. It has often been applied to the Nile Delta and Canal Zone, where, in 1942, 500,000 Egyptian workers in the direct employ of the British plus 1,500,000 employees of civilian contractors backed up the ten or so divisions of the 8th Army and the men of the Desert Air Force. Between 1939 and 1942 some £500,000,000 had been spent on capital projects to create this capacity, which included a new metal industry that consumed *inter alia* 150,000 tons of steel a year. In the same war £250,000,000 was spent on making India a 'base' for the 14th Army. During the Korean War, Japan met the need. A special Japan Logistical Command was established and it estimated that that part of its work eventually being done by local labour would otherwise have tied up another quarter of a million United States service troops.[2] Japan was serving as an operational air base and as a general stockpiling and transhipment area, but a lot of the support activity was manufacture and repair. Since 1953 computer stock-control and air transport have shifted the emphasis towards replacement from home rather than repair on the spot, but it is still very desirable to have a complex of workshops close to the battle area if fighting is prolonged.

Because Southern England lies fifteen to twenty degrees north of the main base areas of the United States Strike Command, British troops being committed from their homeland are much more liable than American ones to suffer from lack of acclimatization. High afternoon temperatures associated with cloudless skies make the Persian Gulf in midsummer an area of especial difficulty, though usually the strains are greater if the troops leave Britain in winter, because it is then that the thermal contrasts between the tropics and the Northern temperate zones are greatest.

[1] See Chapter 6, Section II
[2] Dr. H. A. Houston in *The Military Review*, February 1957

Despite its relevance to any contingency planning a marked complacency persists in British military circles about this question. It is nurtured by the feeling that affluent societies neglect the spartan virtues, and the consequent fear that each endeavour to give the individual fighting man's problems more sympathetic consideration will, at least from the esoteric military standpoint, represent a step towards decadence. No doubt in certain respects the dilemma is real, but not in this one. Although a myth persists to the contrary, no one can train soldiers to survive on an inadequate water supply. Neither can he induce them to adapt to a major salt deficiency in their bloodstream. It is true that fit and enthusiastic men will acclimatize more quickly than debilitated and apathetic ones, but the differences are subtle and marginal rather than conspicuous and basic.

Such interest as has been displayed in the problem by non-medical people has been focused on the danger of 'heat illnesses', since on certain occasions in the past their incidence has been alarmingly high. In 1942 one of the divisions that were sent out from the United Kingdom to build up the Iraq and Persia Command lost nearly a hundred men from heat within a few days of landing and was decimated by non-fatal casualties.[1] Of the troops that moved direct from England to Kuwait in July 1961, 10 per cent were withdrawn from their units with heat disorders in the first five days, whilst many more were taken to Regimental Aid Posts or treated themselves.[2] These figures are rendered the more significant by the fact that the temperatures and humidities in Kuwait at the time were lower than are often experienced during July. Moreover, such statistics are not the whole or even the central part of the story. Actual clinical cases are invariably the result of inadequate salt or water consumption and for that reason can always be prevented. What is much more serious from the standpoint of planning large scale movement is the general enervation that is universally and unavoidably displayed until physiological adaptation is complete.

If men are sent from a truly temperate climate to a tropical one, the extent and variety of the physiological adjustments re-

[1] Letter in *The Times* from A. C. F. Jackson, Esq., July 31, 1962
[2] *The Times*, July 23, 1962

quired are quite surprising. The throughput of the heart in a given time trebles as the volume of blood markedly increases and the rate of flow nearly doubles; meanwhile the capillary network near the skin will expand to help absorb the extra volume; the lung beat will also go up. This whole process of circulatory adaptation only takes about seven days, but the retraining of the sweat glands so that they dilute their salt concentration, raise their maximal and sustained flow rates, and become able to produce fluid more readily, takes something of the order of two to three weeks. The times usually given for overall acclimatization corresponds closely to those for circulation and sweat gland adjustment respectively, being a week to ten days for a high degree of adaptation to be achieved and three weeks for adaptation to be completed.[1] Until it has occurred skin and body temperatures, blood pressure, and heart beat will be too unstable and, on the average, too high. In consequence the soldier will be much too prone to physical and mental fatigue. If, however, he becomes acclimatized and then returns to a northern climate the problem is encountered in reverse. In most cases 'deacclimatization' proceeds very slowly for the first fortnight or so and then more quickly, taking altogether some one or two months.

All the indices of climatic stress are unsatisfactory, because it is impossible to introduce all the required variables into a formula and to give them their correct emphases. However, one that has been employed a fair amount despite its obvious limitations is that of effective temperature. The 'effective temperature' of any environment is defined as being that temperature of completely saturated air, which would produce the same subjective sensation of comfort as the particular combination of temperature and humidity observed assuming that, in both cases, the air was still. This last condition is important, especially if the air is far from saturated and so potentially able to produce fast evaporation by flowing over skin surfaces, or if the ambient temperature is above that of the human body, in which case advective heating will occur. Saturated still air at 62°F is said to be equivalent to saturated air at 73°F flowing at 8 m.p.h. If the relative humidity is 20 per cent in each case, still air at 68°F is said to produce the same feeling of comfort as

[1] J. M. Adam in *Brassey's Annual*, 1961

air at 77°F flowing at 8 m.p.h.[1] The 'effective temperature' concept does not embrace the factor of direct insolation, which can, however, be critically important under operational conditions. Soil surface temperatures beneath high suns and cloudless skies are often 60°F or more above shade values, and inside the turret of a battle tank roasting in the Persian Gulf a reading of 160°F would not be exceptional. Little climatic data on parameters like direct insolation exist and, in any case, it would be utterly impossible to measure, tabulate, and predict all the effects due to everlasting changes in weather and minute local differences in climate.

Despite all these qualifications average 'effective temperatures' do provide some indication of climatic contrasts, as Table I shows. One thing the statistics imply, which is essentially correct, is that a very hot dry régime may be equivalent, from the comfort standpoint, to a quite hot and moist one. Therefore, it makes sense climatically to hold troops in, say, Aden who may be required to fight in, say, Laos.

TABLE I
Average Midday Effective Temperatures °F

	Jan	July		Jan	July
Wilmington (N.C.)	55	81	Bangkok	81	84
Louisville	43	80	Singapore	83	83
London	44	69	Pusan	43	78
Malta	57	78	Perth	77	61
Amman	52	78	Nairobi	71	66
Aden	77	78	Leopoldville	82	76
Kuwait	59	89	Darwin	82	80
Teheran	45	85			

Some Pittsburgh experiments on men working at a rate of 90,000 foot pounds per hour in varying effective temperatures showed that the rises in pulse rate and body temperature (two good indices of strain) grew suddenly and dramatically greater from 90°F Effective Temperature upward. In environments at or above 100°F E.T. subjects could not sustain the work for more than half an hour. To interpret Table I in the light of

[1] C. E. A. Winslow and L. P. Herrington, *Temperature and Human Life* (Princeton University Press, 1949), p. 105

these investigations it is probably best to regard 80°F E.T. as the critical limit rather than 90, so as to make allowance for wind, sunshine, and all the other local and short-term variations in temperature and humidity referred to above. If this is done the conclusion emerges that low-lying localities within the tropics take a bit of getting used to at all times of the year. This is not a finding that will cause much astonishment or give rise to fierce controversy. A much more instructive implication of the table, thinking particularly of a possible Anglo-American base in Australia, is that Perth, unlike Darwin, would be no use for tropical acclimatization during the Australian winter. It is perhaps worth noting at this stage that the obverse side of having commando ships made more comfortable by having them fully air conditioned is that our troops lose some of the advantages of local acclimatization. The effective temperature in the mess decks of a commando carrier at sea in the Persian Gulf in July would probably be about 75.

Air conditioning of land vehicles could, of course, be used to lessen the discomfort felt by mechanized troops ashore. It is intended that the *Mauler* self-propelled anti-aircraft weapons shall be air conditioned, and so when *Mauler* becomes operational a technique will be applied to military equipment that has been employed in civilian motor transport for some time past. Another approach that is being considered to the problem of helping men to adapt themselves quickly for service in the tropics is that of inducing artificial acclimatization by 'cooking' troops in hot chambers and following that up by flying them to their destination in heated aircraft. It has been found that if an individual is subjected, in a chamber that simulates the environment anticipated, to about eight exposures of one or two hours each spread over a period of about four days, a considerable amount of acclimatization will occur. This will persist for two or three days even if no further conditioning occurs. A strong belief grew up in wartime Britain that this was how units of the Afrika Corps prepared themselves for the desert heat. This was not, in fact, the case. They normally did so by spending several weeks in the toe of Italy immediately before departure.

There are other kinds of climatic adjustment which may present difficulties. As Indian troops were finding in the

Himalayas in 1962, above seven thousand feet the attenuation of the atmosphere produces effects which are especially acute in men who have not been living at such altitudes for at least several weeks. Other places in which this could be an important consideration include the Federation of South Arabia, Turkey, Persia, Basutoland and some of the Andean republics. In some of these areas and in certain other ones, too, such as North Norway, cold-weather acclimatization may be necessary. However, optimum adaptation to cold normally occurs more quickly than it does to heat. To say this is not to deny the acute feelings of discomfort that various combinations of low temperature and high wind can induce: it is merely to contend that in physiological terms troops get as seasoned as they will get after a comparatively short period of time.

As far as navies are concerned the strategic arguments are in favour of having all fighting units as far 'forward' as possible. The economic cruising speed of warships is still such that for a typical task force to move six thousand miles would take about a fortnight. Soldiers and their equipment travelling in, say, a S.C.5/31 *Belfast* could cover such a distance in about eighteen hours and a crisis would have to break very fast indeed for them to arrive too late to deal with it even if we allow them a day or so to be briefed and kitted up prior to departure.

In any case what soldiers and airmen in strategic reserve lose through having slower initial reactions they gain by possessing greater flexibility. This is largely because they are free from all the political obstacles that would inhibit shifting of troops from, say, Germany or Korea. In the case of the American strategic reserves, it is because they are located in what is a nodal area geographically. How much importance we attach to this classic advantage must depend on our assessment of the risk of local wars starting in widely separated places almost simultaneously, for if those risks appear to be high little is gained from retaining the option of an eastward or westward deployment.

The slow mobility of sea-power has been mentioned as constituting a powerful case against keeping a high proportion of Western fleets in home waters. Moreover the practical arguments which have been listed in favour of basing army units overseas apply also to the distribution of tactical airpower as well. Against them must be set, however, the two important practical considerations that favour the locating of Western combat strength at home, except during actual emergencies—the maintenance of morale, and the prevention of excessive currency losses. The former is too fundamental to human nature to have much prospect of dwindling in importance in the foreseeable future, whilst the latter would probably only do so if some formulae for sharing costs among allies were worked out. Such formulae would always be hard to construct because of the fundamental impossibility of making precise comparisons between the strains involved in expenditures by nations within their respective economies and those that take place outside them.

Even in theory, however, the choice does not lie simply between strategic reserves and overseas garrisons for there remains another alternative in the form of theatre reserves. As compared with a more dispersed pattern they offer certain advantages in respect of training and administration. Conversely they are more acclimatized and can evoke faster re-actions than strategic reserves can. The actual world-wide distribution of Anglo-American forces always, in fact, reflects a compromise between these three patterns of deployment.

Chapter 3

Dispositions and Commitments

I—BRITISH OVERSEAS BASES—THE IMPERIAL NEXUS

MOST Britons would feel too coy to reiterate at the beginning of 1963 the Victorian boast that they ruled an empire on which the sun never set because although the claim is still valid the empire in question is now a mere skeleton of its former self and it is generally recognized that the process of imperial withdrawal is bound to continue steadily. Nevertheless, many people in Britain are determined that the country shall maintain some sort of military presence in most if not all of her traditional spheres of influence. This is partly because for some years to come we are going to have to fulfil some very important imperial obligations particularly in Southern Africa and Malaysia. It is also because of a feeling that our influence within the Western alliance is related in no small measure to our willingness and ability to participate in collective action. Yet another motivating factor is the extent of British trade outside Europe. Britain will continue to occupy a position unique among the six or seven largest countries of Western Europe both in respect of the percentage of her gross national product that is involved in foreign trade and in respect of the proportion of that trade that is conducted with countries in other continents.

The string of island bases and coastal enclaves over which Britain as yet retains sovereignty are knit to each other and to the home country by the air and sea routes across the Near and Middle East. The strategic concept that these hinge areas between Eurasia and Africa serve as the main corridor for British deployment dates from the opening of the Suez Canal in 1869. The air links are today more important for purposes of rapid reinforcement than the sea one is and so if they disappear as a consequence of political change a new 'lifeline of Empire' will have to be constructed.

At present, however, the Mediterranean remains the first

major sector of the lifeline as well as being a sea around which are five countries towards which Britain has treaty obligations. Four of them are NATO members and the other is Libya, with whom the United Kingdom has signed a defence pact due to last until 1973. Additionally Britain is pledged to help guarantee Israel's frontiers. Although the list of nominal commitments is large, it is improbable that Britain will be called upon to honour them in the immediate future, and in any case units in that theatre can always be rapidly augmented from home. For these reasons the forces kept permanently within the area today are comparatively small.

The Mediterranean Fleet usually consists of a cruiser, about ten escort vessels and a squadron of submarines. It operates chiefly from Malta, where there is also a RAF aerodrome that can be used as a Transport or Bomber Command base, a Royal Naval Air Station, and an Army garrison of one infantry battalion. Malta is no longer officially regarded as a suitable point of departure for mobile operations by the Army and the Air Force and from that standpoint the chief United Kingdom base in the Mediterranean is now Cyprus.

The British Sovereign Areas in Cyprus, which include the large RAF station at Akrotiri, cover only 99 square miles but Britain also has free access for military purposes to roads and ports and a share in the control of Nicosia airport. Training grounds are made available in other parts of the island, but exercises involving more than 500 men can only take place on a limited scale. Outside labour may be brought in under certain circumstances but the 1959 agreements stress that the labour force must normally be exclusively Cypriot. About 1,000 Cypriot citizens live in the British area and over 10,000 come in to work each day.

The base includes a stockpile for one or more brigade groups, a NATO early warning station, a wireless station that is officially regarded as constituting an essential link in Britain's global radio network, accommodation for the three infantry battalions and their supporting units, and Akrotiri, at which some tactical aircraft are permanently located and which is used periodically by transport planes and V-Bombers. At present the British forces number 15,000 and some millions of pounds are still being spent annually on developing new service installations, although the number of infantrymen is expected soon to be reduced to the minimum considered necessary for garrison duties. If so Cyprus will join Malta and also Gibraltar and Tripolitania as being a place where 'penny packets' of British infantry are held isolated from any other fighting units. It is often said that such a dispersion is administratively uneconomic, but as long as each contingent is maintained at battalion size, which it is in these cases, this is probably not a very serious consideration. What is more to the point is that it virtually rules out combined arms or brigade group training unless the units are very frequently rotated. On the other hand, as long as these smaller 'bases' survive, which in the case of Malta and Libya might not be very long, they can serve as sources of acclimatized troops. During the Jordan crisis of 1958 a cruiser took the Royal Sussex regiment from Gibraltar to Malta and thence to Libya and Cyprus. Against this it can be argued that no crisis in the Eastern Mediterranean would be likely to break so fast that there would be no time to fly out strategic reserve units and get them acclimatized before any fighting occurred. It can also be argued that the most useful kind of aid to send to Greece, Turkey, or Israel would be tactical air squadrons and anti-aircraft batteries rather than infantry units. It is likewise quite possible that Libya could be defended by means of air interdiction in the improbable event of an Egyptian attack.

Aden, at which 7,000 servicemen are stationed, is currently regarded as a vital base by the British government. This is because it can accept transport aircraft and V-bombers, has a naval shore establishment of 100 men which serves as a headquarters unit for the amphibious warfare squadron, is the headquarters of Middle East Command, has an Army stockpile, and is being equipped, at a cost of some £10,000,000 to accommodate a theatre reserve of brigade strength in anticipation of a British withdrawal from Kenya. Since the civil port employs a mere 10,000 of the colony's population of 220,000 and is dependent on an entrepôt trade which is inevitably declining, and since the oil refinery employs less than 2,000 people and is not scheduled for expansion, the defence installations are important for the local economy. Local labour is prominent, for example, in the water distilleries, laundries, canteen and cleaning and sanitation services maintained for the military and a complete strike lasting more than several days could immobilize the base unless thousands of extra troops were rushed in to maintain essential services. To try to forestall such an occurrence the British authorities have recruited more Aden Arabs than Yemenis. Also, during 1962 some hundreds of dismissals of the existing labour force took place in an attempt, apparently, to purge it of dissident elements.

The British government is trying to insure against the future by promoting the colony's accession to the Federation of South Arabia. This recently formed association is at present composed of some of the states in the Western Protectorate. The Protectorate are a collection of sheikdoms that receive 85 per cent of their governmental revenues—namely about £3,000,000 a year —from the British. Their security is guaranteed by treaties with the United Kingdom and more specifically by that country paying £4,000,000 a year to keep the four battalions of local levies in being. Aden joined the Federation in 1963, but the colonial governor has retained control in respect of defence, external affairs, and internal security and Aden will have the opportunity of seceding in 1970 if two-thirds of her legislative council so wish. Britain retains the right to keep under sovereign control any pieces of land she feels she needs for military purposes.

The value of the link from the British standpoint is that it will be with an area which is the source of much of Aden's water and an important hinterland for its port and which is currently ruled by people who treasure the British connection. The danger is that the local resentment that the scheme is engendering will produce recurrent incidents necessitating repressive measures that will lead to another slump in Britain's already none too secure reputation within the Arab world.

Already it is proving essential to push the scheme through before the colony's next general election, which has now been postponed till 1964. Defenders of this policy point out that the new proposals command very general support within the present legislative council and that this is a body with an elective majority. However, there was an almost complete Arab boycott of the last general election and, in any case, the franchise is confined to 20,000 people, all of whom have to be from Commonwealth or British protected territories. Thus, all the 80,000 resident Yemenis are excluded, which is highly significant, for they form the cement of the alliance now existing between the trade unions and the newly formed Peoples Socialist Party, which is opposed to accession and also, according to its leader, to British bases. Now that a radical nationalist régime is in power in Sana the long-standing Yemeni demand for Aden is likely to command increasing support within the colony. This is because of the facts of economic geography as well as those of nationalist politics. The Yemen has far more potential than the Federation of South Arabia.

The notion that Aden is indispensable to Britain derives partly from the position it occupies at one end of the Libya–Sudan air corridor although, as implied above, that route may not remain viable indefinitely. Other considerations being borne in mind are the clear moral obligation that Britain has to render assistance to Jordan if it is asked for, and the treaties and agreements that exist between her and the sheikdoms of the Persian Gulf. Since, however, it is nearly 1,500 miles by sea from Aden to Aqaba and over 2,000 from Aden to Kuwait, it would require a very large force of big transport aircraft permanently attached to the brigade that is being built up in Aden to make it able to reach either destination in less than several days. Even then it would not be possible to respond either as rapidly or carefully as would be possible with seaborne forces hovering near the coastlines in question. In the case of Kuwait such fast and flexible reactions might be crucially important because of the weight and speed with which the Iraqis could concentrate along her northern border.

The current British defence plans do, in fact, envisage a strengthened and modernized Amphibious Warfare Squadron that, it is assumed, will continue to operate from Aden. It has to be admitted, of course, that Aden would be the most convenient of the bases that such a seaborne task force might possibly use, but it is by no means the only one. The force in question will have a range and endurance that will permit it to operate from much farther afield should that prove desirable.

Although the one or two fleet carriers, the twelve or fifteen other warships, and the squadron of submarines attached to the Far Eastern Fleet are available for deployment westward, the only combatant naval vessels permanently on station between Suez and Singapore are the members of the small frigate squadron in the Persian Gulf. Likewise no British fleet bases are located within this sector, though in Ceylon a Royal Naval wireless station is maintained under a leasehold arrangement and at Karachi a lot of repair work is done for the Royal Navy. On the other hand, the proportion of total British effective naval strength that is located somewhere beyond the Red Sea is greater today than it was twenty-five years back, and so to that extent the process of imperial withdrawal has affected the Navy less than it has the Army. In pre-war days a dominant feature of the balance of power between the Near East and the Orient was the British Indian Army, but the only battalion the United Kingdom now has stationed between Aden and Malaya is an airborne one in the British-protected oil state of Bahrain. It is most improbable that even this garrison could ever be expanded except on a temporary basis.

Nevertheless, should Britain wish to develop fresh land, sea or air base facilities of different kinds in or around the Indian Ocean, the opportunities exist. In addition to the real and attractive possibility of an Australian base there are many British-controlled islands within the area, and some of them are both technically suitable and politically eligible for a certain amount of development. Thus around the southern flanks of the Arabian peninsula are Kamaran, Perim and the Kuria Murias, which are all British owned and which will be permanently excluded from the Federation of South Arabia. Kamaran and Perim each have a small harbour and an airstrip and, at a price, these facilities could be developed, but the Kurias Murias are precipitous and almost uninhabited. Socotra, sometimes mentioned in this connection, belongs to one of the local rulers from the Eastern Protectorate. It has a difficult terrain and is subject, during the summer, to frequent high winds.

The second group of British-protected islands nearest to Arabia is the Maldives. They include Gan, on which there is now a major RAF station that was built for £5,000,000 and that now handles twenty-five aircraft including *Comets* and *Britannias* on the average day. The construction of this airstrip aroused bitter resentment in all the Maldive islands except Gan itself, where, on the contrary, there was great enthusiasm for the scheme on account of the economic benefits that accrued. As a result of this difference in attitude the inhabitants of Gan revolted against their own central government who, by way of retaliation, organized first a food blockade and then a rather sanguinary punitive expedition. The situation was temporarily stabilized in 1960 by the signing of a new agreement between the British and Maldivian governments that gave the former a twenty-six year lease on Gan and the latter complete control of their own internal policy. But anti-British feeling is again waxing, except of course in Gan, and since November 1962 a British warship has been standing by continuously at Male. Gan is one of the islands on the perimeter of Addu atoll whose lagoon could constitute an excellent fleet anchorage but, politically, it seems clear that it could never be used as such, except, perhaps, on a very provisional basis.

A different political atmosphere prevails in Mauritius, and the fact that she is advancing fast towards sovereignty does not rule out the possibility of Britain retaining base facilities at least as extensive as those she now enjoys, which consist of a Transport Command staging post with a 6,000-foot runway and some naval installations. Mauritius is not much influenced by all the political considerations that help make emergent African states reluctant to make defence agreements with Western powers. Furthermore, she has a strong vested interest in the British connection, especially since ambitions to enter into some kind of political association with either India or the East Africa Federation seem unlikely to be realized, and since Madagascar has firmly turned down suggestions that she should absorb part of the rapidly increasing Mauritian population surplus. About 1,300 miles north-east of the main island lies the dependency of Diego Garcia, which has a good deep harbour and a site for a large airfield. The prospects of a request to establish some kind of base there being granted are enhanced, both by its remoteness from Mauritius itself and by its being sparsely peopled.

The Seychelles, like Mauritius, have a 6,000-foot runway that is used on routine flights by RAF Transport Command and it is a runway that could, if necessary, be extended. The port of Mahe is small, and the best place for a naval anchorage would be the undeveloped lagoon of the Aldabra atoll, which lies well apart from most of the members of this island group: this lagoon is large and could take ships up to cruiser size.

The Cocos Islands are the only other ones within the Indian Ocean at present being used by Britain for military purposes They belong to Australia, but the Royal Air Force are allowed to make use of the 9,000-foot runway available. Even assuming that there were no political inhibitions, it is doubtful whether much more capital could usefully be sunk in this particular base. It is not very conveniently positioned and only vessels drawing less than 24 feet of water can enter the lagoon.

If the Federation of Malaysia does come into being Britain will lose her sovereign rights in Singapore. However, she will be allowed to retain military installations, at least for the time being, for the purpose of assisting '. . . in the defence of Malaysia, for Commonwealth defence, and for the preservation of peace in South East Asia', which is, of course, a formula copied from the Anglo-Malay defence pact of 1957.[1] Even the moderate party at present in power on the island is mandated to remove them as soon as economic circumstances permit, but when, or whether, these circumstances will so permit can be a matter for considerable conjecture. The Royal Navy alone keeps some 10,000 people in work and the Army and the RAF about another 30,000 between them. Total official and private spending by the British Services in Singapore averages £70,000,000 a year.[2] Such expenditure must be critically important to a community of 1,600,000, who are increasing at the rate of 50,000 a year and who already include a hard core of unemployed amounting to 10 per cent of the working population around whom there is a wide penumbra of underemployed. The entrepôt trade is declining here as in most other places, and whilst it is true that local manufacturing industries have expanded in recent years and now maintain 70,000 workers, their markets are directly or indirectly dependent to a considerable degree on the presence of the British forces. In fact, it seems that if the British withdraw completely at any time during the next few years Singapore's only hope of avoiding starvation would lie in the election of a government sufficiently left wing to be prepared to accept indefinitely large-scale

[1] Cmd. 1563; 1962
[2] *The Observer*, November 12, 1961

financial support from the Sino-Soviet Bloc. The official opposition party—the Barisan Socialists—is strongly against the Malaysia scheme and would therefore stand to gain prestige if it collapsed. It is also unconditionally opposed to the British base. A rapid rise in its influence within the trade unions recently has coincided with a marked increase in the number of strikes.

If, through the accession to power of a virulent opposition group, the British connection was terminated, the biggest loss to the United Kingdom would be the naval base. In addition to acting as headquarters for the striking force of the Far Eastern Fleet and its associated auxiliary vessels, it is at present supporting both the commando ships and is garrisoning the two Royal Marine commandos associated with them. The naval dockyard, which is used by the 7th Fleet as well as by the Royal Navy, extends over 4 square miles and has four floating docks and the *King George V* dry dock which can accommodate *Forrestal* class carriers. Its major drawbacks are that 60 per cent of its skilled workers are Chinese and so of uncertain political persuasion and that it lies on the north side of the island, just over a mile from the mainland. The exit channels therefore lie through the narrow and shallow Straits of Johore and so could readily be mined or otherwise blockaded. The whole area is, in any case, dominated by the Indonesian islands immediately to the south and is dependent on the mainland for part of its water supply.

The six Army battalions on the island are held ready for internal security operations, but Singapore also contains a brigade group stockpile and the headquarters of the 28th Commonwealth Brigade in Malaya. The international airport has over 100 arrivals a week and since two other large airfields exist the risk of flying being completely curtailed by thundery weather is remote. The main RAF field is another of those exercised as a V-bomber dispersal base. Any troops assembled in the island could be moved on by air or through the civilian port, which has 4,000 vessels berth per year. These ships take on board or discharge 5,000,000 tons of cargo.

The garrison in Hong Kong and the associated squadron of inshore minesweepers are now concerned only with internal security. Consequently the only British Far Eastern theatre reserves outside Singapore are the British components of the 28th Commonwealth Brigade and the units at RAF Butterworth. There is, however, much uncertainty about the circumstances under which either the air or ground forces stationed in Malaya could be deployed outside it without precipitating a political crisis. As the phrase quoted above demonstrates, the 1957 agreement is deliberately vague on this point, and the ambiguous position of the Commonwealth forces in the Federation was underlined in 1962, when the RAAF *Sabre* squadron dispatched to Thailand had to stage through Singapore, to preserve the fiction that it was not using Malaya as a jumping-off point for SEATO operations.

Until recently, the standard British reaction to inhibitions, such as those they now experience in respect of Malaya and may soon experience in respect of Malaysia as a whole, has been to regard them as proof of the consequences of not having all their installations abroad under sovereign control. This line of reasoning led British Conservative governments to maintain, throughout the nineteen-fifties, that certain of the smaller colonies could never hope for full independence because of their strategic importance. The signs are that this view is now giving way in favour of one that looks upon genuine local support as being the key factor in the maintenance of a base and not nominal sovereign control.

II—AMERICAN OVERSEAS BASES—THE CONTRACTUAL NEXUS

There is a striking contrast between the legal status of most British bases and garrison posts outside Europe and that of most American ones outside the United States, for the latter are nearly all on sites leased rather than owned by the United States government and people. The reasons are clear enough. Britain built up her empire at a time when many Western statesmen felt no inhibitions about colonizing the areas peopled by the black, brown, and yellow races and when there were no forces of nationalism to deter them from so doing. Furthermore, throughout the nineteenth century Britain enjoyed a naval supremacy between Gibraltar and Shanghai far more absolute than any great power could ever secure today. Added to all this is the strong anti-colonial tradition of the United States herself.

When discussing American overseas commitments it seems natural to turn first to the mainland of Europe, whereas when discussing those of Britain it seemed natural to look initially at the Mediterranean. This reflects a major difference in what may be termed geopolitical perspective that derives from the fact that strategically Britain is part of Western Europe. It therefore follows that for the British the stationing of troops in Germany is for a purpose separate from that which is being fulfilled by maintaining them in the Afro-Asian area. The distinction is analogous to that once made between Metropolitan and Imperial defence and it is one of great practical significance. This is because in respect of manning levels, research, development, procurement, and the formulation of doctrine British Army of the Rhine and the attached RAF squadrons are in competition with units held available for extra-European service. The American VIIth Army in Germany and the United States Air Force in Europe, on the other hand, are in a similar position to the forces in Korea in so far as they help protect an area that is physically remote from the United States. All the same, Western Europe is regarded as both vital and vulnerable and so the VII Army has been built up to consist of five full divisions and three armoured cavalry regiments.

Iceland and the Azores are mid-ocean air staging posts that would still play a vital part in any fast and large-scale reinforcement of Germany, but the 4,000 American servicemen in Iceland are not just concerned with facilitating air movement. They have various other roles and some of these relate to possible conflict situations short of general war. Thus they keep the old wartime fleet base at Hvalfjordeur in a state of reasonable preparedness and, since this lies only 1,000 miles from Narvik, it could have a special value in the event of a threat to Northern Norway. The three squadrons of Airborne Early Warning *Super Constellations* that now fly from Keflavik are part of the North American strategic early warning system.

The Communist Party, which can still command 20 per cent of the votes in a general election, remains something of a threat to the American links with Iceland, but in recent years its power has declined, as indeed has the direct influence of the Soviet Union within the country. Politically the Iceland base facilities are at present more secure than those in the Azores, which were built for $80,000,000 and are now manned by 2,000 men, and whose position has been made precarious by Portuguese resentment at American liberal criticism of the less savoury aspects of their domestic and colonial record. The current agreement was due to end on December 31st, 1962, but at the very last moment, and following six months of what seem to have been exceptionally wearisome negotiations, its expiry was deferred for a year to enable the talks to continue.

In September 1963 the ten-year agreement with Spain for the use of bases will automatically expire unless in the meantime an extension of it has been formally decided upon. Preliminary discussions about this have taken place, but so far they have only served to reveal that the Spanish government hope for much more beneficial terms, implicit as well as explicit, in any new bargain struck. This is embarrassing, because the United States has already tarnished its own image by identifying itself with the Franco régime, for, as its repeated failure to get Spain accepted as a member of NATO shows, the memories of the way in which General Franco gained power are dying hard in Western Europe.[1] Among other things that the United States has to bear in mind is the risk that too much cooperation with the present Spanish government may make any such bilateral arrangements anathema to the more liberal administration that will probably follow it.

Another factor to be considered is that the utility of Spain to American strategic striking forces is diminishing. The B-47 medium-range bombers are soon to be withdrawn from the three airfields built for them and the idea that they might be replaced by *Polaris* submarines operating from Rota near Cadiz has now been abandoned. Since ballistic submarines are going to patrol the Mediterranean there are strong arguments on grounds of economy in favour of basing them in or near that sea, but there are a number of other countries that could and probably would offer the United States good sites if asked to do so. Nevertheless Rota will continue to play an important role

[1] Arthur P. Whitaker, *Spain and Defense of the West* (New York, Harper & Bros, 1961), p. 389

by ministering to the needs of the 6th Fleet. About one-half of
the $535,000,000 invested in American military installations in
Spain since 1953 has been spent there, and the results are to be
seen in such facilities as a large air station, a long breakwater,
and a 1,000-foot pier alongside which the largest warships afloat
can tie up. There are also some naval oil bunkering depots at
El Ferrol and Cartegena.

The 6th Fleet is comprised of some fifty ships, including three
attack carriers and including also a small amphibious task
force that has on board a contingent of 2,000 Marines. Although
Rota is the fleet's most important logistic centre outside the
United States, it has extensive servicing facilities in Naples as
well, and that port also houses its administrative headquarters.
A specialist command ship serves as the tactical headquarters,
and this vessel is the only unit that is not rotated between the
6th Fleet in the Mediterranean and the 2nd Fleet in the
Atlantic. Each of these fleets has a dual function. The 6th Fleet
is earmarked to become NATO Striking Force South if the
alliance itself is involved in war. Meanwhile it serves as the
immediately available instrument of United States power
within the Mediterranean. It was so used during the Suez
crisis in 1956, the Lebanon crisis in 1958, and the Algerian
crisis of 1961, when President Kennedy made it clear that the
United States Navy would be used to help forestall any rebel-
lion organized against President De Gaulle from Algeria.
Although a few of the smaller warships occasionally deploy
south of the Suez Canal, the main force never does: the larger
carriers would not be able to get through and the remainder
would take two or three days to make the passage even assuming the Egyptians gave them absolute priority. The 2nd Fleet
with its 370 ships is available to back up the 6th Fleet in local
emergencies, but it also performs a deterrent role in its own
right within the Atlantic basin, as was shown during the Cuban
blockade. It is earmarked to form up as NATO Striking Force
Atlantic in the event of a threat to the alliance as a whole.

Apart from the 6th Fleet the United States 'presence' in the
Near and Middle East and around the Indian Ocean has
always been very thin and patchy. At the moment it is provided
by several small warships, in the Indian Ocean, some maintenance crews on Military Air Transportation Service staging

posts, and military missions in the CENTO and SEATO countries, India, Ethiopia, and Saudi Arabia. The patrol area of the powerful 7th Fleet nominally extends from the Western Pacific half-way across the Indian Ocean, but it is rarely to be seen in much strength west of Singapore, and the dispatch of a 7th Fleet carrier to the Red Sea during the Lebanon crisis must be looked upon as exceptional. The strongest of the USAF contingents referred to are in Wheelus Field, Libya, and in Adana: they amount to one or two thousand men in each of these places. Dhahran in Saudi Arabia used to be the other big MATS establishment in that part of the world, but it has now been closed down. It is true that the military missions are one or two thousand strong in some of the countries and that they generally have a good scale of mechanized transport and to this extent they could always provide good permanent frameworks within which expeditionary forces could expand. All the same military missions do not in themselves constitute combat formations and by their mere existence they do not refute the proposition that those areas around the Iron Curtain that are farthest removed from the United States herself are the ones that are least adequately covered by theatre reserves and garrison units.

The United States has long been the most influential of the Western democracies in shaping events in the Pacific, and it was in that ocean that, between 1942 and 1945, she gave a unique demonstration of the effectiveness of sea mobility, by launching a series of amphibious assaults across waters controlled by a naval armada that eventually consisted of over 100 battleships and carriers, 600 cruisers and escort vessels, and several thousand other ships. Today there is a chain of bases in the Western Pacific which derives from the bilateral Mutual Defence Treaties between the United States and the Philippines, Formosa, Japan, and South Korea and this constitutes a dramatic application of Mahan's principle that the homeland is best defended by dominating the actual or potential enemy's coastline. The fleets that ensure the command of the sea that make such a policy viable are the 7th and the 1st. The 7th Fleet is normally composed of 125 ships and is backed up by the 1st Fleet with 300 ships, the individual ships being rotated in the same way as those based on the Eastern Seaboard are.

The 7th Fleet is responsible for all sea areas west of longitude 160°E.

This chain of bases is linked to the continental United States by a string of islands that make it possible to travel to Tokyo or Manila from San Francisco without doing more than 2,400 miles over any one stage. These intermediate islands are the major exceptions to the rule that the United States is not able to establish overseas bases on her own sovereign territory, for Hawaii is now one of the states of the Union, whilst Wake and Guam are unincorporated territories. The Hawaiian islands accommodate an army and marine theatre reserve of divisional strength and provide it with a 150 square mile jungle mountain training ground. This group is also the location of several air-fields and of the Pearl Harbour naval station. The continuing usefulness of the latter was demonstrated clearly during the Korean War. By 1952 up to fifty ships were being overhauled, repaired, or converted there at any one time.[1] Wake and Guam both have operational airfields and Guam also has extensive naval installations which are little used at present, but which are, as already implied, likely to be employed more intensively in the near future when the island becomes a *Polaris* base. By the middle of 1945 these installations were able to maintain about one-third of the great wartime naval armada.

Forward from Guam lie the Philippines, a country with very close ties with the United States formed during her experience as an American colony; these have been maintained with the help of allocations of foreign aid of well over $300,000,000 which are supplemented by a large flow of private investment. Despite this the United States had difficulty in negotiating the 1959 revision of the 1946 Treaty and only succeeded by making substantial concessions.[2] But certain important sites have been retained on a twenty-five year lease including the Clark Field air station and the Subic Bay naval establishment with its large stocks of fuel. In nearby Taiwan there are no United States troops available for strategic redeployment, but there are very large stockpiles. These are nominally intended for the Chinese Nationalists, but they could presumably be drawn on by Americans in most contingencies. The islands of Japan have

[1] *New York Times*, August 11, 1952
[2] *New York Times*, October 14, 1959

40,000 American servicemen stationed on them in fifteen different establishments, including a vehicle rebuild centre and an army port. Though intended as part of the rear area support for the two-division garrison in Korea, these men could obviously provide some logistic backing for operations elsewhere in the Western Pacific.

In the centre of the network, and serving as its linch-pin, is Okinawa. This island bears three large aerodromes supporting some twenty squadrons, two-thirds of a Marine Division Wing, 2,000 soldiers who man, among other things, *Nike*, *Hawk*, and *Mace B* missile sites, and huge supply dumps. It is said that the total 'base' cost $1,000,000,000 to develop.[1] It contains 45,000 servicemen and employs directly 50,000 of the 400,000-strong Okinawan labour force. One result is an average annual income for the Ryukuans of $300 per head which is over 60 per cent higher than their pre-war income, though in Imperial times these islands were poorer than any prefecture in Japan itself.[1,2] In spite of all this comparative affluence all the parties at present represented in the local legislature are explicitly in favour of eventual reversion to Japan and the United States herself is committed to such a policy under the Japanese Peace Treaty.

Meanwhile there are recurrent protests about many aspects of the military occupation. The way in which a dyarchy of two generals—one styled a High Commissioner and the other a Civilian Administrator—effectively rule through the exercise of such powers as the right to veto the legislature's choice of chief executive is much disliked, as is the fact that the penal code is based on military law. Moreover, although high compensation is paid, bad feeling is caused by the confiscation of land to build things like bowling alleys, swimming baths, and nuclear missile sites. These sources of conflict result from the 'cultural aggression' of a Western affluent military group set among a people whose roots lie deep in a traditional Oriental peasant way of life. Such tensions between indigenous civilians and foreign soldiery have, of course, been experienced since the dawn of history and have occurred in plenty of places where the social contrasts are nothing like as great as obtain in this

[1] *Reporter*, October 13, 1960
[2] John Barr in *World Today*, May 1961

example. The problem even had to be anticipated when the decision was taken to establish a *Polaris* servicing base on the west coast of Scotland, and the decision was taken to locate it at Holy Loch partly so that sailors on shore leave could merge into the large cosmopolitan population of the Clyde Valley. In a congested island in which one adult male in five is a serviceman no such assimilation is possible and however liberal the administration and however upstanding the conduct of the troops there must inevitably be a fair amount of resentment. Such resentment will be sustained, too, by memories of the 'liberation' in 1945, when the island was devastated and 100,000 of its inhabitants killed. Admittedly there is no danger of a physical eviction of the American military, for the thesis that a foreign base is untenable if it is set amid a hostile population does not hold true for this compact and isolated island. In any case there is no physical resistance movement and the militant neutralists, though vocal, remain a small minority with only one seat in the legislature. Furthermore both public and politicians in Japan remain as yet apathetic about the reversion question. All the same there may be situations in which the continued use of Okinawa by the United States would be a grave political embarrassment to her.

In 1903 the United States signed with the Republic of Panama the treaty permitting her to build and operate the canal that now links the Atlantic to the Pacific, and with Cuba an agreement that, among other things, gave her an indefinite lease on Guantanamo. Four years later the first round-the-world cruise by an American battle squadron demonstrated the fact that the United States now possessed a large two-ocean navy that had become the chief guarantor of western hemisphere security and which would be dependent for its strategic mobility on uninterrupted passage through the projected canal. Those propositions were dramatically reaffirmed by the official opening of the canal on the day that Germany invaded Belgium in 1914. A belief became rapidly and firmly established that the security of the Americas was dependent upon the ability of the United States to retain effective control of the Caribbean, and that this could only be done if she maintained, perhaps in conjunction with her ally Britain, an arc of naval bases along its oceanic flank. This tradition still

flourishes and the extent to which the importance of Guantanamo is publicly discussed in terms of its position close by the
Windward Passage is quite remarkable.

The 1934 treaty revision of the 1903 agreement confirmed
that Guantanamo Bay would be returned to Cuba ultimately,
but indicated that this could not happen until desired by both
parties. If the United States ever did decide on such a reversion
it would be giving up a base in which a great deal of real estate
has been sunk. The nominal figure is said to be $76,000,000,
but a lot of the expenditure occurred when prices were lower
than today and so this figure must be multiplied three or four
times to get a correct contemporary order of magnitude. The
greatest asset of Guantanamo consists not of a work of man,
however, but of the deep fjord-type natural harbour. The naval
ditty, about '. . . sixteen battleships all in a line, in Gitmo
Bay . . .' looking mighty fine, belongs to a bygone age in terms
of naval architecture, but the impression it gives of physical
geography remains valid enough, for up to fifty large warships
can use the anchorage simultaneously. West of the anchorage
there is a large airfield and east of it a medium-size one. The
total shore establishment is normally manned by about 3,000
sailors who are assisted by 4,000 Cuban workers who come in
daily, and it is protected by a garrison of a few hundred
Marines. The main water source lies outside the perimeter, but
arrangements exist for supplies to be brought in by tankers in
the event of it being cut off. Merchant vessels have the right to
pass through the anchorage to and from points upstream, but no
Russian ones have done so as yet.

The naval base at Roosevelt Roads in Puerto Rico was extended during the last war and the one at Chaguaramas in
Trinidad begun then. The former is politically secure for,
although President Eisenhower committed his administration to
allowing Puerto Rico complete independence when a majority
of the inhabitants desired it, in the 1960 elections only 2.7 per
cent of the votes were cast for independence.

Chaguaramas was wanted by Trinidad as the site for the
capital of the abortive West Indies Federation, but a recent
agreement has given the United States a lease on it till 1977.
Together with smaller sites on Jamaica, Antigua, and St.
Lucia, it is all that remains of the string of bases leased for

ninety-nine years by Britain in 1941 in exchange for fifty old destroyers. The others are now small areas used entirely for missile tracking and other research activities, with the exception of the large airfield on St. Lucia. However, Sir Alexander Bustamente, the Prime Minister of Jamaica, recently said that the United States could have a military base in his country any time they wanted it without having to offer the bribe of extra economic aid.[1] Meanwhile the Canal Zone itself remains United States sovereign territory and is guarded by an army battle group and one or two squadrons of fighter aircraft.

The United States Navy has recently formed a South Atlantic Command, though few ships have as yet been attached to it. The only sizeable body of American troops stationed ashore there helps keep open the staging post on Ascension Island which MATS shares with RAF Transport Command.[2] Ascension would be difficult to transform into a more extensive kind of base, because the meagre port facilities it has are incapacitated for about six days in each month by powerful rollers.

III—AUSTRALIA AS A BASE?

The political leaders of Australia have long been conscious of her strategic isolation as an underpopulated, white country on the oceanic fringe of South East Asia, and this consciousness has deepened in recent years with the military emergence of China and Indonesia. This has coincided with a recognition on the part of governmental and public opinion in Britain that overseas bases are only worth having if they are politically secure. Therefore, there has been some thought in Britain about the possibility of the United Kingdom being accorded permanent facilities in Australia.

At first sight such a prospect would appeal to many Australians. It would give them added security without forcing them to raise defence expenditure above its present very modest level, and without obliging them to reintroduce conscription.

[1] *The Guardian*, August 8, 1962
[2] MATS is the Military Air Transport Service of the United States Air Force, the equivalent of Britain's RAF Transport Command

It would be good business, both as a direct source of British sterling and as an advertising medium for the immigration authorities and private commercial interests. Its attractiveness particularly to older Australians as a concrete link with 'home' is too obvious to bear emphasis. However, a major difficulty would be that of persuading Australians that such a move was in their own long-term interests. If they could not be so persuaded it would be most unlikely that it could be sold to them simply by playing on their sentiment or their sense of short-term material advantage.

Australians are aware of the progressive decline of British power and influence east of Suez. Faith in Britain's ability to guarantee unilaterally the integrity of Australasia was shattered irrevocably twenty years ago when the sinking in a few short hours of the battleship *Prince of Wales* and the battlecruiser *Repulse*, which together constituted the core of the British Pacific Fleet, was followed within months by the fall of Singapore. All this happened at a time when the bulk of Australian and New Zealand field armies had been dispatched to the Middle East on the basis of assurances that Singapore was impregnable and the Royal Navy absolutely capable of protecting the Pacific Dominions. More recently doubts have been more and more frequently expressed about whether Britain will want to maintain a 'presence' east of Suez indefinitely. The Common Market negotiations are regarded as proof of a steady political re-orientation towards Europe which, it is felt, is likely to affect not only British deployments but also the relevance of her equipment and doctrine to Pacific conditions. A recent piece of 'evidence' that the British are gradually but definitely contracting out of what remains of their Pacific and Indian Ocean commitments was the announcement that sometime after 1967 the Royal Navy will withdraw the three submarines it has for some years based on Sydney.

Of course, there is still a lot of functional co-operation on defence between Australia and Britain especially in naval matters, but the American connection has steadily become more important. The American signature of the Anzus Treaty in 1951 and, to some extent, of the Manila Treaty in 1954 derived from an Australian desire to formalize this connection. Since then, Australian army organization has been re-modelled along essentially American lines as witness the pentropic battalion structure. In 1961 the Minister for the Navy in Canberra said that the placing of orders for two American-built guided missile destroyers would probably lead to equipment standardization between the RAN and the USN. He contended that comparable British ships would have lacked the duration and air-conditioning required for the Pacific.[1] In May 1962 the Prime Minister, Sir Robert Menzies, announced an agreement whereby the United States will build and operate a naval communications centre at North West Cape. The main transceiver is to be one of very high power and very low frequency capable of communicating with totally submerged submarines across wide areas of the Pacific and Indian Oceans. The projected cost is £A33,000,000 for the operational equipment and about as much again for housing and amenities. Under this scheme, the old American wartime submarine base at Exmouth Gulf and landing strip at Learmouth are to be redeveloped to accept large tankers and *Hercules* transports respectively. It is intended that construction will be complete by 1966. Sir Robert Menzies considered that the plan marked '. . . an important step in the steadily increasing defence collaboration between the two countries'. Mr. Calwell, leader of the Labour opposition, said his party was suspending judgement until the legal status of the American garrison had been decided upon.

Paradoxically, and in spite of the remarks of the Prime Minister, it is possible that the proposed establishment at North West Cape may remove the inhibitions which the authorities in Canberra apparently feel about strengthening or even preserving existing defence links with London, for fear that in so doing they might seem to relieve Washington of a moral commitment to send immediate and massive help in time of trouble. Australians may henceforward feel that, since they have at last got American forces physically committed to their continent, they can concentrate more heavily than in recent years on increasing their diplomatic status and flexibility by forging fresh strategic links with the senior member of the Commonwealth. Even so, they would still want convincing that Britain had a positive desire to maintain these links as long as the need for strong deterrent forces within the area remained.

[1] *The Guardian*, July 1, 1961

There would be a natural suspicion that the programme was a short-term one designed to alleviate the discomfort of imperial decline or intended as a kind of insurance in the British Commonwealth ideal against the risk of Britain being permanently excluded from the European Economic Community.

Another question, which itself could become complicated by inter-state politics within Australia, would be that of exactly where any base installations should be. As far as naval establishments were concerned, Sydney would be on intrinsic merits easily the most attractive site. It is a thriving industrial city of 2,200,000 people with considerable shipbuilding and repair yards. Like the Williamstown Yard at Melbourne, they construct warships of up to destroyer size. Sydney also possesses a dock that can accommodate capital ships of up to 50,000 tons. By comparison other possible locations lack the presence of large urban complexes and the skilled labour pool and recreational amenities that are part and parcel of them. In the aftermath of Suez, Cockburn Sound was suggested by the West Australian government, but although nearby Perth and Fremantle have a combined population of 450,000 the district would suffer from a marked shortage of the kinds of skilled labour needed for the construction and operation of comprehensive base facilities.[1] Darwin is even worse off with a population that still only numbers 10,000 whilst North West Cape has practically no indigenous inhabitants. Darwin suffers from the added disadvantage of a 26-foot tide. On the other hand North West Cape, for example, is only 1,600 nautical miles from Singapore and 5,100 from Aden compared with Sydney's 4,300 and 7,900 nautical miles respectively. The best compromise would probably lie in developing further, on an Anglo-American-Australian basis, the present Sydney naval station and in establishing or extending forward operating bases elsewhere.

IV—RESERVE FORCES OF THE UNITED STATES AND BRITAIN

The term 'strategic reserve' is normally employed to mean a body of regular soldiers held available within the home territory

[1] *The Times*, January 26, 1957

of a nation ready for rapid movement to trouble spots anywhere in the world. The definition is sometimes and quite logically stretched to include air force units maintained in a similar way for a similar purpose.

The only countries that currently have large land and air forces organized to be strategically mobile, together with substantial air and sea transport organized to carry and support them, are the United States and Britain, and for this reason attention is largely confined to them. It is worth noting, however, that when the impending reorganization of the French Army is complete one of the six regular divisions to be formed will be stationed in Western France ready for movement overseas. The kind of overseas movements the French authorities have in mind are those that might follow urgent requests for assistance from one or more of the Community nations in West Africa or possibly in the Indian Ocean. This division will probably be the only one available to meet such contingencies, since all the reservist ones are likely to be earmarked for tasks within Western Europe. It will be spearheaded by squadrons of AMX-13 tanks and almost all the other organic equipment will also be airportable.

It seems useful to discuss, concurrently with the British and American 'strategic reserves', all non-regular forces that might be mobilized and dispatched to crisis situations overseas. In certain respects such organizations are not comparable with regular strategic reserve forces. They are often called upon to provide individual rather than unit reinforcements and in such cases obviously do not influence the nominal order of battle within the theatre concerned. Also they can never display the speed of response that regular forces can: one of their functions is to serve as a safeguard against general war. On the other hand, certain part-time volunteers already play a major part in the American preparations for mobile operations and play some part in the British. Even if this were not the case they would obviously constitute a second-line strategic reserve available after the first had been committed.

In September 1961 the United States began a dramatic adjustment to the needs of the present and the future by the formation of Strike Command. This was created by the amalgamation, after the Navy and Marine Corps had asked not to be involved, of the Strategic Reserve Army Corps and the Tactical Air Command. A command headquarters was formed which is composed half of Army and half of Air Force officers and which, except for a small rear echelon, is completely air-portable. Meanwhile, the Strategic Reserve Army Corps was increased to eight divisions under two corps headquarters. The first is to command the two airborne and two infantry divisions of the 18th Airborne Corps based in North Carolina, Kentucky, Kansas, and Georgia respectively. If 25-ton M-41 tanks with 76-mm guns are substituted for 45-ton medium tanks with 90-mm guns in the infantry divisions, all the equipment will be airportable except for the 8-inch and some of the 155-mm howitzers and some cranes and tank recovery vehicles. It can be assumed that the 18th Airborne Corps will remain at the same sort of alert status as it has been at for some years. This has involved a 250-man rifle company always being ready to leave at one hour's notice and a 1,800-man battle group at four.

The other major army element in Strike Command is 3rd Corps, which comprises two armoured and two infantry divisions. One of each kind is a regular division—one being garrisoned in Louisiana and the other in Georgia—whilst the other two are National Guard ones and are thus the first reserve units ever to be assigned to a strategic striking force in peace-time. By the middle of 1963 there will be five *Hawk* anti-aircraft battalions in Strike Command as whole and it is expected to receive also some of the *Davy Crockett* mortars that can fire either high explosive or sub-kiloton nuclear warheads over ranges of one or two miles.

The Kennedy Administration is also reorganizing the National Guard and the Army Reserve. This policy partly derives, like the creation of Strike Command, from a general desire to improve America's limited war capability but it stems particularly from the bitter experience of mobilization during the 1961 Berlin Crisis. Although the two National Guard divisions activated then had been singled out as being the most efficient, they were initially only 60 per cent manned, they had had grossly insufficient integral training, and they were far below their full equipment authorization. It has been said that the 32nd Infantry Division was not rated as good as a regular unit until it had been on active duty for three months.[1] Congressional investigators have criticized the Army for a bad mobilization scheme, saying that too many old veterans and too many 'completely unqualified' young reservists were recalled, and that the authorities revealed a complete inability to identify the skills of individuals in the latter group.[2]

It is felt that the remedy for such ills lies in drawing a firmer distinction between formations assigned as prospective reinforcements in a sudden limited war emergency and those maintained against the threat of more general war following a period of high tension. Six National Guard divisions and eight National Guard and Army Reserve brigades each with a 4,500-man establishment are to be kept permanently at 75 per cent to 80 per cent of full strength as compared with a maximum of 70 per cent in the past, and an even higher state of preparedness is to be maintained by a number of independent battalions with specialized artillery, signals, engineer, medical, and transportation functions. All these formations are to have 100 per cent equipment scales as against an upper limit of 71 per cent hitherto but, of course, many of the major items will be a generation older than their counterparts in the regular army. The intended result is that these divisions and brigades should be ready eight weeks after any alert and the independent specialist battalions four weeks earlier. About one-third of the total manpower will be allocated to a lower priority reserve that will contain seventeen National Guard and six Army Reserve divisions. These figures imply a reduction of eight in the present aggregate divisional strength which is a compound of twenty-seven in the National Guard and ten in the Army Reserve. President Kennedy had hoped to exploit that fact to reduce authorized force levels by 10 per cent, but, as President Eisenhower did before him, he has given way to the resistance offered by those who, reared in the Jeffersonian tradition, still see the National Guard as a check and counterbalance against federal military power, and also by those who see it as a source

[1] Testimony by Mr. McNamara during hearings in the Department of Defense Appropriations for 1963 before a Subcommittee of the Committee in Appropriations, House of Representatives, 87th Congress, 2nd Session, PT. 2, p. 31
[2] *New York Times*, August 27, 1962

of social amenities and status symbols. All the same, officials feel that the total of reservists will inevitably drop back from 700,000 to around 640,000 as a result of an insistence on better physical, mental, and training standards and so surplus funds will become available to help procure the new equipment needed, raise the minimum number of drills from twenty-four to about forty-eight a year, and enable more people to complete their statutory obligation of fifteen days' annual training.

As has been said, Tactical Air Command has become the air element in Strike Command. It is being built up to forty regular squadrons several of which will fly tankers. It includes forty-eight squadrons of the Air Reserve Forces of which thirty-six are tactical. Three ARF tanker squadrons are being formed. The Air Reserve Force units concerned have won widespread praise for the efficiency with which they obeyed the call to active duty on October 1st, 1961. Twenty thousand men and 650 planes were federalized out of a total complement of 55,000 men and 1,500 planes and a contingent equipped with 300 F-84s flew across to Europe. The experience of the 102nd Fighter Wing has been cited as typical.[1] Four weeks after being recalled, it received movement orders to France and eight days later was in position at Phalsbourg. After another eight days it was declared fully operational. This is a slow movement compared with what a specially tailored and equipped Composite Air Strike Force is capable of, but it was adequate for that cold war situation.

Nobody associated with Tactical Air Command would suggest that operational reserve units are inferior qualitatively to regular units in terms of training, experience or morale, but it is inevitable that they should be in respect of the relative obsolescence of their aircraft. On the other hand, this is not a critical handicap with transports and it is a matter of some controversy whether it is with close-support aircraft. During the Berlin crisis the authorities deemed it a virtue in disguise because they felt they wanted some rather slow but steady F.84s to compensate for what they regarded as a deficiency of ground-attack

[1] Testimony by Mr. McNamara during hearings in the Department of Defense Appropriations for 1963 before a Subcommittee of the Committee in Appropriations, House of Representatives, 87th Congress, 2nd Session, PT. 2, p. 31

planes. However, the idea that slowness is a recommendation in such machines is a throwback to Korea, when stately old *Thunderbolts* and *Mustangs* were reintroduced to ferret out well-camouflaged targets of opportunity. It may well already be an out-of-date notion as far as the NATO front is concerned and even if not will rapidly become so as Soviet light anti-aircraft artillery improves.

A Marine Corps Reserve of 120,000 exists and is intended, among other things, to fill out the skeleton 4th Marine Division in time of trouble, but no part of it was called up in 1961. However, about 8,000 United States Navy reservists went on active duty out of a total of about 120,000. Of these some were employed to bring various combat vessels from a peacetime manning strength of around 80 per cent up to full war establishment. Others were employed to provide about one-third of the crew of thirty-five vessels being commissioned from the Reserve Fleet. Ships in this fleet are held in a state of preservation by stripping or covering installations on the weather deck, by air conditioning the lower decks, and by liberal applications of rust-preventives, desiccants and anti-fouling paints. A cruiser, for example, can be put into 'mothballs' for around $50,000 and the subsequent upkeep costs are very moderate. The speed at which such a ship can be prepared for sea is normally between two and four weeks, but then it usually requires several months of seatime before all the 'bugs'—in the form of leaky steam pipes, corroded wires, and the like—have been ironed out. In any case the vessels built in thousands after Pearl Harbour have basic designs largely incompatible with modern requirements. Therefore, the Reserve Fleet is being allowed to decline from 1,288 ships in 1958 to 550 in 1965. In that latter year it will probably require a total maintenance personnel of around 2,000.[1]

Since late 1961 the British Army's Central Strategic Reserve has been divided into two main components. The first, which is called 3rd division, consists of the 19th and 51st British Infantry Brigades and has been earmarked for the reinforcement of British Army of the Rhine. It has permanent bases about 200 miles from Transport Command's main airfields, but

[1] *Department of Defense Appropriations Hearings*, part 3, *op. cit.*, p. 261

it can deploy to positions near them in twenty-four to thirty-six hours. The other component consists of the headquarters and two of the battalions of the 16th Independent Parachute Brigade, together with one or two infantry battalions which boost the total strength to 6,000. It is on light scales with an emphasis on Landrovers and other equipment with a high degree of airportability.

All British army reservists are in either the Regular Army Reserve, the Army Emergency Reserve, or the Territorial Army. The first is, as its name implies, composed of men who have finished their periods of service as full-time soldiers, but whose terms of engagement include a reserve obligation of some years. The Army Emergency Reserve consists of volunteer civilians who are specialists in certain skills and whose chief purpose is to supplement the administrative services of the regular army. Thus some members of the reserve Port Task Force are AER men, though most are in the Territorial Army, which is also essentially a volunteer force, although it does still include on paper some conscripts fulfilling a National Service obligation. Each of these organizations include some groups who can be called out without a Royal Proclamation ordering defence against an actual or apprehended attack on the United Kingdom. Thus those in Section A of the Regular Army Reserve, which is composed of those who have left the army in the previous twelve months together with other ex-soldiers who volunteer, and which has a maximum permitted strength of 45,000, are liable without a proclamation as are the several thousand reservists in the AER Class I. Up to 1962 the government needed a proclamation to embody any part of the Territorial Army, but since then the TA has included a force of 'Ever Readies' who are fully efficient soldiers who must be always instantly available to reinforce, as individuals, troops overseas. A ceiling of 15,000 has been fixed for this category and by the end of 1962 4,000 applications had been received.

All the metropolitan air force is in principle available to be directed overseas and, as indicated below, parts of it are frequently exercised to this end. However, among the RAF groups based in the United Kingdom No. 38 is of special significance, since this was reconstituted in 1960 to work in close conjunction with the advance guard of the Strategic

Reserve. It includes two squadrons of ground-attack fighters, two of helicopters, and one of light aircraft. It also has some *Beverley* tactical transports and is getting some *Argosies.*

Some of the men of the 12,000-strong Royal Naval Reserve man the several RNR squadrons of coastal minesweepers. Rather over 100 minesweepers and about a score of coastal craft are kept 'mothballed' in the Reserve Fleet. Of these six coastal minesweepers are at Aden. Various ships in other classes are also kept in a state of preservation. The purpose is to keep the operational fleet up to strength and to provide it, in emergency, with additional afloat support.

There may well be increasing speculation over the years ahead about whether it is worth while to keep in being large non-regular reserve forces. They would be of a certain amount of value in general war, but some of them at least are superfluous to any limited war contingencies that can reasonably be envisaged. It can also be argued that in so far as recruitment to them is voluntary they provide a way of experiencing many of the pleasures of service life without encountering any of the drawbacks and to that extent tend to undermine regular recruitment. Also, of course, all such forces in Britain and the United States are strategic reserves if we are thinking in terms of limited operations, and so there is little point in keeping them unless an expensive airlift capacity is provided as well.

All the same, there is not much doubt about their comparative cheapness reckoned on a simple actuarial basis. In the 1962 fiscal year the United States federal government spent $860,000,000 on the upkeep of the thirty-seven reserve divisions, including the two called to active duty during the Berlin crisis, and $108,000,000 on new equipment for them, whereas it spent $4,550,000,000 on the upkeep of the sixteen divisions and ancillary units of the regular Army and $2,390,000,000 on their procurements. During the same twelve months a high percentage of the 55,000 men in the Air Reserve Forces were on active duty and so upkeep comparisons between them and the regulars are not very meaningful. Nevertheless it is worth noting large differences in procurement costs per head which reflect the fact that, as in the case with the Army reserves, a great deal of ARF equipment consist of items which have been handed down from regular squadrons. The ARF had $59,000,000 spent on new aircraft and $15,000,000 on other kinds of equipment. The 880,000 regulars in the USAF absorbed over $3,700,000,000 of the American taxpayer's money on new aeroplanes alone.

In this day and age, however, any discussion about the usefulness of fighting formations must revolve around the question of how soon they can become combat ready. The answer is generally fairly obvious with air force units, but is less so in the case of army ones, for the simple reason that the potential fighting ability of an infantryman is harder to determine than that of a pilot. Some would contend that no reservists could possibly become ready for operations against a first-class army until they had completed a 'refresher course' of full-time training, just because they will not have had the repetitive indoctrination necessary to assure that they will be able to carry out certain key operations semi-automatically in situations of acute stress. The Swiss and the Danes, on the other hand, can call nearly all their reservists to active duty within twenty-four hours and regard the units as combat ready as soon as they have assembled. It must be remembered that these claims have never been put to the acid test of war and also that citizen armies are not the same thing as strategic reserves, but it is significant that the Swiss and Danish authorities feel able to advance these claims at all.

A crucial point is that the concept of preparedness must be related to the use to which the troops are liable to be put. If they are intended to hold static defensive positions they will not require such elaborate training as if they were required to engage in more mobile and aggressive warfare. Some commentators have suggested that if we ever decide to plan a purely conventional defence of Western Germany it should be arranged on the basis of having unmechanized brigades or divisions dug in the forward areas to act as blocks that would divert enemy thrusts into channels in which they would become vulnerable to counter-attacks from highly mobile formations poised in the rear.

The reaction times envisaged in the latest American army reserve plans are rather slow, but this is more a reflection of what the United States Administration thinks is necessary than of what it regards as practicable. Mr. McNamara has, in fact, said that they originally contemplated getting two divisions on to a three-week availability, but were persuaded that the build-up of the full-time Army rendered this superfluous. No comparable statistics have been published for the British Territorial Army, but it must be assumed that its state of readiness is much lowered by the fact that, with the end of National Service, it will include a progressively higher proportion of young men who will never have done more than two weeks' continuous training, whereas a minimum of twelve months is generally considered necessary for the production of a fully trained soldier. Added to this is the legal complication, referred to above, that no Territorial unit can be called up without a Royal Proclamation.

Germany has been mentioned several times in the course of this discussion and this reflects the fact that for some time past the reinforcement of the NATO armies in that country has been regarded as the most important task British and American reserve forces might be dispatched abroad for. This preoccupation will probably grow stronger, partly because more conventional forces will be required in Central Europe if, as is likely, inhibitions against the use of tactical nuclear weapons increase. But it will be partly because the experience and the equipment that reservists will have will come to be regarded as only suitable for temperate lowland areas when the requirements of tropical or mountain warfare become closely linked to air mobility.

Chapter 4

Our Recent Experience

I—SUEZ

THE Defence White Paper of 1957 revealed major changes of emphasis in British strategic planning, for it announced the abolition of conscription and the allocation of the resources thus released to building up the independent thermonuclear deterrent and the creation of mobile non-nuclear regular forces. In the United States different conclusions were drawn by most observers about the desirability or even the feasibility of any further large-scale military actions by Britain or France, acting upon their own initiative, and about the desirability of these countries keeping strategic striking forces in being in order to underwrite such operations. Nevertheless, the point about the need for more mobility was fully taken and the Suez campaign was an important part of the background to all the agitation for larger airlifts and more streamlined strategic reserves that made up a good proportion of the American defence debate in the subsequent four or five years. In the history of the Suez operation there is a wealth of evidence about the nature of mid-twentieth-century limited war, and about the way in which its aims and methods are governed by a complex of military and political factors. However, the biggest single lesson that emerges is that mobile forces that are large enough to cope with any likely contingency must be kept in being, and that they must be capable of being deployed with speed and flexibility.

It was necessary that any military action following the Egyptian nationalization of the canal in July 1956 should be swift and sure. The longer the agony was drawn out the more time world opinion would have to mobilize against the British and the French, the more time the Egyptians would have to block the canal, and take reprisals against the many Anglo-French nationals still in their country or against the enormous British stockpiles and military installations located in the Canal Zone. The threat, which of course materialized, to the waterway itself was rendered the more potent by the fact that Western Europe's reserves of oil were equivalent to three or four weeks' normal consumption.

The British and French governments did not have at their disposal enough forces of the required kind to intervene immediately the crisis broke. They spent several months building up their strength, and meanwhile trying to seize the diplomatic initiative. They eventually mustered forces whose order of battle looked impressive, but which were only capable of launching an amphibious assault in a slow and ponderous manner, and against an Egyptian defence already hard pressed by Israel. Even this assembly of strength had constituted a desperate race against time and particularly against the Egyptian build-up of Soviet arms. By November a third of her 750 tanks and track-mounted guns and nearly two-thirds of the 250 jet aircraft were of Soviet origin.[1] Egyptians still almost totally lacked experience in handling Russian equipment, but they would soon have been trained on its use by the rapidly expanding Soviet military mission. The mission itself might have been formed into operational units. As it was, London suspected that the skilful interceptions of reconnaissance overflights that took place on October 29th had been carried out by Soviet pilots.[2] An even more immediate factor that the planners had to bear in mind was the end of the American Presidential elections on November 6th. Climate was another, for conditions in the Eastern Mediterranean during the winter are often very unsuitable for amphibious operations. As it was, the margin left was desperately fine. One well-informed opinion has been offered to the effect that a freshening north-easterly breeze would have rendered the landings hazardous eight hours later and impossible if attempted the following day.[3]

After some equivocation the Libyan government finally vetoed, on November 4th, any movement of the British 10th Armoured Division out of their country against Egypt. A landing at Alexandria would have raised political complications by

---

[1] Edgar O'Ballance, *The Sinai Campaign* (London, Faber & Faber, 1959; New York, Praeger, 1959), Chapter II

[2] Anthony Eden, *Full Circle* (London, Cassell, 1960), p. 254

[3] Bernard Fergusson, *The Watery Maze* (London, Collins, 1961), Chapter XVI

virtue of the vast local population and the recurrent visits of ships of the 6th Fleet. The only other possible point of application was Port Said, which was devoid of cranes or furnished quays and which was connected to the mainland by a twin road causeway twenty-five miles long. The prospective opposition chiefly consisted of two divisions east of the canal and two more, plus an armoured brigade, west of it. There was also an irregular National Guard whose 50,000 men were mainly in Sinai and a 3,000-strong Frontier Force. In addition to items already listed the Egyptian armoury included 200 field and anti-tank guns and at least as many anti-aircraft pieces as well as hundreds of armoured personnel carriers.[1]

It was early in August that an Anglo-French command in London began preparations for any hostilities that might take place. Twenty thousand reservists were recalled in Britain following a Royal Proclamation on August 2nd. Resentment among these men at being kept 'hanging around' sparked off criticism of the government for calling them up, but some did use their skills and experience during the landing, notably in the Port Task Force that was improvised. Some landing craft being used by private firms were requisitioned as were some merchant ships, including the 20,000-ton emigrant liner *New Australia*. Other warships were taken out of reserve, troopships diverted, and aircraft operators asked to earmark capacity. Likewise the French government commandeered over fifty merchant ships for varying periods. They included some nine tankers that were fitted out as water-bowzers lest the Port Said waterworks was immobilized. The French, like the British, had been using their paratroops for internal security and the men needed a fortnight's refresher course in jumping. All in all, it was not until mid-September that the joint command felt ready for a large-scale triphibious operations.

International negotiations broke down on the issue of whether Egyptian ownership of the canal was to be regarded as a *fait accompli*, and on September 12th Britain and France announced the formation of the User's Association to collect transit dues. The United States acceded, but, unlike Britain and France, explicitly ruled out an ultimate resort to force.

[1] Edgar O'Ballance, *The Sinai Campaign* (London, Faber & Faber, 1959; New York, Praeger, 1959), Chapter II

Meanwhile, Israel was getting acutely frightened. The only worthwhile response to the mounting Arab guerilla campaign was occasional 'massive' retaliation, and yet the Israeli army of 12,000, although able to expand to 100,000 men and women in twelve hours and 250,000 in two days, was in immediate danger of being overtaken in power by the Egyptians.[1] For instance, Israel had some 400 field guns and about as many tanks, which were enough to match the existing Egyptian strength in those categories, but which would soon have been dwarfed had the Egyptians long maintained their current rate of expansion.[1] In any case the Israeli Air Force had not the numbers of planes or depth of airspace to protect her cities and, at the same time, adequately support her armies.

All the same, Mr. Ben Gurion was determined not to involve his country in an anti-Arab tripartite alliance. He publicly approved of the act of nationalization in July and then defied Britain again in early October by launching a retaliatory raid against Jordan. Although during September and October the Israelis were carrying on staff discussions with the French and were accepting *Mystère* fighters, they were hoping that when they struck the only direct help they would get would be a guarantee of air protection. They did not want a seaborne landing.

The meeting of British and French premiers and foreign secretaries on October 16th took place against the background of an impending Israeli attack. A secret mobilization began as soon as an Egyptian-Syrian-Jordanian joint command was formed on October 25th after the pro-Nasser swing in the Jordan elections on the 21st.[2] Though complete tactical surprise of the Egyptians was to be achieved on the 29th the mobilization was reported to the British government as soon as it started and was noticed, too, by the Americans, who started evacuating nationals from Alexandria on the 28th.[2] Meanwhile the French forces in the Western Mediterranean were putting to sea.[3] However, the British government was most anxious to

[1] Edgar O'Balance, *The Sinai Campaign* (London, Faber & Faber, 1959; New York, Praeger, 1959), Chapter II

[2] Merry and Serge Bromberger, *Secrets of Suez* (London, Pan Books and Sidgwick and Jackson, 1957), p. 191

[3] *Ibid.*, p. 64

avoid creating an impression of direct collusion with Israel. Therefore, there is no reason to doubt the statement that the British units in Malta had no notice of the twelve-hour ultimatum sent to Egypt and Israel on the 30th telling them each to pull back ten miles from the canal and allow the joint task force to occupy positions in the buffer zone.

The Egyptians had disposed themselves in the Sinai on the assumption that they would only have to fight on one front. Several brigades with stockpiles that included 7,000 tons of munitions lay dug in across the metalled north coast road in the Rafa-Gaza sector. Their immediate flank was guarded by the fortifications of Abu Agweiba, but the line southward was thinly held. It was expected that the air force together with mobile army reserves from the Delta would be able to intercept and smash any enveloping movement. However, the threat of the amphibious landings deterred the Egyptians from sending more than their armoured brigade, which numbered 10,000 men and 200 tanks, east of Suez and induced them to order the withdrawal of many of the troops already forward of the canal. Meanwhile, the Anglo-French air offensive made it at first seemingly inadvisable and then utterly impossible to fight for aerial control of the Sinai. Also, sixty French *Mystère* pilots and their planes arrived in Israel on October 28th and, in conjunction with the Israeli squadrons, they soon began devastating Egyptian mechanized columns with guns, rockets, and napalm.[1] The heavy French naval bombardment of Rafa, which was just behind the Gaza strip and which was crammed with 200,000 Palestinian refugees, obviously helped bring about the surrender of that centre. Another form of assistance was that rendered by the French transport planes that, flying from Cyprus, dropped supplies to combat formations and, in particular, to the parachute battalion that from the evening of the 29th held the nodal Mitla Pass forty miles east of Port Suez.[2] Permeating all these tactical and strategical effects of the intervention of two major industrial and imperial powers was its psychological impact. But for it Egyptian morale would surely have been much higher. As it was, determined resistance was

[1] Erskine Childers, *The Road to Suez* (London, MacGibbon & Kee, 1962), pp. 242, 295
[2] *Ibid*, p. 243, and Brombergers, *op. cit.*, pp. 71, 87

offered in places and, had this been rather more universal and sustained, the Israeli attack might have collapsed ignominiously. Their 5,000 vehicles were so unsuited to the poor desert tracks that during a mere five days' fighting 2,000 of them broke down beyond immediate repair.[1]

The British and French forces included seven carriers and battleships, sixty Landing Ships Tank and Landing Craft Tanks, five hundred aircraft, and four divisions, one of which remained in reserve in Britain, and two independent brigades of troops and marines. Some RAF bombers were based on Malta, but the rest, together with five squadrons of strike aircraft plus all the airborne assault planes, were crammed into three airfields in Cyprus that remained very inadequate in spite of the extensive reconstruction of that summer.[2] Cyprus was very deficient in port facilities and so the British half of the invasion fleet had to proceed at a steady ten knots from Malta whilst the French came in from various points west. As each steamed east the planes, submerged submarines, and ships of the 6th Fleet caused them much inconvenience.

Allied aerial operations began ninety minutes after the ultimatum had been rejected. At first the emphasis was on the elimination by bombing of air opposition and preventing blockships being sunk in the canal. By November 2nd it was clear that the first aim had been attained and the latter frustrated. Henceforward, the main object was to isolate Port Said from reinforcements, especially of armour, and the subsidiary one, which was easily accomplished, was the immobilization of Cairo Radio. Although the Egyptian anti-aircraft shooting steadily improved, it was not much of a deterrent. The one hundred and fifty planes of the Fleet Air Arm flew 1,600 sorties and only two were lost.[3] The RAF bombers operated above the 'flak', but they ceased operations on the 4th for lack of appropriate targets.

On the morning of the 5th a battalion of British paratroops landed on Gamil airfield west of Port Said, whilst two French

[1] O'Ballance, op. cit., Chapter III
[2] C-in-C's Dispatch. Published as a supplement to the London Gazette, 10.9.57
[3] Bernard Fergusson, The Watery Maze (London, Collins, 1961), Chapter XVI

ones secured the waterworks and a key bridge over the canal south of the town. Above them a 'cab-rank' of strike aircraft responded to support requests with swiftness and efficiency. The Egyptian garrison of about 4,000 men resisted stubbornly for some hours, but in the afternoon the Governor surrendered, although that night his decision was overruled by Cairo.

Around dawn the next day two British and two French battalions with tank support landed at Port Said and Port Fuad respectively. The leading British LVTs touched down on a 600-yard front immediately after a forty-five minute naval bombardment, which had been reduced drastically as compared with the original fireplan in order to minimize civilian casualties.[1] As they did so the first of twenty-two helicopters touched down near the pier to begin a vertical envelopment in which 400 men were landed in ninety minutes.[1] The Egyptian army fought back fiercely, but within six hours a link with the French at the waterworks had been made and within twelve systematic resistance had ceased. A race down the causeway and beyond then began, and when a general cease fire was announced nineteen hours after the seaborne forces had landed El Qantara, which was twenty-five miles south of Port Said, had been reached.

Local military opinion and the French higher command had expected Suez to be reached the next day, but the British War Office had thought five more days would be needed. This last figure would have made the whole operation take twelve days, which was the figure given in the original planning estimates. Lord Avon (then Sir Anthony Eden) has stressed that it might have needed more time.[2] It is a moot point whether effective control over the whole waterway could ever have been established at all. Thousands of Egyptian soldiers coming out of the Sinai were merging with the 400,000 or so civilians of the Canal Zone, many of whom, like hundreds of thousands of their compatriots elsewhere in the country, had been given arms by the government in the previous few days. Even in 1954 the British forces tied down in anti-guerilla operations in this very area had numbered 80,000.

[1] C-in-C's Dispatch. Published as a supplement to the *London Gazette*, 10.9.57
[2] Anthony Eden, *Full Circle* (London, Cassell, 1960), p. 254

In many ways the British and French behaviour during their intervention was marked by a commendable circumspection and restraint. Clear radio warnings preceded attacks on airfields and firm guarantees were always given before strikes against land forces that civilians and their property would not be molested. It is absurd to imply that the calm that prevailed in Cairo and elsewhere just betokened a simple willingness on the part of the people to martyr themselves and was in no way due to their accumulated respect for British assurances.[1] The fact that the Egyptian army respected such assurances is demonstrated by the way it scattered itself among the populace as much as possible.[2] Similarly, although it must be acknowledged that the British official estimate of the number of civilian casualties in Port Said as being 650 is probably several times too low, the reduction of the naval bombardment undoubtedly saved many Egyptian lives by putting some Allied ones in jeopardy.

On the other hand, certain aspects of the record show that at that time many senior officers still had a lot to learn about the controlled use of force for specific and limited political ends. For example, an absolute prerequisite for such action is a good communications system. In fact, on the critical day of November 6th a very bad one existed. Links were bad between the task force commander and his deputy and between them and Cyprus, Paris, London, and the front line. This particular source of a 'fog of war' could have been eliminated if a well-equipped combined tactical headquarters had been established ashore during the late morning in place of a British one on an 11,000-ton depot ship and a French one on a 3,000-ton depot ship.[3] Better radio links would also have given newspaper correspondents a fair chance of sending copy out. This might in part have compensated for the way they had languished in Cyprus, under a censorship wholly inconsistent with the honourable conduct of a 'police operation'.[4] The propaganda services in Cyprus were also guilty, in the opinion of the writer,

---

[1] As does Erskine Childers, *op. cit.*, p. 265
[2] *ibid.* pp. 242, 295
[3] Brombergers, *op. cit.*, p. 169
[4] Paul Johnson, *The Suez War* (London, MacGibbon & Kee, 1957), pp. 112–13

of a gross lapse of judgement when they decided to shower Egypt with leaflets depicting scenes like Colonel Nasser cowering in a trench whilst swarms of bombers came screaming overhead. Such wild nonsense displayed a thoroughly unchivalrous attitude towards a leader whose physical courage had been amply demonstrated at Falluja and elsewhere and it achieved nothing. In any case it was in conflict with the claim that our war aims were limited and did not include a political reconstruction of Egypt.

The cease fire on November 6th ended prematurely a campaign on which the British taxpayers alone had spent at least £100,000,000.[1] Some would claim that Bulganin's notes of the night of the 5th threatening by direct implication the use of strategic rockets was a prime cause of the cease fire. However, these notes were not sent until it had become practically certain that the Soviet Union would never have to implement such a threat. The basic fact was that world opinion rapidly mobilized behind Egypt. One consequence of this was a flight of capital from Britain that was so fast that within a few days a devaluation of the pound would have been inevitable. Another was that the United Nations evolved a Middle East policy more positive than anything it had possessed hitherto. Twenty-five hours after the Israeli attack began the Security Council met to consider a United States resolution urging her to refrain from using force. Early on November 2nd, after the Security Council had been blocked by an Anglo-French veto, an emergency meeting of the General Assembly voted for an immediate cease fire. That same day Mr. Lester Pearson of Canada suggested that a United Nations peace force should be established and on the 4th the Assembly decided by 57 votes to nil to instruct the Secretary-General to produce a report on how this should be done. Two were submitted and they said that no great powers should contribute to the force, that the Secretary-General should be allowed a certain discretion in deciding its actions, that it should operate in no country without that country's consent, that it should be immune from local criminal law proceedings, that a contributing nation should only have to find money for the equipment and salaries of its troops, and that

[1] Eden, *op. cit.*, p. 556

units in the force should only fire in self-defence. The second report was adopted by 64 votes to nil at 7 p.m. Eastern Standard Time on the 7th. Meanwhile, four countries had offered troops on the 4th, three on the 5th, and five on the 6th. The number of nations who had made such an offer eventually rose to twenty-five.

As far as the question of mobility is concerned, the most interesting aspect of the story after the Anglo-French cease fire was the rapid organization and dispatch of the United Nations police force. At 10 p.m. on the 8th the Secretary-General, Mr. Dag Hammarskjold, was ready to ask the Italians for air staging facilities. The following morning he was offered Capodichino and on the next day soldiers started landing there in American aircraft. All troops were asked to bring with them sidearms, tents, and ten days' supplies. Millions of dollars worth of 'C' rations from American stores in Leghorn, Metz, and Dreux were purchased, and from Leghorn came also some helmet liners to serve as distinctive United Nations headgear. Tons of sky-blue paint were purchased from the British and French in Port Said. One spot of bother was caused by one contingent which turned up with wooden prefabricated dwelling units instead of tents. A more serious one arose out of Egypt's refusal to admit the Queen's Own Rifles of Canada, who had already paraded and embarked, because of their outward resemblance to British troops. Nevertheless, Egypt gave permission for the rest of the force to enter on November 12th and on the 14th an advance party of ten men arrived at Port Said. The following day Swiss aircraft, chartered by the Swiss government at their own expense, began landing the main force at Abu Suweir.[1]

In 1957 the United Nations Emergency Force patrolling the Egyptian side of the armistice line with Israel numbered 6,000 men from ten countries. Since 1959 there have been 5,000 from seven countries. In 1962 these were (in decreasing order of the magnitude of their contributions) India, Canada, Yugoslavia, Brazil, Norway, Denmark, and Sweden.[2] In January 1962 it

---

[1] W. R. Frye, *A United Nations Peace Force* (New York, Oceana Publications Inc., 1957), Chapter III
[2] *The Times*, January 1, 1962

was costing the United Nations about $1,500,000 a month.[1] A special fund had been established to meet this expense and thirty-four countries had paid their full contribution for 1961 by the end of that year. No Soviet Bloc state was giving any financial assistance. Since 1956 the volume of frontier incidents has been much reduced, but it is uncertain as to what extent this is an effect of rather than the cause of the continued presence of the UNEF.

II—LEBANON

Before 1956 Lebanese politics were reminiscent of those of the Italian Renaissance. The President had large executive power, but his position was in practice heavily dependent on the continuous support of the most important of various groups of merchant bankers, urban commercial potentates, and rural feudal leaders. The perquisites of office were divided according to a 1943 formula between the various communities with the Maronite Christians commanding the lion's share.

However, in the year after Suez this unstable equilibrium was exposed to new stresses. Against a background of a progressive Moslem erosion of Christian supremacy, in terms of total numbers and of political experience, the Sunni Moslems of the big cities became increasingly opposed to the pro-Western policy of President Chamoun, symbolized by his acceptance of the Eisenhower doctrine, the signing of a United States/Lebanon defence agreement, and the presence in Beirut of part of the 6th Fleet during the Jordan purge of the spring of 1957. Shortly afterwards a bitter election campaign was waged in the Lebanon at the height of which the opposition staged an armed riot in protest against the rejection of their demand for a caretaker government to ensure an impartial conduct of the poll. The elections themselves passed off peacefully and produced a strong majority of 'loyalist' deputies, but this in turn gave rise to a 'National Front' alliance of frustrated opposition deputies united in their determination that President Chamoun should resign when his first term of office came to an end in 1958.

A resurgence of tension occurred early that year when some

[1] Alan James, in *The World Today*, September 1962

of Chamoun's parliamentary supporters tabled a motion enabling him to stand for a second term. Then on May 8th, ten
days before this motion was due to be debated, a journalist
working for an opposition newspaper was assassinated and
within three days strikes had been called and barricades erected
in the opposition-dominated areas of Beirut, Sidon, and Tripoli.
Fighting broke out in these towns and in many other localities
also and, although the facts are obscure partly because of the
existence of a tight government censorship, it seems that in the
course of the next ten days several hundred people were killed
or injured. During this period the rebels held their urban
strongholds and established control over wide areas of the
interior and, to all intents and purposes, this territorial balance
between themselves and the government was preserved
throughout the summer. The government claimed that rebel
strength was due to an infiltration of arms, money, and men
across the Syrian border, which it said had been going on ever
since Suez, becoming massive in recent months. It was stated
that 500 armed men had been involved in one attack on a
frontier post. In the second week in May it was announced
that the United States was stepping up arms supplies to the
Lebanese government and that eighteen *Globemasters* were
being dispatched to Germany against the possibility of having
to evacuate the 2,500 American nationals residing in the
Lebanon. It was also announced that an extra seaborne
Battalion Landing Team was being dispatched to the Mediterranean, but official circles in Washington were at pains to
emphasize that this was in no way connected with the Lebanese
situation. Then on May 19th the news came that a NATO
exercise scheduled to take place in the western basin of the
Mediterranean would now be transferred to the eastern
basin.

On May 27th the Beirut administration gave an assurance
that President Chamoun would not seek re-election, but by
this time the rebel attitude had hardened and they were now
demanding his immediate resignation. Consequently tension
persisted into June, but the outbreaks of fighting were now
more sporadic. The most serious incident of the month occurred on the 26th and 27th, when a rebel attack in Tripoli,
supported by machine-gun fire and grenades, was repelled with

the aid of artillery, about a hundred houses being destroyed. Meanwhile, after an attempt by the Arab League to formulate a positive attitude towards the crisis had failed, a discussion began in the Security Council which resulted on June 11th in a decision, which neither the Lebanon nor the United Arab Republic opposed, to dispatch a United Nations Observation Group. The advance echelon of the servicing element, which was recruited from the staff of the United Nations Truce Supervision Organization in Palestine arrived in the Lebanon the following day. A month later there were 135 observers on duty, including forty-four from Scandinavia, fifteen from Italy, ten each from the Netherlands and Canada, nine from India, and smaller numbers from Burma, Chile, Ireland, New Zealand and Peru respectively. They were maintaining road patrols by means of jeeps using two-way radios, ten fixed wireless and observation posts in strategic positions, and a headquarters unit that included a specialist evaluation unit. Aerial reconnaissance was also being used.

The reduction in the number of incidents in June may well have been largely due to the presence of the observers, but it cannot be claimed that the group succeeded in its more specific aim of establishing the truth about the alleged infiltrations. The first observer group report, published on the 4th July, reveals that of the 278 kilometres of frontier between Syria and the Lebanon only a sector 18 kilometres wide across the Beirut–Damascus road was in government hands. The opposition very frequently prevented access to remaining sectors. Nevertheless the observers saw armed opposition gangs up to 200 strong and saw much evidence of the mining of roads, but obtained no conclusive proof of mass infiltration of men or arms. As soon as the report came out it was fiercely attacked by the Chamoun authorities, who asserted that European observers were not competent to determine the countries of origin of Arabs and that, in fact, at that moment, 3,000 armed United Arab Republic citizens were operating within Lebanese borders. They also said that the number of arms smuggled in now totalled 36,000. If this last figure was anything like correct, one might have expected some identifiable Czech-, Soviet-, or Egyptian-produced equipment to be among the arms the group discovered and examined, but this was not the case.

Nevertheless it would be naïve to assume that the United Arab Republic was subject to powerful moral inhibitions against conducting indirect aggression against her sister state the Lebanon. In any case such a degree of inter-communal tension was prevalent that any violence, whatever its instigation, was liable to escalate into full-scale civil war which neither side could hope to win unaided and which would destroy any hope of a fair and realistic compromise solution. What is more the efficacy of the army and air force as aids to the civil power was very dubious. The air arm was being used for various kinds of internal security operations including the occasional combat strike, but it was obviously not a wholly appropriate instrument for curbing irregular warfare in country that was quite well forested and quite heavily populated. The army numbered about 6,000 men organized as several infantry battalions with a little artillery support. It was not large enough to seal the border and to reduce rebel forces estimated by the government at 12,000 men. Even if such operational limitations had not existed the Chamoun régime would still not have been able to use the military to crush the insurgents, for the simple reason that the army was not prepared to obey unconditionally the orders of those who were supposed to be its political chiefs.

It was in the light of these circumstances that President Chamoun requested American intervention at midday on the 14th of July shortly after he heard of the revolution in Bagdad. At that time, of the three Battalion Landing Teams at sea with the 6th Fleet, one was near Malta and homeward bound, one to the north of Crete, and one on station about twelve hours' sailing time from Beirut. However, the last mentioned BLT lacked its Landing Ship Dock which contained its Marine Shore Party and Naval Beach Group. Furthermore it was not allowed to use the most suitable beach just north of Beirut to land on, because egress from it was through areas of intensive cultivation. The beach exclusively employed at first—which was labelled Red Beach—was of significantly worse quality than aerial photography and intelligence handbooks had led the task force commander to expect. It had very soft sand which few wheeled vehicles could negotiate, whilst a few hundred yards out to sea lay a formidable sand-bar. Nevertheless the 'assault wave' of BLT 2/2 touched down at 3 p.m. on the 15th local time and one hour later forward elements had secured Beirut airport.

At 4 a.m. on the 16th BLT 3/6 which had arrived from the Crete area, started coming ashore and soon relieved BLT 2/2 at the airport, thus enabling it to take over the Beirut port area. The direct road between the airfield and the harbour was dominated by rebel posts and General Chehab at first advised the Americans to adopt a much more circuitous route that would, in fact, have retarded their movements by twenty-four hours. Eventually, however, he agreed to head a long mechanized column of Marines advancing down the road as an ordinary military convoy and by 3 p.m. on the 16th the required port facilities had been occupied. Two days later Yellow Beach was open for off-loading. This was only 200 yards wide and nowhere more than 75 yards deep, but at least it had a firm surface. The same day, Marine Corps aircraft flew in advance elements of BLT 2/8 from the United States and munitions for them from the base at Port Lyantey in Morocco. The following day Military Air Transportation Service and USAF planes staging through Adana delivered the first of 2,000 men of the 24th Airborne Brigade. Initially the soldiers deployed into olive groves near Beirut to form a central reserve. Their 'seatail' began disembarking on the 22nd July and by the 27th 8,000 soldiers and 6,000 marines were in the beachhead, along with 10,000 to 20,000 tons of stores and equipment. The total sealift involved about twenty MSTS and chartered ships, some of which had to stand off for a couple of days or so before obtaining berths in the congested port of Beirut. However, thousands of Lebanese dockers rendered idle by the decline in civilian traffic induced by the crisis were available to aid military personnel in the swift unloading of cargo once a ship had been docked.

It has been revealed that the total weight of stores and equipment within the beachhead at the peak period was nigh on 50,000 tons—a figure which presumably included the reserves of petrol, oil, lubricants and building materials all of which were obtained locally. While the build-up in the Lebanon was continuing, a 'pentomic' battle group of 5,000 men was flown into Adana and held there under the control of the task force commander. Meanwhile, about fifty ships of the 6th Fleet, among them an attack carrier, two cruisers, and twenty-eight destroyers, manoeuvred near the coast and aircraft from the carrier and Turkey reconnoitred, maintained standing air patrols, and launched leaflet raids over all parts of the Lebanon. The first stage in the withdrawal began when BLT 2/2 became a task force floating reserve in mid-August, but the first overall reduction of force levels in the Eastern Mediterranean occurred when two battalion landing teams left for the United States in September. The withdrawals of army units began on October 10th and the evacuation was finally completed on the 25th.

Seven hours after the first Marines had set foot on Lebanese soil on July 15th a formation of twelve F-8os left Langley, Virginia, for Adana as the first wave of a Composite Air Strike Force. Despite the facts that the route had never been exercised and that Morocco and Greece refused over-flight facilities, four of the planes reached Adana at 11.25 p.m. on the 16th and became operational two hours later. Heavy thunderstorms, radio failures, and planning errors caused the remainder to miss the first refuelling rendezvous north of Bermuda and three of the fighters landed in Nova Scotia and five in the Azores, though very marginal weather conditions prevailed in both places. The four luckier ones had another difficult rendezvous near the Azores because of unexpectedly high winds and associated sand and turbulence.

Although it had been developed and prestocked with supplies under a NATO infrastructure programme, Adana airfield soon became seriously congested. Planes '. . . were parked nose to tail and wing to wing at odd angles on every foot of concrete and on the sunbaked plain alongside the railways'.[1] Flight crews and paratroops slept alongside or under aircraft surrounded by piles of ammunition and maintenance equipment. Water, food, and even compressed oxygen became short as the number of American personnel on the station rose rapidly from a pre-crisis total of 300 to 5,000. On the 17th some transports had to be flown out to make way for B-66 reconnaissance bombers coming in.

The smoothness of the operation during both its entry and exit phases was, under all the circumstances, an impressive

[1] Leverett G. Richards, *Tactical Air Command* (New York, John Day Co., 1961) Chapter X.

demonstration of American business efficiency. Nevertheless, room was left for substantial improvement in several important practical matters. For instance, poor health discipline was responsible for an unduly high incidence of dysentery among the ground forces. Negotiations with the local military and civilians were severely impeded by language difficulties despite the fact that the Lebanon is a state in which English, and of course French, is spoken much more generally than is normal across the Middle East. Language difficulties coupled with an ignorance of Lebanese commercial law hampered negotiations over the lease of storage space. One consequence of this was a serious congestion in the vast fuel and ammunition dumps. Also the Logistic Support Group employed was a pure improvisation, being composed of men seconded from battalion landing teams reinforced by headquarters staff flown in from the United States.

The beachhead established was 20 kilometres wide and 15 deep. The deployment of forces with it was in the form of a ring of independent tank and infantry posts served by a main line of communication that was under constant surveillance. General Chehab was obviously apprehensive at first about the implications of the intervention, but once it was made clear that the American tactical posture was to be such as in no way to betoken occupation of the area, he became willing to co-operate to some extent with the United States commander. A few joint patrols were maintained and each American battalion had a Lebanese liaison officer attached. The task force personnel had strict instructions not to open fire unless shot at from a clearly identifiable source, and in fact, apart from a bit of harmless wild-cat shooting near American positions, no violent clashes occurred in spite of reconnaissance by small mechanized patrols far beyond the beachhead. Furthermore the reception that the Americans got, individually and collectively, from the civilian population was very friendly, and after the first fortnight about 2,000 men were on leave in Beirut each day.

In the light of subsequent events it is on the whole fair to claim that the American presence had a stabilizing influence on the political situation. At the end of August General Chehab became President-elect, since he was the man most acceptable to all factions, and with his assumption of office the following month some of the old sources of communal jealousy and mistrust began to weaken somewhat. The archaic 1943 formula for the distribution of the spoils of office still survives, but in the Lebanon today relatively constructive and objective ideological disputes are playing a rather greater part in political life and traditional sectarian attitudes rather less. The Prime Minister and his Cabinet have acquired more real policy-making power, thus partially detaching the President from involvement in day-to-day politics. Also the army is enjoying an enhanced prestige as a symbol of, and a seminary for, a genuine national consciousness. The revolt led by a small group of soldiers at the end of 1961 was easily suppressed, but this revolt, and the confiscation of 600 small arms in the search of Beirut that followed, does, of course, show that the new spirit of harmony is still only skin deep. However, the longer the harmony survives without serious interruption the more genuine it is likely to become.

In evaluating the net results of the intervention one must take into account the large volume of real and simulated suspicion and hostility it evoked in many parts of the world, coinciding as it did with the movement of 2,000 British troops to Jordan. The Soviet government soon announced that large-scale manoeuvres had been taking place since July 7th in Transcaucasia and Turkmenistan. On July 18th about 75,000 people demonstrated outside the American and British embassies in Moscow and on the 19th Peking radio claimed that 2,000,000 had joined a similar demonstration in that city. In diplomatic exchanges and Security Council debates, the Soviet Union contended that the main purpose of the operation was to secure a springboard for the invasion of Iraq. However, it was the United States that requested a Security Council debate and it was the Americans who sponsored a resolution urging the replacement of their troops by United Nations forces. This would have been carried but for the Soviet veto. Nevertheless the United States policy was heavily criticized in the Council by Sweden as well as by Russia. The Swedish delegate denied that intervention in this instance was justifiable under Article 51 of the Charter and demanded the withdrawal of the United Nations Observation Group the formation of which had been a Swedish idea. He contended that the conditions for its proper functioning had now been destroyed. Meanwhile the Observation Group itself was severely snubbing American attempts to liaise with it in the field. The Indian government condemned intervention and there was also considerable criticism from radical opinion in Britain.

The strength of the hostile reaction abroad underlines the need to conduct intervention of this kind with the greatest circumspection and restraint. This being the case one feels that the stockpiling by the task force in the Lebanon was excessive. The scale of the logistic build-up was obviously not responsible for the degree of international resentment evoked, since this resentment had waxed and largely waned before the build-up really got going. Nevertheless, had the Middle East situation taken a graver turn than in fact it did during that summer, the Russian accusation that the Americans were preparing a base from which to attack Syria and then Iraq might have gained a very wide and sympathetic hearing. Furthermore the Russians might have become convinced of it themselves and acted accordingly. The most important moral of the Lebanon emergency of 1958 is that the armed services must always be restrained from inflating small-scale precautionary moves into full-blown mobility exercises.

III—THE CONGO

Belgium acquired no colonies until the very end of the long era of European expansion and so she had no George Washingtons to teach her at an early date lessons sufficiently sharp to be remembered. Her period of colonial rule was punctuated by two world wars, in each of which she was herself occupied for several years at a time. The Congo basin is quite the most difficult region in Africa to govern and develop. It is not hard to understand why Belgium was not a very constructive imperialist.

All the same the precipitate haste of her withdrawal from the Congo takes a lot of accounting for and, whether it can be accounted for or not, it left behind a situation pregnant with conflict. The nationalist politicians in the newly constituted parliament included a majority party under Patrice Lumumba, who favoured the creation of a unitary socialistic state, and several smaller parties of which the most important were the federalists under Kasavubu and a Leftist group under Gizenga. Outside Leopoldville and Stanleyville no kind of nationalism had any influence before 1960 and tribal loyalties were strong. Also, very few Congolese had been trained in administration or any of the professions.

Such foundations as the new state had were shattered only four days after it became independent on June 30th, 1960, when the 25,000-strong *Force Publique* mutinied against its Belgian officers. Several days of widespread rioting followed, in the course of which many Europeans were assaulted and much European property damaged. Several thousand Belgian troops therefore moved back into the country and re-occupied certain key centres. Thereupon the Congolese government, acting on the advice of President Nkrumah of Ghana, appealed to the United Nations, on July 11th, against Belgian 'aggression'. The previous day they had asked the United Nations for technical assistance in the rehabilitation of the country. At the same time, however, Mr. Lumumba and Mr. Kasavubu were soliciting direct aid from some of the Afro-Asian states and from the Soviet Bloc. Meanwhile tribal fighting was breaking out in many places and the administration of Katanga was claiming that that rich copper-mining province was independent.

It was not until the evening of July 13th that the Security Council met to discuss whether to give the Secretary-General the authority to send troops, and even at that late stage it was by no means certain that the Council would, in fact, do so. Some heavy canvassing of the European members by the Americans and of the Soviet Union by the Africans was necessary in order to ensure that nobody would veto the relevant resolution. This was despite the fact that the resolution explicitly stated that the United Nations was not going to '. . . be a party to or in any way intervene in or be used to influence the outcome of any internal conflicts, constitutional or otherwise'. The principle of non-involvement was further emphasized by Mr. Hammarskjold in the speech with which he opened the debate, in which he argued that it would be unwise to give the United Nations soldiers permission to fire except in self-defence and that contingents should be sought only from countries not politically involved in the situation. In particular he sug-

gested that no non-African member of the Security Council
should send men.

Of course, as during the Suez crisis, Mr. Hammarskjold did
not wait until he had the legal sanction of a Security Council
vote before he started operational planning. On the night of
the 11th July he warned Major-General Van Horn and certain
other officers on the UNEF staff to stand by for Congo service.
The next day he called a meeting of leading delegates of nine
African states and asked that their governments provide police
officers and troops. At the same time he was making other and
more private contacts with Ethiopia and Tunisia—two states
whose African nationalism was of a rather conservative brand
—and made specific requests for two battalions from each of
them. Within several hours Ethiopia had agreed unconditionally and Tunisia had agreed subject to the proviso that
Morocco must contribute also. As soon as he received the reply
from Tunis Mr. Hammarskjold got in contact with the Casa-
blanca government and quickly persuaded them to comply
with the wishes of the Tunisians. That same day Ghana and
Guinea made firm though unsolicited offers and Ghana announced the immediate dispatch of an advanced party of fifty
men under Major-General Alexander, who was a British
officer on secondment. Some friction was occasioned by this
Ghanaian initiative, because the Secretary-General was anxious
that the first units to go on duty should be from French-speak-
ing armies, but on July 15th he formally and unconditionally
accepted the contribution from Accra. Meanwhile the Security
Council resolution had been passed, and as soon as this was
done formal requests for military assistance were communicated
to Guinea, Mali, Morocco, and Tunisia.

On Friday the 18th Tunisian troops began arriving at
Leopoldville in United States Air Force planes and Ethiopian
troops in aircraft belonging to their own national airline. They
were soon followed by Moroccans. Whilst this was going on the
Swedish cabinet was asked if it would permit the redeployment
of the battalion of Swedish troops in Gaza. It said that it would
and the airlift of the men in question began on Thursday the
21st. On the Friday they were followed by police and infantry
from Guinea—whose departure had been delayed by some
United Nations equivocation about what was needed of each

type of unit—and on the Sunday by the first battalion of Irish volunteers. The speed at which the Irish became available was remarkable bearing in mind that theirs was a completely *ad hoc* formation, and that it was not able to leave for foreign service until an amendment to the Irish constitution had been passed. Conversely the Mali contribution was delayed until the beginning of August largely because of resentment on the part of other African states over the participation of several Senegalese units in the Algerian war. Liberia was another African country with very strong ties with the West, but they did not inhibit her from sending a few companies of men towards the end of July. Sudan insisted on sending some infanteers to match the parachute battalion offered by the United Arab Republic, and both these forces were flown in in the middle of August. A similar process of pairing took place later that month when India and Pakistan began to dispatch several hundred men apiece to help remedy deficiencies in logistic support. The total strength of the United Nations military forces in the Congo increased from 3,500 on July 18th to 8,400 on the 26th, and to 15,000 on August 22nd and 18,800 on September 9th. By the last date there were also 120 civilian technicians and technical advisers in United Nations service. At that time the cost to the United Nations of the military operations was just over a quarter of a million dollars a day.[1] This figure excluded basic pay and emoluments which continued to be provided by the respective national governments. Needless to say, the Swedes and the Canadians drew salaries several times those being paid to the men from the poorer countries, but it does not seem that this particular difference was ever a source of friction, presumably because the opportunities for spending money on the spot were pretty restricted.

The Ghana contingent was flown to Leopoldville by planes belonging to three of the great powers. The first to arrive were two aircraft of RAF Transport Command that appeared on the 16th July to carry the advance party. The following day five Soviet *Ilyushin* jets that had been used to run goods supplies down to Leopoldville were made available for one trip only, and then on the 18th part of the fleet that the USAF had earmarked for the Congo operation was directed to Accra and,

[1] *New York Times*, September 12, 1960

working in conjunction with more RAF planes, it completed the initial lift. The USAF delivered during July a total of 600 troops and 100 tons of supplies and equipment from Ghana and the RAF 1,500 troops, 60 tons of supplies and 45 vehicles.[1] Relations between Mr. Lumumba and the United Nations authorities became bad during August because of the refusal of the latter to assist the efforts of the central government to compel the breakaway régime in Katanga led by President Tshombe to submit to their control. The prospects of the central government achieving this unaided were already being progressively diminished by the build-up in Katanga of a *gendarmerie* trained by Belgian officers. As the situation developed the Soviet Union became progressively more critical of the United Nations handling of it and began to devote its energies to the direct support of Mr. Lumumba. The number of *Ilyushins* using Leopoldville airport gradually increased and by the end of the month had risen to about fifteen, and with them was a group of Russian pilots and ground technicians totalling about 200. They were used on internal flights on behalf of Lumumba and on 6th September the United Nations command (ONUC) had to close Leopoldville airport in order to prevent them rushing reinforcements to South Kasai, where his army was fighting Baluba supporters of yet another separatist 'Mining State'. This action obviously helped the United Nations officials on the spot to secure a cease fire there on 12th September. A few days before the temporary bar on flights from Leopoldville other Soviet *Ilyushins* had delivered about a hundred lorries to the Congolese central army, and before and after this other consignments of aid occurred.[2] The Belgian and Soviet policies of rendering aid to particular factions were not ruled out by the wording of the Security Council resolution authorizing intervention, but they were clearly in conflict with its spirit.

In accordance with its policy of preventing the Congo basin becoming a cockpit for the great powers, the United Nations restricted as much as it possibly could internal flights carried out on its behalf by the USAF. Instead it built up a local air

[1] Tarleton H. Watkins, USAF, in *Air University Quarterly Review*, Summer, 1961: Cmd. 1292; 1961, *Explanatory Memorandum On Air Estimates*
[2] *The Times*, September 5, 1960

transport fleet of its own which by September consisted of about
sixty machines whose operation was controlled by Air Commo-
dore Carpenter of the Royal Canadian Air Force. It included
ten C-119 *Flying Boxcars* which belonged partly to the RCAF
and partly to the Italian Air Force, and several helicopters and
cabin monoplanes loaned by the USAF and piloted by nations
of other states. There were also six or eight aircraft on permanent charter and a large number on temporary charter.

Except in the cases of the Ghanaians and Ethiopians all
external troop movements between the middle of July and the
beginning of September were carried out by the United States
Air Force. During the first three months of the emergency, in
fact, it carried 20,000 people, of whom 2,500 were refugees and
1,800 returning Belgian troops, together with 3,500 tons of
cargo, of which rather over half was military equipment and
supplies. The headquarters that organized this effort was that
of the 322nd Air Division (Combat Cargo) of the United States
Air Force in Europe: it was located at Evreux in France, which
was also the home base of its three C-130 *Hercules* squadrons
each with sixteen planes. All these were assigned to the Congo
airlift as soon as it was initiated, and thenceforward USAFE
only had three squadrons equipped with obsolete C-119 *Flying
Boxcars* to carry out its routine work in Europe. Between the
14th and 19th July five Military Air Transportation Service
squadrons equipped with a total of sixty C-124 *Globemasters*
were put under the control of Evreux for United Nations purposes. Most of these planes had to be flown in from the United
States.

It was on 8th July that the 322nd Air Division was told to
put some planes on standby alert ready to evacuate if necessary
the 300 United States citizens then in the Congo. However, no
movement orders were given until the 14th and the first actual
flight to the Congo was that of the two *Hercules* that left on the
15th to take to Leopoldville the fifty men of a Combat Airlift
Support Unit together with some basic equipment. The
numerical strength of this CALSU later rose slightly, but it
never became high enough, particularly bearing in mind the
fact that there was also insufficient handling machinery. The
shortage of manpower was chiefly due to the need for men with
similar skills at the various departure fields, but it may have

been aggravated by the policy of keeping tours of duty in the Congo as low as three weeks.

One general problem was the inadequacy of all kinds of navigational aids. Thus, there were at Evreux to begin with practically none of the relevant maps, radio facility charts, or other flight publications, and the gaps had to be filled by means of loans from the Royal Air Force, Air France, and Sabena. There were also few beacons or other kinds of ground-based aids on most of the routes used and, indeed, over large sections of them there was no means of keeping in contact with ground controllers at all. The gravity of this was emphasized by the lengths of the individual stages which were often in excess of 1,500 miles, which made it dangerous to depend on dead-reckoning, and by the lack of cities and significant terrain which more or less precluded the use of visual or radar navigation.

By the 25th July the USAF had flown in 4,120 troops and 850 tons of food and equipment and by 10th August 9,190 troops and 1,100 tons of material. Even the second figure only represents one short-range simultaneous lift on the part of the aircraft concerned, which suggests that once again the military allotted a much higher proportion of their resources to the task in hand than proved necessary. Nevertheless quite a lot of allowance has to be made for the fact that these figures do not represent a routine haulage operation conducted from one well-established airport to another. They were a series of movements of small parties from many widely separated places and under the most difficult navigational conditions. The ground-based landing aids were good on the international airports, but elsewhere tended to be poor. Within the Congo, air traffic control facilities had largely been manned by Belgians, who left their posts as soon as disorders broke out, and so it was necessary to improvise auxiliary services. There was also a general need for better radio communications, and so in the course of the first week of operations the USAF established single side band permanent stations in Chateauroux, Kano, and Leopoldville, and prepared three mobile units that were subsequently to be employed in such places as Kamina, Addis Ababa, and Dakar.

The exodus of the Belgian experts was an especial nuisance as far as the meteorological services in the Congo were concerned for accurate forecasting was, if not essential, at least highly desirable in a country in which masses of shower cloud built up every day and in which diversionary airfields were always few and far apart. At the beginning, the only forecasts available were those issued by the Strategic Air Command weather centre at Torrejon in Spain, and they were based entirely on climatological averages. To help remedy this state of affairs a USAF meteorological unit was sent out to Leopold-ville and by the end of the second week was broadcasting terminal airfield forecasts from there.

As has been the case in most of the air mobile operations of recent years, the physical dimensions of the departure and terminal airfields were to some extent limiting factors. The *Globemaster* squadrons were unable to use certain aerodromes because the runways were too short or weak, or because the engines of their aircraft were not able to adapt themselves to the particular grades of aviation fuel locally available. The men in the *Hercules* squadrons were not affected by any of those considerations, but they experienced problems caused by inadequate parking space and insufficient reserves of fuel. The most acute bottleneck was that which developed at Kano in Northern Nigeria. This was an airfield that normally handled 150 outgoing flights and at which bulk stocks equivalent to three weeks' average consumption had been built up under the terms of the Anglo-Nigerian defence agreement. With a rise in the number of departures to a peak of over 500 a week these supplies were rapidly depleted, and, since the only means of replenishment was a single-track railway running 500 miles from Port Harcourt, many of the *Globemasters* were re-routed through Dakar and Accra—two airfields lying on the coast. Leopoldville was not accessible to ocean shipping, but aircraft carriers and tankers were able to keep its reserves well topped up by means of one of the two pipelines from Matadi.[1]

By early September about thirty United Nations members had some kind of military representation in the Congo. One reason for so many states becoming directly involved was that they wanted to in order to gain military experience and to get more influence over the formulation of United Nations policy. Another was that the African contributors suffered from

[1] Watkins, *op. cit.*

military inadequacies especially in signals, transport, and administration that could only be remedied by their being rendered some support by states whose armies and air forces were
better provided for. Similar influences are likely to affect in
much the same way any large United Nations army assembled
in, say, 1970 or even, perhaps, in 2070. Therefore the early
history of the Congo operation is well worth studying for the
insight it gives into the problems that must be overcome in
organizing an international armed police force from scratch.

The discipline of almost all the contingents was excellent
during this initial period, despite the fact that they were working to the excruciatingly difficult brief of stabilizing a very
complex and explosive situation merely by the exertion of their
moral influence. They could not usurp local political authority
and they could not fire except in self-defence, and yet they were
required to dissuade mutually hostile factions from indulging
in open warfare and to persuade certain of them, namely,
various tribal groups and the *Force Publique*, to disarm. This was
a great deal to ask of small units widely scattered across a predominantly jungle landscape in a strange land to which they
were not at first even acclimatized let alone mentally attuned.
Physical courage was obviously needed less than on a battlefield, but greater premiums were placed on self-control, tact,
and judgement. That the United Nations troops had achieved
as much as they had by the end of August, and had only suffered
five deaths from hostile action in the process, says a great deal
for their general quality.

Their conduct appears the more creditable in the light of the
unsuitable arrangements made in many cases for the personal
comfort and fitness of the men. It is true that all units were
advised to bring with them, in addition to light arms, food for
fifteen days, equipment for purifying water, field stores, and
tents, but such advice was not always heeded and, in any case,
it touched upon only a few aspects of the welfare problem.
After their basic rations were exhausted many units were issued
with American 'C' packs which proved repellent to many
Afro-Asians on religious as well as upon more subjective
grounds, and distasteful even to Scandinavians, who eventually
made arrangements to be fed on a diet containing plenty of
fish and cheese. Also, as time went on more and more troops

were able to purchase local food to make their meals more varied and to reduce their transport requirements. Another source of acute discomfort initially was that of inappropriate clothing. The first Irish battalion arrived in winterweight khaki shorts and trousers and with blankets rather than sheets for use at night. It had very few tents and its men were suffering from the effects of having been vaccinated with a smallpox lymph that was too strong for African service.[1]

A most encouraging aspect of the whole business was the way in which the Commonwealth association helped to diminish the inhibitions of Africans, Asians and Canadians and fostered the growth of a club feeling that was described by one observer as being that of '. . . the whisky and Sandhurst set'.[2] The Irish shared this sense of common heritage, as was evidenced in their dress, insignia, regimental marches and drill movements, and they and the Liberians also shared with the Commonwealth members a command of the English language. The other West and North African nations had comparable links derivative from their mutual experience of French rule, whilst the Canadian signal unit was the more able to improve communications all round on account of its being bilingual.

There was for some time a general shortage of signals equipment which was felt all the more because of the great distances between adjacent company or battalion headquarters and the poor reception conditions induced by a jungle landscape and innumerable thunderstorm cells. Battalions like those from Guinea that arrived with no wireless sets had to be provided with American ones and this took several weeks. By September the Canadians had established links between ONUC and most of the territorial commands, but what was left of the civilian radio network was still being relied upon in places. One of the arguments advanced in favour of the Irish was that Erse constituted a code that no cryptographer could crack.

Some supply bottlenecks were caused by the motley collection of Swedish, Czech, French, Soviet, British, American, and other kinds of equipment in use, but the chief source of logistic trouble was that there were nothing like enough vehicles. In the middle of September a total of three hundred trucks be-

---

[1] *The Guardian*, September 8, 1960
[2] *New York Times*, August 1, 1961

longing to the United Nations were in the Congo, a country as large as Western Europe. The Chief of Staff Logistics said then that he needed 1,400 trucks and if the scales of establishment of Western infantry battalions and brigades are any guide that was a fair estimate.[1] The United Nations air fleet was of some help, but they were of little value for tactical movement or re-supply below battalion level. Some movements were carried out by water, but this was a slow and awkward process. It was estimated that it would have taken forty-four days to send supplies by water from Leopoldville to the Irish troops in Kivu Province. Measured in a straight line this was a distance of 900 miles.

In September 1960 there was one United Nations soldier in the Congo for every 700 inhabitants. If the United Nations force had been spread evenly over the country there would have been one soldier every $6\frac{1}{2}$ miles. The *Force Publique*, which had been the military power behind Belgian rule, had been well provided with personal equipment, wireless sets, trans-portation and heavy infantry weapons. It knew the country and had the full authority of the law behind it, to say nothing of the Belgian army. It never had to cope with all the fears generated and tensions released by a complete collapse of the civil authority. It never had to cope with powerful separatist move-ments or with the presence of thousands of troops under foreign national command or, for that matter, with a mutiny of the *Force Publique*! Nevertheless the Belgians had considered it necessary to keep it at a steady strength of 25,000, which sug-gests that even the United Nations peak figure of 20,000 was much too low. The United Nations also started off with far too flimsy a command structure at what we might call divisional level. One result of this was that local outposts often received instructions that were altogether too vague. Major-General Horn did not arrive at all until July 19th, owing to a series of ridiculous transport muddles, and for two or three crucial days the commander on the spot was a civilian official, Dr. Ralph Bunche.

Like Suez, the Congo operation suggests that United Nations forces will not have much difficulty in achieving strategic mobility if the operation in question has the support

[1] *New York Times*, September 12, 1960

of the great powers and, in particular, of the United States. On the other hand, tactical mobility, which is crucially important to the success of a police operation, is obviously much harder for an international force drawn from a number of small countries to achieve. The United Nations would find it quite uneconomic to maintain large numbers of short-range aircraft, ground vehicles, and wireless stations even if such a plan were agreed to by the member states. It would seem that the only way of reducing this problem would be to establish a small but highly expert staff at the New York headquarters which could engage in a wide range of contingency planning and acquire a detailed knowledge of the relevant resources available in countries that might offer contributions.

One point to note is that Britain, France, and the United States between them still provide the Afro-Asian and Latin American states with most of their training and equipment. Therefore, the more these three countries standardize their infantry battalions and basic signal units the more homogeneous is any international police force likely to become.

IV—KUWAIT

In the first few days after Kuwait became fully independent on June 19th, 1961, she received a number of cordial messages from other countries, including some from her sister Arab states. Furthermore Iraq had at different times in the recent past negotiated with the sheikdom on the basis of sovereign equality. However, on June 25th, General Kassem made a speech reviving a claim that Kuwait was part of Iraq and announcing that the Ruler of Kuwait was a lieutenant-governor in the Iraqi administration who '. . . would be severely punished if he did not do as he was told'. Three days later a statement by Lord Home and an inspired leak from Cairo made it clear that Britain and the United Arab Republic were prepared to support Kuwait in the maintenance of her sovereignty. Nevertheless, following reports of Iraqi troop movements, the Ruler formally asked Britain and Saudi Arabia for military assistance on June 30th. At that time the British theatre reserve consisted of a tank regiment and an armoured car regiment based on Aden, and of five battalions of infantry—one based on Aden and four on Kenya. Two squadrons of *Hunter* fighters constituted the main hitting power of RAF Middle East.

On June 29th the commando carrier HMS *Bulwark* left Karachi in accordance with a two-months-old programme and two days later disembarked forty-two Commando Royal Marines in Kuwait. The same day two LSTs of the Amphibious Warfare Squadron, which had been at Bahrein taking part in a normal Aden–Bahrein standing patrol, disembarked a squadron of tanks. Also the first elements of a lorry-borne contingent of a hundred Saudi Arabian paratroopers drove in over the desert. RAF movements on July 1st included those of eight *Canberras* from Germany to Bahrein and a *Hunter* squadron from Bahrein to Kuwait. On the 3rd Fighter Command began fitting a *Javelin* squadron with in-flight refuelling equipment to enhance its strategic mobility. Transport Command resources east of Gibraltar were by this time mobilized to the fullest extent possible for the purpose of the build-up. By the end of the previous day about seventy planes (out of the total of 200 in Transport Command) had been diverted to the operation.

Sunday the 2nd saw the arrival by air in Kuwait from Kenya of two infantry battalions (less two companies that had been serving as the Bahrein garrison and came up from there) and a brigade headquarters. At the same time another commando flew in from Aden and the Amphibious Warfare Squadron put ashore an armoured car squadron from the Trucial Oman, whilst it was announced in London that some intended manoeuvres in Portugal by the 19th Infantry Brigade of the Central Strategic Reserve had been cancelled.

On July 3rd, Transport Command planes flying down the Turkey–Persia air corridor brought up a parachute battalion from Cyprus and an artillery battery from Aldershot. On the 4th another battalion arrived from Kenya to be followed by yet another in the middle of the week. Also on the 4th the news came that two battalions of infantry and one field battery from the CSR were going to be airlifted to Kenya and relifted to Aden respectively. It was intended that the gunners should draw their artillery from the Aden stockpile. The airlift of the infanteers from Britain began on Thursday, which was the day the air movement into Kuwait itself began to slow down. The last major unit to arrive was a Royal Engineer field squadron which came in from Kenya on the Wednesday. By July 7th, 5,700 British troops and marines were in the sheikdom, as were two *Hunter* squadrons. The first to arrive was a ground-attack squadron and this was followed by a fighter reconnaissance one. During the eight days of the build-up both Khormakshar and Bahrein dispatched about 4,500 men and 700 to 900 tons of freight, although ordinary civilian traffic was accorded precedence at Bahrein. The uncompleted Kuwait new civil airport with its 9,000-foot runway was used as the Transport Command airhead and as the *Hunter* base, despite the fact that it had no Ground Control Approach and was often closed on account of sandstorms. Its peak acceptance of transport planes was about five an hour. Obviously the air freightage totals mentioned above imply drastic deficiencies of stores and equipment in comparison with the force levels of personnel. These deficiencies were partially remedied by utilizing *Bulwark*'s helicopters, impressing motor transport in Kuwait, and by drawing on stockpiles of stores and equipment in Kuwait and Bahrein. The Amphibious Warfare Squadron was kept busy bringing items from the Bahrein stockpile up for operational service in Kuwait. They were assisted by some LSTs manned by merchant seamen and under War Office operational control.

It seems that the precautionary assembly of naval forces began on June 29th, when one of the three frigates under the control of Flag Officer Middle East prematurely left Mombasa. More or less simultaneously sailing orders must have gone to another of the frigates doing self-maintenance at Karachi, because she left on July 1st ten days ahead of schedule. By the following day the warships in the immediate vicinity of Kuwait included *Bulwark*, one frigate, one LST, and a headquarters ship from the Amphibious Warfare Squadron. The last named had wireless sets capable of maintaining a direct link with the United Kingdom. Meanwhile the fleet carrier HMS *Victorious*, together with an escort of one destroyer and three frigates, was proceeding from the Hong Kong area at the maximum speed compatible with endurance. She arrived in the Gulf on the 7th and immediately assumed air defence control for the whole expedition. During the night of Wednesday, the 5th, the fleet carrier *Centaur* made the Suez transit *en route* for Aden in company with three destroyers and one LST. Two days later a minesweeping squadron began passing through also heading for Aden. The naval strength in the Kuwait local area was not increased, but by July 10th a total of forty-five ships were under the command of the Flag Officer Middle East, and his ships on station in the Gulf were receiving 600 tons a day of logistic support from three Royal Fleet Auxiliaries.

It is even more difficult to evaluate the potential opposition in this case than is normal in a cold-war situation. In the Arab-Israeli war of 1948, as during the 1941 revolt, Iraqi troops did badly. In fact, their performance in Palestine was appalling, bearing in mind the unique opportunities they had for cleaving the Jewish-held territories in half, the extent of their build-up in Jordan before the fighting developed, and the atavistic enthusiasm shown by the government in Bagdad throughout the hostilities about the prospect of driving the enemy into the sea. A major weakness seems to have been an inbred tradition of cynicism and disdain among the officer class. As has been remarked earlier, the events of 1956 showed that Colonel Nasser had been unable to do very much about it in a few brief years and we can assume that the same was true of Kassem in 1961. In fact, this negativism was probably even stronger within the officer cadre in Iraq than in Egypt, because poverty and illiteracy were even more prevalent among the other ranks. Another factor that must have sapped the dedication of the officers was political intrigue, and tribal jealousies, too, must have affected them as well as their men. The effect of the latter must have been exceptionally marked during the summer of 1961, because throughout that season the Kurdish community, from whom the army drew a goodly proportion of its other-rank volunteers, was in revolt in the north. The Kurdish revolt would obviously have had the more direct effect of involving one or two divisions in continual internal security operations. Therefore, since it would have been necessary to keep another division or so in the centre of the country in support of the civil power, out of a total army strength of four or five infantry divisions and a couple of armoured brigades, only a small margin would have been available for offensive operations beyond Iraq's borders.

On the other hand, the volumes of extra equipment acquired by the Iraqi army during the 1950s had obviously increased its firepower and mobility and must have raised its self-esteem.

The motor transport available by 1959 probably permitted the mechanization of two of the infantry divisions to a degree that would have made them usable in mobile operations. The armoured brigades shared between them about 110 *Centurions*, 40 American M-24s, and perhaps 100 to 150 Soviet T-54 tanks. There were also a fair number of tank transporter vehicles available. The first of the Soviet tanks had arrived in late 1959, so that their crews had had good time in which to become familiar with them. Other army equipment included American 8-inch howitzers towed by caterpillar tractors and some Soviet howitzers, rocket launchers, and 100-millimetre mortars. Administrative support has always been a major weakness of the Iraqi army and its supply problems must have been intensified by the phasing out of Western equipment in favour of Soviet. However, logistics alone would not have prevented the Iraqis from reaching Kuwait town.

The other two services of Iraq's armed forces both constituted a substantial potential threat. Apart from a small flotilla of river gunboats, the navy consisted of about a dozen twenty-year-old Motor Torpedo Boats supplied by the Soviet Union in 1959. They retained their twin 20-inch torpedo tubes and naval base facilities were being developed for them at Um Qasr. Despite their age their value might have been considerable had hostilities developed. Likewise, the Iraqi air force was a significant factor in the local balance of power. In 1959 the first-line element had been comprised of one squadron each of *Hunters*, *Venoms* and *Vampires*. In 1961 the *Hunters* were still in commission, but the majority of the fighters were MIG-17s and MIG-19s. Other Soviet planes in service included IL-28 bombers, MI-4 helicopters and AN-12 transports. The air force station at Shaibah and the civil airport at Basra provided actual or potential jet-fighter bases within striking distance of Kuwait. Also it is safe to assume that the pilots were, by that time, fully conversant with their machines. It is, of course, true that the aircraft supplied by the Soviet Union were obsolescent, but this was more than offset by the fact that they were conceded the right of first strike. It would not have been difficult for them to have taken some of the RAF *Hunters* based on Kuwait New Airport or some of the ships lying inshore by surprise. The depth of airspace available to the British was very inadequate for early warning purposes. The early warning radar was largely shipborne and not completely effective in providing cover against low-level attack from a landward quarter. Also, the whole operation of air surveillance was much complicated by the need to monitor a continual stream of traffic into Basra and into Kuwait itself.

In aggregate the military power of Iraq was quite impressive and it cannot be taken for granted that the British forces eventually assembled would have repelled an invasion without difficulty. For one thing the desert climate undermined the efficiency of troops and their equipment in various ways. Electronic equipment became overheated. Abnormal lapse rates of temperature with height seriously disturbed radio communications. *Whirlwind* helicopters were called upon to perform well above their official ambient temperature limit of 104°F. It is reasonable to argue that such technical difficulties must have embarrassed the British more, since they were more dependent on electronic gadgetry and more dependent on helicopters. In any case the British had a special acclimatization problem. In the first week about a hundred cases of heat exhaustion were treated at Sabbah hospital and many more were handled in *Bulwark* by the Field Ambulance Unit or within the squadrons and battalions.

Another climatic effect that was obviously of major importance was the recurrent 'Shermal' sandstorm. The 'Shermal' that blew with general wind velocities of 15–25 m.p.h. for the first week raised thick dust to 5,000 feet and reduced surface horizontal visibilities to around 200 to 500 yards. Such reduction of vision would have made desert navigation far from easy and would have inhibited the long-range use of tank guns against dug-in infantry positions. However, what is probably more important is that it would have precluded the aerial strikes on which the defenders of Kuwait would have largely relied to redress the balance between their forty tanks, half of them Kuwaiti, and the estimated Iraqi total of about 250.

The defence plan adopted was that of having light mobile screens of jeeps and armoured cars patrolling the frontier, while the main force lay back fifty miles down the Basra–Kuwait road along the bottom of the only reasonably continuous natural tank barrier—a crumbling sand and stone

escarpment which faced south-east and had a general height
of about twenty feet. A coastal indentation opposite this Jal az
Zaur escarpment closed the British right flank and although
an inferior lateral track existed which would have somewhat
facilitated Iraqi deployment to the south-west, the limited
cruising range of the tanks and their dependence on wheeled
logistic support would have precluded them developing a front
of manoeuvre of more than, say, fifteen to twenty miles. On the
frontier, however, deploying on both sides of the road axis
across a desert surface generally quite tolerable for wheeled
traffic, they could have advanced on perhaps a thirty-mile
front. Also positions on the frontier would have been vulnerable to tactical surprise. However, the Jal az Zaur position
offered no protection whatever against the most likely form of
military challenge. It is most improbable that General Kassem
would ever have initiated a blitzkrieg offensive to smash south-
wards to Kuwait town and 'liberate' it in an orgy of gory street
fighting. The canons of Arab nationalism dictate that Arabs
do not kill other Arabs in large numbers. What would have
been more likely than an unrestricted 'war of liberation' was
a limited advance across the frontier to lay symbolic claim to
one of Kuwait's northernmost group of oilfields. The guardians
of Kuwait would then have been obliged to go over to the
tactical offensive to eject the invaders.

Kuwait town can be regarded as having been secure against
all threats except that of physical occupation. During the crisis
there was some talk about the vulnerability of its freshwater
distillery, situated by the shore of the sea, upon the throughput
of which the 300,000 inhabitants of the state largely depended.
In fact, however, Iraq would never have dared to destroy the
water supply of a sister Arab community even if she had
wished to. Furthermore, there was no internal security problem
in Kuwait town. General contentment based on material
prosperity prevailed everywhere, not least among the 40,000
resident Iraqis.

Of course, in evaluating the potency of the scratch brigade
group the British brought together we must bear in mind the
ground support it was receiving from the Saudi and Kuwaiti
armies. The Ruler's defence force numbered 1,600 men organized into a tank squadron, a field battery, and several com-

bined groups of jeep-mounted infantry and armoured cars. The soldiers' morale was high and they knew their countryside backwards. This contingent, which was led by a young Sand-hurst-trained brigadier, joined the British troops under a joint command headed by Brigadier Horsford. The small Saudi unit present was not prepared to do this.

Taking the overall picture it seems reasonable to conclude that at any time after July 9th, which was the date on which the arrival of HMS *Victorious* ensured British air supremacy, any conceivable Iraqi military challenge would have evoked an adequate response. However, it is still very debatable whether the British presence was a major reason why aggression did not occur. One would have thought the prospective hazards involved in aggravating simultaneously the oil companies, the other Arab states, and Persia would have been adequate deterrents in themselves. It is, in fact, doubtful whether Iraq made any serious preparations for an early attack. The mechanized armoured brigade permanently based on Basra did not deploy beyond it and the armoured movements towards that town from the north really prove nothing about General Kassem's intentions *vis-à-vis* Kuwait. In December 1961 the British response to several days of armoured reinforcement of the Basra garrison consisted merely of flying 200 men belonging to air movement parties out to the Middle East and ordering the carrier *Centaur*, two frigates, and three RFAs to sail from Mombasa into the Indian Ocean. It is true, of course, that from the 20th of August Kuwait was a member of the Arab League and that by December 2,000 to 3,000 Arab League troops were on duty within her territory, but in most respects the circumstances of the December crisis were similar to those of the June one. The arguments used in June about the necessity for a strong local deterrent force because General Kassem's policy decisions tended to be hasty and irresponsible, and because he was a rather volatile personality at the head of an unstable dictatorship, must have been as applicable six months later. On 31st December, General Kassem made a speech more chauvinistic than any he had delivered in June.

The contrast between the two reactions illustrates the special difficulty about going to aid Kuwait. The Iraqis do not need to telegraph a major blow more than a few days ahead. On the other hand, Britain cannot undertake a large-scale strategic redeployment every time a few T-54s go careering across the desert. A statement in the House of Commons on July 25th gave the cost of the build-up and partial withdrawal (of 2,000 men and some ships) conducted during that month, at about £1,000,000, and finance is by no means the only embarrassment that such a commitment entails. Furthermore, it hardly seems that the Arab League is willing or able to take over Britain's special responsibility for the sheikdom. The Egyptian, Saudi Arabian, and Jordanian contingents have now been withdrawn from the joint force leaving only the 100 Sudanese. It is clear that the withdrawal of the Saudis was due to deep distrust between the Kuwaitis and themselves resulting from the claims their country also has made on Kuwait. In the years ahead occasions may well arise again when Kuwait has to ask for British protection.

V—CUBA

President Kennedy did not make his radio and television statement to the effect that the United States proposed to blockade Cuba in order to prevent it from becoming a Soviet strategic missile base until the late afternoon of Monday, October 22nd, 1962; but for six days past extensive preparations for some such action had been in hand.

The preparations began as a result of a Lockheed U-2 overflying Cuba on October 14th and bringing back convincing evidence that long-range missiles were being imported and emplaced and that Russian IL-28 medium bombers were being added to Fidel Castro's inventory of manned aircraft. The U-2 in question had been carrying out one of a series of weekly reconnaissances intended to supplement patrols along the Cuban coasts by planes using oblique photography techniques. The particular flight in question had apparently been postponed for several days because of bad weather, and this made its findings even more sensational than they might otherwise have been. As a result of them, the aerial surveillance of the island was stepped up on October 17th and the same day a brigade of Marines moved into the Key West naval station which lies on the extremity of Florida Keys about a hundred miles from Havana. Twenty-four hours later a crack naval fighter squadron had joined the planes already available at Key West airfield. By Friday the 19th Tactical Air Command had already completed a large part of a deployment into the South Eastern States that was eventually to involve 7,000 men, over 1,000 planes, and some 3,300 tons of support equipment. Over the week-end Strategic Air Command started to vacate its Florida bases to leave them free for incoming Tactical Air Command, Air Defense Command, and Military Air Transportation Service planes and in order to disperse its own aircraft. Simultaneously, it was creating a continuous airborne alert and bringing its long-range missiles to a state of readiness. It reached the required level of preparedness in less than two days and maintained it throughout the emergency, although this involved most of its men doing twice their normal working hours during this period. Other developments in the course of the week-end included the arrival in the theatre of operations of the first of the extra Air Defense squadrons, and the unscheduled departure from Norfolk, Virginia, of six amphibious vessels destined to join a fleet manned by some 20,000 sailors and Marines that had already been assembled in the Caribbean in preparation for a proposed exercise on and around Puerto Rico. Then in the last few hours before the President made his speech warships put to sea in considerable numbers all along the Eastern Seaboard.

The President's speech revealed that several mobile MRBMs with ranges of rather more than 1,000 miles had been observed in their firing positions in Cuba and that it had been found that some sites from which to launch IRBMs capable of travelling 2,000 miles were being rapidly constructed. In announcing the forthcoming blockade President Kennedy made it clear that its purpose was to check the build-up of these and other 'offensive' weapons and to bring about the removal, under United Nations supervision, of those already installed. It was not to be regarded as a device for bringing Cuba to her knees economically. On the other hand, the right was explicitly reserved to use other and tougher punitive methods, which might include economic sanctions, if the naval quarantine did not quickly achieve the required results. Furthermore the gravity of the situation was firmly underlined by the warning that if one nuclear armed missile from Cuba landed in the

United States it would trigger off a full retaliatory strike against the Soviet Union.

The blockade came into force at dawn on the 24th, following a proclamation that designated bombers as 'offensive' weapons as well as surface-to-surface missiles, and it was conducted initially by about fifty ships and submarines assisted by hundreds of aircraft. Strike Command headquarters was not used to control the operation, because it was decided that Task Force 136, as it was designated, was best commanded by a sailor in the person of Admiral Ward—the C-in-C of the 2nd Fleet from which, of course, all the ships and submarines and many of the aircraft had been drawn. On his behalf messages were broadcast requesting all ships passing to or from the Caribbean to avoid the Straits of Florida and the Windward Passage and indicating various enforcement procedures that would be adopted when or if necessary. One such procedure, which never had to be put to the test, in fact, was intended to deal with the problem of communicating with submerged submarines. The plan was to use light explosive charges as sound signals to back up wireless messages transmitted in international code and on a stated frequency. These signals would have ordered any boats found to surface.

When the period of quarantine commenced twenty-five Soviet ships were approaching Cuba and there seemed to be a grave risk of some kind of incidents occurring probably in the course of Thursday morning. However, at what was in some cases almost literally the last moment they all altered course, except for one tanker which was screened by ships and aircraft and then allowed through the cordon. Moscow Radio advised us that the whole of its crew had voiced their determination to defy the 'piratical' American blockade.

On the 26th a statement was made from the White House expressing concern about the fact that site construction was still continuing and indicating that further measures might have to be taken to check this. One was taken at half past nine the following morning when 14,000 Air Force Reservists in twenty-four transport squadrons and six aerial port squadrons were called to active duty. Within twenty-four hours 93 per cent of the men and 75 per cent of their 300 planes were operational.

Whilst this war of nerves was being played out on the high seas the Security Council met and decided to ask U Thant, the Acting Secretary-General, to mediate between Mr. Khrushchev and President Kennedy. U Thant agreed and wrote to the Russians and the Cubans asking them to halt the arms build-up for a while and to the Americans asking them to suspend the searching of ships. This move initiated a trilateral exchange of letters between him and the American and Russian leaders that by Monday the 29th had got close to producing an agreement, based on a supervised withdrawal of the controversial weapons and a guarantee by the United States that she would not engage in hostile operations against Cuba. Some delay in obtaining this measure of agreement had been occasioned by the fact that, during the week-end, the Soviets temporarily insisted that the withdrawal of ballistic missiles from Cuba should be made conditional on their withdrawal from Turkey.

On Tuesday, President Kennedy ordered the lifting of the blockade for forty-eight hours following the visit to Cuba of U Thant. Four days later he said that aerial surveillance was now providing clear evidence that the dismantling of the sites was proceeding apace. The gradual subsidence of the crisis was arrested by a dispute that flared up between the United States and the Soviet Union around November 9th and during the following week a large number of warships and amphibious vessels from the United States Pacific Fleet passed through Panama. The principle issue at stake was that of whether the obsolescent IL-28 medium bombers ought to be withdrawn or not. This obstacle to a return to normalcy was not removed until the 21st when Mr. Khrushchev promised to withdraw all the bombers under supervision within thirty days. As soon as he did this President Kennedy announced the end of the blockade and forty-five minutes later the eight carriers, fifty other ships, and five submarines that by that time were on patrol round Cuba began withdrawing. All Air Force Reservists were released immediately and at the same time the order retaining until the end of February all sailors and Marines was rescinded.

The maintenance of the blockade must have placed a considerable strain on the capacity of the 2nd Fleet which at the start of the crisis would have included about ten carriers, some 150 other warships, and approximately 200 support

vessels. Of the total over one-half would have been undergoing
refits or would have been involved in routine training duties.
Since it is likely that the Denmark Straits and the Faeroes Gap
were patrolled during the period of greatest tension to ascertain
whether an exceptional number of Soviet submarines were
travelling towards the open ocean, it seems that resources must
have been stretched close to the limit, even allowing for the
facts that some reinforcements were sent from the Pacific and
that not all the vessels operating off the Cuban coast were
warships. On the other hand, it can be argued that more than
enough ships were assigned to the blockade bearing in mind
the assistance they were getting from hundreds of United
States Navy and Marine Corps planes and hundreds of USAF
bomber and reconnaissance aircraft. Also, the fact that the
hurricane season had ended meant that there was a very high
expectation of good visibility and moderate seas.

All the same the operation was an impressive example of the
flexibility and subtlety with which sea-power can be exercised.
This was indeed as well, for this was a situation in which any
other course of action might have proved wholly disastrous.
Although the United States President and the half-dozen or so
advisers he selected to help him shoulder the responsibilities of
decision making seem to have been in complete agreement,
they were conscious enough of the supreme hazards involved.
They could not be sure whether the Russians had installed or
intended to install normal nuclear warheads in the missiles or
whether they had modified them to carry large conventional
warheads at the expense of a reduction in range. If they
assumed that nuclear warheads were, in fact, going to be
carried they still did not know whether the Soviet Union was
seeking to win a major diplomatic victory through the ruthless
use of nuclear blackmail or whether their behaviour stemmed
from a genuine fear of another attempt to invade Cuba. The
strategic consequences would have been the same either way
had the missile sites actually been completed, but the problem
at that stage was that of how best to prevent this. An endeavour
to negotiate without the employment of any physical sanctions
would have been disastrous if Soviet policy had been fundamentally aggressive. An immediate bombardment of the sites
would have been catastrophic if this had been seen by a defen-

sively minded but politically misinformed Kremlin as final
proof that the United States had all along been planning
aggressive war against Cuba. Fortunately, the kind of force
brought to bear was of a kind that could be totally effective
without being lethal. It would have been quite possible to stop
any one of the cargo ships without killing any member of its
crew simply by putting a small calibre shot through its steering
gear. A deterrent as controlled and precise as this was exactly
what was needed in so uncertain a situation.

We do not know, and perhaps never shall, how close the
Soviet Union was to raising the stakes, but one factor in the
appraisal she made of the situation must have been the practical
difficulties involved in so doing. She was utterly incapable of
wresting naval control of the Caribbean from the Americans.
She was also incapable of running an effective airlift to Cuba
and thereby forcing the Americans either to concede defeat or
to resort to measures that would have resulted in people being
killed. There were only about six Soviet aircraft—the Tupolev
114s—that were capable of direct flight from Moscow to
Havana and they could not have carried items as bulky as
missiles. Various other planes could have got there if they had
refuelled in Canada, but the possibility of this happening was
eliminated by a prompt Ottawa accouncement of a ban on
Russian aircraft using Canadian airspace to get to Cuba.
Neither did there appear to be much scope for flying through
Africa. Of the seven flights the United States authorities estimated the Russians had made to Havana during the previous
four months only one or two had been through Africa and so
their aircrews were lacking in relevant flying experience. That
this would not have been regarded as an insuperable objection
in itself is shown by the record of their activity during the early
days of the Congo troubles but to it was added the need to
negotiate a large number of over-flight concessions. This need
could almost certainly never have been met.

If this analysis is correct Russia had only two positive
options—to initiate general war or to take reprisal action somewhere around the periphery of the Iron Curtain. The first
solution would obviously have been no solution at all in terms
of constructive politics and there is no evidence that she ever
seriously contemplated it. On the contrary, Mr. Khrushchev

in his reply to U Thant's first letter fairly strongly implied that he did not regard himself as committed to any physical action if any conflict did occur between Soviet and American ships: all the Soviet spokesmen studiously avoided any repetition of the hints that had been dropped occasionally during the previous two years or so to the effect that any United States 'aggression' against Cuba might invoke the use of Russian strategic rockets. Nevertheless certain steps were taken to increase Soviet preparedness for total war. All leave was cancelled and all demobilization from the strategic rocket, submarine, and anti-aircraft services halted, and the submarine fleet began to disperse.

Although Turkey was the only country specified in any kind of threat, it was announced that the Higher Command of the Warsaw Pact was bringing its forces to alert status, and Western newspapers were full of speculation about the possibility of a hostile move against West Berlin. Meanwhile the governments directly concerned took a number of precautions. On Tuesday, October 23rd, American governmental officials discussed contingency plans with the Germans, French, and British ambassadors in Washington. Soon afterwards some British troops attached to the Berlin garrison were prematurely recalled from exercises in the German Federal Republic and all members of the Bundeswehr were ordered not to travel more than eighteen miles from their barracks.

The United States response to the Soviet attempt to run missiles into Cuba did not have to be controlled and cautious only in order to dissuade the Soviets from taking matters further. There was also the need to ensure that a strategic success was not at the same time a first-class political reverse. It easily could have been, for around the world there were a lot of people who, craving for a postponement of war at any price, were quite prepared to regard the whole business as part of the Democratic Party's campaign for the mid-term Congressional elections. They readily remembered that it was not beyond the wit of man to fake an odd photograph or two and their scepticism was in no wise discouraged by Mr. Zorin, then Soviet delegate to the Security Council. In Britain, for example, all the more vociferous members of the Campaign for Nuclear Disarmament took up an unequivocally anti-American attitude, whilst even the official Labour Party reaction to the blockade proposals stopped well short of enthusiasm. In what was the most sensitive area of the free world on this issue, namely Latin America itself, the reaction, at least at governmental level, was very favourable. President Kennedy's policy was approved by a delegate conference of the Organization of American States by nineteen votes to nil with one, apparently accidental, abstention. Furthermore, there was a tolerably good response to the Pentagon request of October 23rd that all Latin American nations should ascertain what practical assistance they could offer the United States in support of its current policy or any extension of it. Within thirty-six hours Honduras had volunteered an infantry battalion and some fighter aircraft, Costa Rica some base facilities, Peru part of her armed forces for any action approved by the OAS, and Argentina the use of her navy in certain circumstances. Various offers were also made by Columbia, Dominica, Guatemala, and Venezuela.[1]

Had the United States felt obliged to initiate hostilities it seems clear that she would have done so by means of aerial strikes with conventional bombs against the missile sites and bomber bases and that these strikes would have been delivered after a Cuban rejection of a final ultimatum for, as Mr. Robert Kennedy said, his brother had no wish to play the part of a Tojo. The procedure of issuing a warning before any resort to air action was, in fact, adopted by the Department of Defense on October 26th, when, following the loss of a Lockheed U-2, it announced that if any more planes were shot down it would order counter-attacks against the anti-aircraft defences responsible. Unfortunately a strike following explicit warnings might not have been effective against the mobile MRBMs, for these could have easily been camouflaged and they could have been moved to fresh locations and rendered operational in them in periods of less than eighteen hours.

It was fully recognized that any invasion of Cuba that proved necessary would have been, from the tactical standpoint alone, a most hazardous undertaking. Fidel Castro commanded an army of 80,000 men and a militia of 200,000 and both these organizations had very many Soviet weapons. The

[1] *The Times*, October 25, 1962

ground forces are said to have included twenty-four anti-aircraft missile complexes and the air force to include 160 MIG fighters, of which forty were of the ultra-modern MIG-21 type. In addition the strength of the IL-28 bomber group was estimated to have risen to twenty. The coast was being screened by twenty or thirty Soviet-built fast patrol boats and unofficial reports have stated that all the more likely landing places around it had been sown with pressure mines.

The consensus of informed American opinion was that in overcoming such opposition 40,000 or 50,000 casualties would be incurred—some estimates put the figure as high as 90,000. How large the sheer physical effort required would have been is shown by the size of the forces made ready. Eventually 185 naval vessels were concentrated of which sixty-five directly participated in the blockade and fifty, being amphibious ships, stood by in readiness for assault landings. One Marine Corps division was detailed to constitute the first amphibious assault echelon. This formation, together with ancillary units, represented a commitment of 45,000 men of which some thousands were actually embarked at the height of the crisis. Altogether five United States Army divisions were alerted, but the one that would apparently have comprised the second seaborne assault echelon was the First Armoured which was moved from Texas to Georgia as soon as the crisis broke. This mass of military might could very possibly have sufficed to vanquish Cuba but it would have been impossible to justify its use except as the sequel to a savage attack by the Soviet Union on a territory such as Turkey or West Berlin.

The great lesson of Cuba was that of the enormous value of being able to make the amount and kind of deterrent power applied fit the specific threat towards which it was directed. The military strength of the United States in that particular context was sufficient to enable the policies she pursued to be flexible and restrained. It is true that the Soviet Union enjoyed the initial advantage of being able to compel her rival to break the international law of the sea but once this card had been played all the trumps were in American hands. Russia had no means of checkmating American actions except by resorting to measures that would have involved a serious extension of the conflict.

Chapter 5

Mobility by Sea

I—AMPHIBIOUS OPERATIONS

THE specialized amphibious vehicles evolved since 1939 are, in most cases, heavily dependent for their efficient operation on appropriate shore conditions. Whilst a very low tidal range may be a nuisance in that it enables an enemy to bunch his obstacles around a near constant watermark, very high tides will often cause the landing forces more trouble because they will be associated with fast and variable currents, and because the fluctuations in the sea-level will make beaching or the construction of causeways difficult and will inhibit the handling of stores on the beach itself. Local variations in the submarine shore profile due to sand-bars, protuberances of hard rock or coral reefs can be major hazards. Sand-bars are characteristic of coastlines which are emergent or that have a pronounced prevailing wave motion from a very oblique angle. Likewise substructures of soft sand or mud, which are usually associated with low beach gradients, impede the passage of vehicles, though this problem can be reduced by the use of plastic or pierced steel matting. Also the low gradients themselves may prevent the beaching of large landing craft and landing ships. This is because the slope of the keel of a large vessel may exceed that of the beach sufficiently to prevent its bows from reaching the 4- or 5-foot depth of water which is the maximum tolerable for the off-loading of waterproofed wheeled vehicles even in a calm sea. A typical landing-ship tank cannot off-load directly over a beach gentler than 1 in 50 or, if it uses a pair of causeways, about 1 in 80. The standard metal causeways in use are each about 150 feet long and a pair of them weighs over 100 tons. They must be strapped on the sides of their LST or alternatively towed at low speeds to the landing area. When faced with gradients gentler than 1 in 80 the British make recourse to Rhino ferries which are propelled by outboard motors and which can be made from pontoons of a kind that a LST can carry internally. The slope of the beach is of less consequence in the operation of Landing Craft Tank and in the case of the minor landing craft it matters little. However, the use of all kinds of amphibious shipping is severely controlled by one other factor and that is the presence of enough treeless moderate slopes to permit ready egress from the beach itself. Linked with the problem of egress is that of storage space. A division typically requires five acres open and five acres covered for its war maintenance reserves.

The importance of shore conditions in combined operations is enhanced by the fact that it is very difficult to discover or predict them with any certainty prior to any assault. Geological science helps little, for although it is known, for example, that gentle gradients tend to be associated with emergent coastlines or tranquil weather conditions, no one could ever quantify all the variables and produce precise equations. The most that anyone can do is to use theory to interpret more rationally random bits of intelligence which may derive from espionage, stereographic aerial photography, pre-H hour reconnaissance by the frogmen of underwater demolition teams, and published hydrographic surveys. The published charts are very inadequate as far as the remoter areas are concerned. Thus it is by no means exceptional for them to rely to some extent on the diaries of eighteenth-century explorers. In any case no chart of a stormbound coast could ever be entirely dependable, because a violent gale can dramatically alter a beach profile.

The weather can, of course, exercise a much more direct influence. Gales caused heavy damage during the Anzio and Normandy landings and serious inconvenience during the Sicily one. They twice wrecked the main causeway at Inchon. Even a fresh breeze can in itself seriously affect the control of minor landing craft and may, in any case, create a dangerous sea state. A wind of 30 m.p.h. blowing for a full day over an unlimited stretch will build up average waves of 5 feet. Waves of this height if coupled with a moderate swell of, say, 12 feet could hamper the lowering of assault craft from davits. Furthermore, waves tend to build up as they approach the shore, although that depends on the angle of incidence, the degree of exposure, and any funnelling effect. If the waves described above came into a straight coastline at an angle of 50 degrees, they would break in water 8 feet deep at a height of 6 feet. If a beach is steep all waves tend to break simultaneously, producing a narrow but intense zone of surf embarrassingly close to the positions from which troops and vehicles leave landing craft. In any case, small landing craft will probably themselves be wrecked by a plunging surf reaching 10 feet or so in height. Two hundred such craft were lost from this cause at Iwojima and their accumulated wreckage severely congested the landing beaches. The effect of sea and swell states is enhanced by the fact that these states are largely unpredictable and unmeasurable and subject to infinite local variations. However, they will always be much less critical in sheltered bays and on lee coasts. As for the future, it does seem that the increasing use of helicopters will make almost all the facets of physical geography less important and that the eventual use of hovercraft will make the width and composition of the beach less so. If either class of vehicle had been the chief medium of ship-to-shore movement during the Suez landings, the British and French would have been able, if they so desired, to go ashore across the long lagoons east of Port Said and so avoid the charge that whilst claiming to be separating the combatants they landed in the rear of one of them. Since henceforward task-force commanders are likely to be much more narrowly circumscribed by political considerations in respect of their exact choice of time and place than in the past, it is a pity that landing craft seem destined to remain, for the rest of this decade at least, the chief vehicles of any assault at brigade strength or above.

The smallest units in any American assault wave today would normally be armoured amphibians and the LVTPX-11 is currently being designed to serve as the principal equipment of the amphibian tractor battalions. It will weigh about 13 tons empty and be able to carry a 4-ton payload or twenty-seven troops. Two varieties of Landing Vehicle Hydrofoil are due to be tested early in 1963. The LVHX-1 will weigh 10 tons and is intended to have a water-speed with foils lowered of 45 knots through 4- to 6-foot waves. It will also have large tyres and an all-wheel drive system producing a maximum land-speed of 50 m.p.h. Larger amphibians have been developed, including the 60-ton unarmoured BARC with twin screws and low-pressure tyres 9 feet high. It can carry 100 tons of cargo. The smallest non-amphibious landing craft are the LCVPs which are the American equivalent of the British LCAs. They can carry half a company of men or one or two light vehicles. The rather larger and sturdier LCM-6s can each accommodate a battle tank. There are also the Landing Craft Utility, as the smaller versions of the old LCT class are now called. The recently constructed LCU 1608 displaces 200 tons light and 375 tons with a full load. LCUs, like the other minor landing craft, can be transferred in and off-loaded into the water from Landing Ships Tank and Landing Ships Dock.

The American Landing Ships Medium, whose specification is closely comparable to that of the British LCT(8), carry up to 300 tons of cargo. They are slow, rather uneconomical, and ill suited to transoceanic voyages and so are now regarded as obsolete. The LSTs generally have a cargo capacity of around 2,000 tons, a full load displacement between 4,000 and 6,000 tons, and a range of about 10,000 miles. Those built in the 1942–5 era have maximum designed speeds of 13 knots, but the modern *Suffolk County* class can reach 17 knots. However, they must always fall far short of this in heavy seas, because, although large ballast tanks can be filled to make them settle lower in the water, their hull configuration is a squarish shallow draught one appropriate for grounding on beaches. The best way of reconciling such conflicting design requirements is by building Landing Ships Dock that can release small assault craft from a well in their hulls. A typical LSD has a full load displacement of 11,000 tons and carries twenty-one LCM-6s, 350 troops and 2,000 tons of cargo. It has a pair of 50-ton cranes and a helicopter platform. A new version called the amphibious transport dock (LPD) displaces approximately 14,000 tons, carries 1,000 troops and 2,500 tons of cargo, and has a much-improved flight deck. Both types can do 20 knots. In December 1961 the Admiralty placed an order for the first of two LSDs for the Royal Navy to be built at a cost of approximately £8,000,000.

These vessels are supplemented by the attack transports (APAs) and cargo ships (AKAs). As their designation clearly implies, these ships are suitable for an assault role, but in fact they would probably be used chiefly during the build-up phase. The modern AKA *Tulare*, which displaces 18,000 tons, can

accommodate nine LCM-6s and fifteen LCVPs and can transport them together with 5,000 tons of assorted stores and equipment for 10,000 miles at 20 knots. It has a flight deck of about
500 square yards and three 60-ton main booms. It can back in
and out of port and has a tactical diameter of 700 yards. The
initial cost was about $15,000,000. Ready for the follow-up
stage of operations, the British are building the first of several
Landing Ships Logistic for an estimated cost of £1,750,000. It
will displace 6,000 tons and will be able to transport a load that
will include several tanks. Its installations will include double-
jointed ramps and fore-and-aft cranes and it will carry some
pontoons and a cargo helicopter.

Various mechanical aids have been devised for over-the-
beach supply during the build-up stage. Since 1955 a series of
NATO Off-Shore Discharge Exercises (NODEXES) have been
held in France and Turkey. During some of them an aerial
tramway has been employed by means of which 10-ton *Skycars*
can shift up to 5,000 tons a day. For more modest movements a
pair of amphibians can tow to the beach a rig that makes
possible high-line ship-to-shore transfers. Also plastic causeways and breakwaters are being developed. For handling
stores in and beyond the beach area the United States Marine
Corps now regularly use small bulldozers, fork-lift trucks, and
3-ton mobile cranes. Meanwhile it is evolving an Airoll vehicle
which utilizes a new principle of locomotion that involves a
system of free-rolling low-pressure tyres secured to an endless
chain or track driven by a sprocket. To help solve the vexed
problem of oil supply *Dracones* have been invented. These are
oil-barges with flexible skins and capacities, so far, of up to 400
tons, though 1,000-ton models are being built. *Dracones*, which
are normally towed at about 7 knots, are a cheap form of
transport by virtue of the fact that their cargo usually constitutes about 98 per cent of their loaded weight. It is relevant to
note in concluding this brief survey of some of the techniques
for build-up across open beaches that all the figures for cargo
tonnage given above assume that ships would be loaded in such
a way as to make the maximum use of their cargo space. However, ships participating in the actual assault would be tactically
loaded which would reduce their capacity by something like
half.

For tactical landings in brigade strength or more, certain other kinds of specialist ships are normally required, including minesweepers, radar pickets, guided missile destroyers, a cruiser, a commandoship, an attack carrier, a Landing Ship Headquarters, which will contain among other things a very comprehensive range of communications equipment, and a group of replenishment vessels. A modern conventional gun-cruiser can perform in a support role in such a situation very efficiently. The 6-inch guns of HMS *Tiger* fire over twice as fast as those of any previous generation and far more accurately.

The modern doctrine of large-scale amphibious assault holds that it should be a synchronized combination of horizontal movement across the coast by troops issuing from landing-craft, and a leapfrog to positions beyond the coast by troops transported in helicopters from what the British call commando ships and the Americans amphibious-assault ships or LPHs. In addition, however, commando ships are regarded as uniquely appropriate for independent small-scale actions and when used in this way have been likened to the gunboats our grandfathers knew. Their radii of action are, however, much greater than those of the gunboats. Even with the present generation of helicopters they are 100 miles or more. That figure may seem small in proportion to the size of continents but, of course, there is a strong tendency, particularly in ex-colonial areas, for the centres of commerce and government to lie near the sea. For example, fifteen of the twenty-one political capitals of Latin America are within 100 miles of it.

The first British commando ships have been the 27,000-ton *Bulwark* and her sister-ship *Albion*. As a light fleet carrier *Bulwark* cost £9,000,000 and she was converted at a cost of £4,000,000. She has now in addition to a ship's company of 1,000, a *Wessex* helicopter squadron of 200 men, and a reinforced commando of 750, which includes two attached troops of Royal Artillery pack howitzers. The troop complement can be expanded to 1,200 for short-range emergency lift. The normal load of vehicles is about 100, including twenty 3-ton trucks: thirty heliportable *Citroen* cars and four LCAs are also carried. She retains her original radar gear and so is capable of directing fighter aircraft. Furthermore, she is able, at short notice and entirely within her own resources, to adapt her helicopters for anti-submarine work. Her United States counterpart—the LPH *Iwojima*—was built from scratch for $40,000,000. She displaces 18,000 tons and does 20,000 miles at 20 knots. She normally carries about twenty-five helicopters, 2,000 Marines, and 500 tons of assault cargo.

Although the combat elements of the US Marine Corps are completely airportable, and although in Korea it fought in a frontal land war alongside the army units of the United Nations Command, it is still overwhelmingly concerned with the problem of amphibious assault to form beachheads on defended coasts in support of naval operations. This mission gives the service a distinctive purpose, is in accordance with all its experience and tradition, and is, in fact, formally assigned to it as its primary task by the National Security Act of 1947. Current doctrine within the corps about an assault by a Fleet Marine Force envisages landing over about six different beaches. One notional beach of about 1,000 yards in extent would constitute the initial front of a battalion landing team. The object would be to establish a perimeter perhaps 20 miles wide and 30 deep, to carry out helicopter raids up to 50 miles beyond that, and aerial surveillance about 300 miles beyond. It is felt that naval shore fire support to 75 miles would be desirable if missile development made it possible. It is felt too that all operations must be conducted against the background of the nuclear threat. The Fleet Marine Forces themselves have a large and versatile nuclear capability.

The organization of the Marine Corps clearly reflects its dominant interest in establishing and holding beachheads. The basic element in a FMF is the 19,000-man division which is still built on the triangular principle. The extra mobility and capacity for all-round defence that a pentomic arrangement offers are thus sacrificed in favour of simplicity, tight control and staying power. Likewise the choice of equipment is governed by the same preoccupation, with, for example, an emphasis on automatic and recoilless rifles and a standard scale of only 1,100 self-propelled vehicles. Also a large variety of supporting arms and services are kept as force troops in the FMF echelon. They include the extra logistic support necessary to sustain operations for more than about a fortnight, the amphibian companies, all the armour, all the artillery more powerful than the 105 millimetre howitzer, the anti-aircraft battalions, and many other kinds of unit. The intention is to add force troops as required so as to make a division self-sufficient in any situation except perhaps deployment a great distance inland. In that circumstance, the main logistic support would probably come through army channels as it did in Korea. This is partly a question of resources and partly too one of skills. Only the army has experience, for example, of maintaining railroads and long-distance pipelines. Such joint supply is quite practicable because the vast majority of user-items are the same. Certain types of wireless currently constitute an important group of exceptions.

Attacks on stoutly defended beaches are generally costly and chaotic and tend to be handicapped by inadequate armour and artillery support. There is therefore a premium on requests for close air support and tactical air supply being met with great speed and precision. Because of this each Marine division has a Marine Air Wing organic to it. All the men in any such wing have had a basic infantry training and throughout their careers commissioned aviators remain line officers capable of filling a wide range of non-flying posts. There is as much integration as possible between a division and its wing in matters like ad-ministration, messing, and recreation. These Marine Air Wings tend to be exceptionally large. Current thinking favours eight attack and fighter squadrons, six helicopter squadrons, a photo-reconnaissance-cum-electronic warfare squadron, three air con-trol squadrons, and a service group consisting of a dozen C-130s.

The Marine Corps totals 200,000 men and contains three divisions of the kind described above. One is stationed on the Atlantic coast of the United States and one on the Pacific coast, whilst a third is located in Okinawa. To provide these landing forces with a ready sealift the United States Navy maintains a large fleet of assault shipping in being. In the middle of 1961 this included the *Iwojima* and three other LPHs, one of 10,000 tons and two of 38,000 tons. In 1961 there were also two LPDs, thirteen LSDs and seventy-nine LSTs. Both the LPDs, eight of the LSDs, and twenty-two LSTs have been built since 1950. More representatives of each of these classes have been

planned, as have some more headquarters ships. About fifteen
attack transports and cargo vessels were also attached to the
assault fleet in 1961. The total simultaneous lift capacity was
then equivalent to one and a half Marine divisions and one and
a half Marine Air Wings. They are married up with the landing
forces, two-thirds being with the Pacific Fleet and one-third
from the Atlantic. The building programme is intended to
replace the older ships being progressively withdrawn from
active service, and so the aggregate lift should remain constant
for several years. When not involved in Marine Corps training,
the Navy conducts many amphibious exercises with United
States Army divisions.

The Royal Navy operates nine LSTs and twenty LCTs
together with a hundred or so smaller craft. There are another
seventeen LSTs on charter to the War Office or on loan to
civilian contractors and these could be made available in an
emergency. Of Royal Naval vessels two LSTs and three LCTs
are in the Amphibious Warfare Squadron now based on Aden.
This also contains four frigates and one headquarters ship. All
the present assault shipping is due for replacement and by the
end of 1964 the assault echelon of Amphibious Warfare Squadron will probably consist of two commando carriers and two
LSDs and will thus have about double its present capacity.
With several LSLs in support, such an echelon would be capable of moving a complete brigade group in one lift. Such a
group would probably include at least one Royal Marine
commando which is more or less equivalent to an infantry
battalion. At the present time there are two commandos in
Britain and Singapore respectively and one in Aden. A sixth
could probably be formed from the units of the Royal Marine
Force Volunteer Reserve.

One question which merits much more vigorous examination
than it has yet received is whether the future will offer much
scope for amphibious assaults. Commentators draw attention
to the flexibility such techniques have always afforded to those
who are able to exploit them, and seem to assume that history
is necessarily going to repeat itself. However, in the completely
novel world situation of today, an inherent tactical flexibility
cannot be exploited if that involves extending the area of conflict beyond politically unacceptable limits. The Communist

heartland, in particular, is not a Festung Europa upon which we can descend at will. For example, it would be absurd to land at Canton in order to check a Chinese advance into Laos. The force levels necessitated would be well above what the Western powers would feel inclined to spare and would probably be more provocative to our opponents than, say, a very selective use of tactical nuclear weapons within the original battle zone. The use of Chinese Nationalist troops would relieve the manpower problem, but would much increase the political complications. In any case what would one do next if one did occupy Canton? It would not be possible to exploit the situation militarily, because final solutions are ruled out in modern war. To remain in possession of an isolated and useless enclave would merely be to preclude the possibility of a political settlement. Aerial interdiction would always be a more effective way of persuading the Chinese to desist from aggression, because it would hurt them physically without involving them in loss of face through loss of territory. Of course, it could be said that a special case might arise in favour of establishing a deep beachhead on the north banks of the Red River in Vietnam in the event of Chinese aggression in South East Asia. Such a lodgement could block the supply routes of a Chinese expeditionary force deployed to the south. However, the establishment of such an enclave would be a major and very hazardous undertaking.

The degree of political flexibility a task force affords depends upon its composition and the circumstances in which it is being employed. If, as at Suez, it consists largely of landing craft of limited endurance slowly proceeding to a hostile shore from a fixed base 1,000 or so miles away, flexibility becomes the least of its virtues. If, on the other hand, it is made up of large vessels like commando ships and LSDs, it becomes as subtle an instrument of deterrence as a carrier task force with which, in practice, it would often be co-operating. One uncertain factor is that of the length of time troops could be kept on board ship during a period of tension without seriously impairing their combat efficiency. The British suggest one or two months. The Americans speak of six, but envisage one or two brief exercises ashore in the course of that time. It is perhaps worth remembering that Nelson's ships lay off Toulon virtually continuously for eighteen months between 1803 and 1805.

Leaders of amphibious forces have usually had to be men of cavalier spirit, because, however meticulously planned, the operations they have conducted have generally had an exceptional element of chance in them. The cavalier tradition in this sphere is reflected even at Inchon in MacArthur's remark before the landing that he was taking a 5,000 to 1 chance. However, though this tradition is most attractive it is becoming dangerously anachronistic because of the premium placed by modern conditions on guaranteed success. What might be, by historical standards, a moderate tactical reverse could constitute a political catastrophe at the present stage of the cold war. It is therefore doubly unfortunate that in many ways the odds against success have widened over the last fifteen years or so. The paramount position of politics in limited war strategy might well preclude the winning of the absolutely unconditional aerial superiority that is practically mandatory. For example, it would not be possible to guarantee complete control of the skies over North Vietnam without massive interdiction against the airfields of South China and this might not be politically admissible. Political considerations might, as at Suez, dictate a complete sacrifice of tactical surprise and, in any case, military security would be virtually impossible to maintain during a long-distance movement. The technical advances in naval mine warfare amount almost to a revolution and, if revolution it be, it is one that strongly favours the defence. Furthermore we do not eliminate the nuclear threat just by acknowledging its existence and by expanding the dimensions of the hypothetical beachheads outlined in staff college précis. A beachhead is by definition almost a point target under conditions of nuclear war and a concentration of unarmoured ships would be totally destroyed by even a small nuclear air burst. Moreover, small task forces are by definition more exposed to the loss of some vital component. At Okinawa there were eight headquarters ships and at Kuwait there was one.

This is not to say that an amphibious assault will never again be launched. Many of the technical and political difficulties enumerated above would not apply if a coastline were lightly held. Also in one or two places in the Middle East and several in Latin America circumstances could well arise in which it would be appropriate to use a seaborne hook to check aggression. All the same, whilst training for opposed landings must naturally continue, it seems likely that the chief purpose of amphibious forces henceforward will generally be that of conducting land operations based on a friendly country whose ports are too few, small, or vulnerable to offer adequate support. It is to this end that equipment, organization, doctrine and training should largely be geared.

11—CARRIER TASK FORCES

A major element in the limited war posture of the Western powers are their Carrier Vessels Attack. The United States is still using in this role seven of the 33,000-ton *Essex* class, though these vessels, which are now about twenty years old, are scheduled for conversion to anti-submarine work. Her more modern carriers include three ships of the 51,000-ton *Midway* class, which were completed in the 1945–7 period, the six 60,000-ton *Forrestals* built between 1955 and 1961, and the 75,000-ton nuclear-powered CVAN *Enterprise* completed in 1962. Like the other 830 ships of the active fleet, the attack carriers are divided about equally between the 2nd and 6th Fleets based on the east coasts and the 1st and 7th based on the west coast. The 7th Fleet, which patrols the Pacific West of the 160°E meridian, and the 6th Fleet in the Mediterranean normally have two or three attack carriers apiece. The Royal Navy has two light fleet carriers of 22,000 to 23,000 tons, the *Victorious* of 30,000 tons, and two larger units of 43,000 to 44,000 tons. Canada has the 16,000-ton *Bonaventure* in service and the Netherlands the *Karel Doorman*. Both these vessels have old keels, but modern superstructures. France is in the process of commissioning two new 22,000-ton carriers and these ships will form the backbone of the French surface fleet for the rest of this decade. They are intended for use in protecting the sea routes to and from the homeland and for service in *forces d'intervention* serving farther afield. In all the above-mentioned navies except the American one all carriers have both an attack and an anti-submarine role.

Naval aviation has certain inherent advantages over that which is shore based. Within the tropical zone heavy cloud is less prevalent over the sea and, in any case, ships can steer towards good weather. An air station on land can usually be readily attacked because its co-ordinates are known, whereas a carrier can lose itself at sea—especially when it is not operating aircraft. Radar reconnaissance can be frustrated by jamming and by fitting large reflectors on the smaller ships, whilst visual reconnaissance remains an unreliable, imprecise, and hazardous means of establishing a ship's position. Another consideration is that surface clutter on radar screens is far less over the sea and so low-flying planes can be more easily detected. This may be an embarrassment to naval aircraft intruding over a hostile coastline, but it will much facilitate the air defence of their parent ship. An air group attacking it might well have to accept an attrition rate of 80 to 90 per cent. Submarines are, of course, a special hazard, but a carrier, unless hit in an exceptionally sensitive spot like a propeller shaft, should be able to absorb a number of hits from torpedoes, and for that matter from bombs, without being crippled. On the other hand, various small but vital components of a task force such as the air-direction frigates are much more vulnerable.

Over the last decade improved landing aids and other advances have virtually eliminated the traditional difference in performance between sea- and land-based aviation. The A3J *Vigilantes* and F4D *Phantom* IIs entering the United States Navy today are superlative machines by any standards. Night flying from carriers is now quite routine. Also with modern steam catapults installed on board elaborate manoeuvres to enable aircraft to be launched downwind are not so often required. Another important point is that with the widespread introduction of better hull designs, automatic boiler controls, and stabilizers the different units in a task force are more able to keep station in heavy seas.

American naval authorities are convinced that these gains in efficiency are closely associated with the commissioning of larger aircraft carriers. Their published statistics on the meteorological factor show that in the Norwegian Sea and Straits of Taiwan, for instance, a *Forrestal* can reckon to fly its aircraft for 345 days of the year, but an *Essex* for only 220, and they point out that even under ideal weather conditions the latter has difficulty in handling the larger of the modern jets. They stress, too, that concentration in big units avoids duplication of many elements and give this as the reason why each of the *Forrestal* ships carry three times the aviation fuel and one and a half times the ordnance that the *Essex* class do and why their attack aircraft can be generally larger and almost twice as numerous. The difference in jet fuel reserves, for example, cannot be more than very partially explained by the fact that the larger vessels represent a later basic design. The proportion of the ships' full load tonnage that is represented by fuel and lubricants is the same in both cases—about one quarter. The differential is created by a *Forrestal*'s own engines consuming less in proportion to the work they do. Additionally it is likely that for a long time to come nuclear propulsion will exhibit considerable economies of scale favouring its employment on big ships. Of course, in strict economic terms marine nuclear propulsion is still not a proposition at all. The CVAN *Enterprise* at $435,000,000 cost exactly twice as much as the *Forrestal*. Mr. McNamara has stated that, even allowing for the extra logistic support it needs, a carrier driven by chemical combustion involves capital and operating costs only 65–75 per cent of those incurred by a nuclear-propelled one. This disparity should, however, gradually be reduced and, in any case, nuclear propulsion confers certain special advantages. A Carrier Vessel Attack Nuclear can sustain 33 knots on long global voyages, whereas at such speeds the range of a CVA would probably be cut down to about 3,000 miles. Alternatively if it kept company with the kinds of fleet oilers in service today it could not average above 20 knots. It is said that an all-nuclear carrier task force could be fully self-contained for twelve days. It is worth noting in this connection that the 9,000 tons or so of aviation fuel the *Enterprise* carries is said to be about twice that a *Forrestal* can manage.

Of course, large attack carriers have got certain drawbacks apart from inherent vulnerability. They cannot be economically converted to commando, anti-submarine, or logistic ships. Those of *Forrestal* size and above cannot negotiate the Panama and Suez Canals. No ship can recover more than one plane at a time and, although ideally this means one every fifteen seconds, battle damage or accident could cause major disruption. All the same, it is reported that the Admiralty is urging a

50,000-ton specification for the design study that the British
government have embarked on for a ship that might replace
the *Victorious* when she is withdrawn from service in 1970. This
vessel would carry an aircraft type common to the Royal Navy
and the Royal Air Force. The United States laid down a
64,000-ton CVA in January 1961 and another attack carrier is
due to be built under the 1963 programme.

Advocates of naval air power always point out that attack
carriers are part of the strategic deterrent, since they have on
board very fast attack aircraft capable of delivering thermonuclear weapons, but, as an extra argument in favour of
keeping them in being, this is only of marginal importance. In a
pre-emptive strike about half of them would be caught in port
whilst even those at sea would constitute large unhardened
objectives whose capacity for evasion and concealment would
avail them little against multi-megaton air bursts. What is
more about two-thirds of the carriers controlled by the Western
Alliance are normally at least several days' steaming time from
any positions from which they could deliver a strategic counter-
strike. Furthermore, their aircraft lack sophisticated electronic
equipment and so would have to accept higher attrition rates
when engaged in general war missions than, say, a B-52 would.
Last but not by any means least, a carrier-based strike aircraft
is, if all the respective supporting elements are weighed in the
balance, several times more expensive to procure and maintain
than a long-range heavy bomber and many times more expensive than an intercontinental ballistic missile.

However, the fact that carriers are becoming less and less
suitable for general war purposes does not mean that they have
ceased to be subtle, flexible, and powerful instruments of local
deterrence. Their deployment can take place without the consent of third parties and does not imply a prior commitment on
policy in the same way as the movement of land-based elements
does. Potential aggressors will always be aware of a task force's
presence, but it will not hurt their pride and thereby impair
their judgement as much as the arrival of troops might. Its
tactical reaction time is short and the latest generation of aircraft afford very good radii of action, particularly when in-flight
refuellings are possible, as they will be when the aircraft are
overflying friendly or undefended territory. Assuming high-level

approach to the target, the F4H can operate over a radius of 900 miles even without being refuelled whilst the A4D *Skyhawk*, if it is refuelled in flight, can deliver a 3,000-lb. bomb over about the same distance. An A3D *Skywarrior* if refuelled by one of its own kind could probably hit targets over 3,500 miles away. A carrier task force patrolling off some coast would always be a good means of guaranteeing immunity from sudden attack for United Nations forces operating in the hinterland. If, on the other hand, a limited war involving large powers breaks out, the strategic mobility of such task forces might be a considerable asset. A 30-knot carrier group can travel 500 miles more quickly than the ground echelon of an air wing. No doubt naval air enthusiasts make too much of this advantage, which could not be exploited without escalating a local conflict. If Chinese troops were being engaged in Vietnam, then to indulge in indiscriminate carrier strikes along the Chinese South Coast would be to invite Chinese attacks on Hong Kong, Quemoy, Matsu, and perhaps South Korea. It would also enhance the risk of Soviet intervention. Perhaps the most that should be claimed is that the strategic mobility of the task forces would be a restraining factor on the Chinese taking the initiative in escalating the conflict.

One of the drawbacks of carriers is that they are large and conspicuous ships whose individual identities are usually widely known. Therefore the sinking of one would become a prestige issue to a quite disproportionate extent. Another is that a large task force composed of two or three attack carriers, fifteen to twenty cruisers and destroyers and other supporting vessels extends over a box some 200 miles square when deployed for action. It is, moreover, desirable to leave 100 or 200 miles between the task-force perimeter and a hostile coastline and to have several hundreds of miles of depth for manoeuvre in other directions. Fleets of such a size are ill adapted to the dimensions of say the Aegean, the Red Sea or the Persian Gulf, though several such groups could operate simultaneously in the South China Sea, which is the area where such a concentration is likely to be required. If they did so they would very probably, at any time during this decade, be able to dominate any airpower China was able to mobilize against them in that particular theatre.

III—PORT CAPACITIES AND SEALIFT[1]

The intensity with which small ports and beaches have some-times been used to meet the needs of armies in the field is, to the layman, staggering. Shortly after its capture in 1943 Tripoli was accepting 6,500 tons a day, although its quayface had been blown in with characteristic German thoroughness. Dieppe was handling 7,000 tons a day one month after its liberation and Ostend 5,000 after a slightly longer interval. In June 1945, 20,000 tons a day was being deposited on the Okinawan beaches despite the heavy seasonal rains.[2] An average of 1,500 tons of supplies a day was being put across the beaches of Quemoy and Matsu towards the end of that period in 1958 when the United States Navy was making itself responsible for the logistic support of those islands in order to discourage the Communists from continuing their artillery bombardment.

From such evidence, formulae have been derived for estimat-ing the traffic a port or beach could cope with if provided with as much experienced labour and movable specialized machi-nery as it required. These formulae assume that the ships being worked are the *Liberties* and *Victories* of last-war fame, and on that basis it is reckoned that in a twenty-hour day up to 1,200 tons could be cleared per 1,000 linear feet of wharfage if the vessels were tied up alongside and up to 1,800 tons if they dis-charged to lighters.[3] Whether these figures could ever be reached would depend upon the width of quays and piers, the amount of open and covered storage available, and the land-ward exits from the port area. The strength of the wharfs would also be relevant, as that factor controls the maximum unit weights that might be handled. Many wharfs are not built to take strains in excess of 500 lb. per sq. foot and many piers have piles that cannot stand loads greater than 20 tons or so. Above all, of course, even small-scale enemy action such as the laying

[1] (a) Unless otherwise indicated all details of port facilities in this section come from Sir Archibald Hurd *Ports of the World* (The Shipping World Ltd., 1959)
    (b) Throughout this book a ton capacity is taken as being 2,000 lb.
[2] Edward Pinkowski in *United States Naval Institute Proceedings*, November 1946
[3] FM 101–10. US Department of the Army, February 1959. Part I, p. 349

of one or two mines could wreak havoc. Indeed, the mere threat of it could cause major inconvenience by inducing wholesale desertion of local dock labour and by necessitating ship dispersion and blackouts. The datum figures given above imply that lighters constitute the best way of utilizing restricted wharfage. This is true, but lighterage inevitably involves a double handling, is usually ruled out for heavy loads, and is very slow and difficult, if not impossible, in a choppy sea or heavy swell.

No general formulae have much relation to beach capacities in specific situations, because so much depends on the local facts of physical geography and also on what proportion of the cargo is wheeled. However, for what it is worth an average of 3,000 tons per mile per diem is given for reference purposes.[1]

In the following examination of several stretches of coastlines belonging to countries to which Britain and the United States have treaty obligations, it transpires that there are generally one or more ports with high nominal capacities, but that acute difficulty would be experienced in achieving them because of the lack of such handling equipment as cranes and lighters resulting from the light and unsophisticated nature of much of the peacetime traffic. Another problem in most places is the stringent upper limit that exists on the size of ship that can either anchor in the harbour or tie up alongside any wharf. This is illustrated by considering whether in each case high-speed destroyer transports, large *Forrest Sherman* class destroyers, *Victory* ships, or *Essex* class carriers could be accepted—to take a range of types in order of increasing draught.[2] Neither *Forrest Sherman* destroyers nor *Essex* class carriers would normally be used for logistic support, but they are specified because their lengths and draughts approximate to the smaller kinds of ocean-going cargo vessels and some of the larger modern passenger liners respectively.

Salonika in Greece was serving in 1917 as a main base for up to 600,000 Allied troops and it is still by far the most important port in Macedonia and Greek Thrace. It could take about eight *Forrest Shermans* alongside and has a potential throughput of well over 5,000 tons a day. Unfortunately at certain times

[1] FM 101-10. US Department of the Army, February 1959. Part I, p. 349
[2] See Table II on p. 127

persistent 'Northwesterlies' seriously impede operations. Farther east lie a chain of usable beaches and the ports of Kavalla and Alexandroupolis. The former could take three *Victory* ships and two *Forrest Shermans* alongside and be made to handle several thousand tons a day. The latter has one or two lighter quays, but the anchorage would be too shallow for much except APDs.

The best ports on the Aegean and Mediterranean coasts of Turkey are Izmir and Iskenderun, which could handle about 5,000 and 3,000 tons a day respectively. Izmir has three berths that destroyer transports could use and a deep sheltered anchorage within which nearly 150 tugs and lighters ply in normal times. Iskenderun, which is being developed under CENTO programme, has at present just one pier and this could take a pair of destroyer transports and a pair of large destroyers alongside. Some forty lighters are locally available to work ships anchored in the roadstead which would easily be deep enough to accommodate an *Essex* class carrier, but which is, unfortunately, rather exposed. Of the six or seven other ports south of the Dardanelles at only one could even a destroyer transport come alongside a wharf, and only two can provide deep sheltered anchorages, which is a great drawback, since during the winter gale force winds blow for five or ten days a month producing heavy surf and swell.[1] Of the smaller ports Mersin is the most developed, but even it has an optimum daily capacity of well under 1,000 tons and is hampered by wind and swell one hundred days a year.[2] Along the whole of this coastline there are said to be only three cranes able to lift at least 6 tons each, and only one that can manage 30 tons. Fortunately there are plenty of small beaches in sheltered gulfs and from most of them at least one roughish road leads inland. Many of them have served as sites for one or more of the NATO offshore discharge exercises.

At Abadan four assault transports could use the largest cargo jetty which has a 10-ton crane and there is available also a 200-ton floating crane. Otherwise, the only quays on the south

---

[1] Mediterranean Pilot (London, Admiralty Hydrographic Department), Vol. IV, 1955, p. 238; Vol. V, 1950, p. 18

[2] B.R. 507A. Turkey, Vol. II (London, Naval Intelligence Division, 1943), p. 102

coast of Persia that might take anything as large as *Forrest Shermans* are one or two at Bundar Shahpur and Khorramshar. Neither of these places has any cranes and like Abadan are rendered the more vulnerable by being placed some distance up shallow estuaries. Farther down the Gulf are Bushire, which has two small cranes, and Bundar Abbas, which has no cranes at all. Both are entirely dependent on lighterage. Nearly everywhere along the north-east shore of the Gulf high mountains lie steep to the coast, so that decent beaches are few and far between and exits from them are very generally abominably poor.

In Thailand there is only one recognized port, namely Bangkok, which has a normal throughput of around 6,000 tons a day, and which has 5,000 or 6,000 feet of quayside, much of which is concreted and has mechanized handling machinery installed. This includes a 15-ton crane. Unfortunately the tidal bar prevents any ships drawing more than about 22 feet from entering. Similar sand bars block most of the string of tiny estuarine harbours on the western side of the Gulf of Siam, which are, in any case, virtually closed for several months by the north-east monsoon: even in sheltered Bangkok this reaches gale force one day in ten in October and December. On the other hand, the west coast does have some reasonably firm and flat beaches, though, of course, they are even more exposed to monsoon winds than the harbours are. In the Bight of Bangkok itself mangrove swamps and soft mud together with a range of waterways in the immediate hinterland preclude 'over-the-beach' supply. Farther east there are some good beaches but exits are bad, because of jungle vegetation and steep gradients.

A mechanized infantry division weighs over 20,000 tons and an armoured division almost twice as much. This is apart from the minimum 5,000 or 10,000 tons supplies each of them would wish to accumulate within the combat theatre in order to be able to conduct sustained operations.[1] The figures dwarf the amount that would have to be shipped in each day for replenishment purposes, which would rarely exceed 1,000 tons. It is true that after two or three weeks, depending on circumstances, the leading Western nations involved would have to accept the responsibility of resupplying the armed forces of the alliance country being supported and that although the civilian import

[1] See Chapter 7, Section II

trade could be halted at the start of an emergency it would generally have to be resumed after about the same period, but neither of these factors is likely to alter the picture fundamentally. The weight of the first responsibility would be reduced by the relatively low firepower and mechanized mobility of the armies of most non-Communist countries outside Western Europe and North America which would result in any one of them having very modest logistic requirements. Then again, imports, too essential to sacrifice even in wartime, would normally constitute a small proportion of the usual overseas trade, and all the ports, unless any had been captured or had suffered heavy and irreparable damage, would eventually be working substantially faster than in peacetime. It seems almost certain that the pressure on the sea terminals available will be greatest at the beginning of an operation unless, of course, a high percentage of the initial movement is done by air.

When the mass of material involved in an initial build-up of divisional strength or more is compared with the capacities of most of the ports referred to above, it is clear that in many situations there would be a grave danger of congestion and delay. The problem is further complicated by the fact that it is during the opening stages that local labour shortages are liable to be at their worst and that the defences against air and submarine attack are likely then to be at their least adequate. The theoretical case studies made above are, in fact, borne out by the experience of Suez and the Lebanon when even comparatively well developed terminals like Port Said and Beirut were hardly capable of supporting large-scale seaborne mobile operations, although in neither case were the landings interfered with by aircraft or submarine.

Behind all else lurks the nuclear threat, for we cannot rule out the possibility that the Soviet Union might, if she felt her vital interests were at stake, use such weapons in limited war situations. By so doing she would imply a rejection of the views she currently holds about the inevitability of escalation of a conflict to a world scale once nuclear warheads are used at all, but a change of outlook on this question is not inconceivable. As I have already remarked, it is logically possible to conceive of targets against which tactical nuclear weapons could be used without involving a great risk of escalation and a port might, under certain circumstances, constitute a good example. Suppose, for example, the Soviet Union did send troops into Iran and the West, then promised the Persians assistance in defending themselves. Moscow Radio might then announce that in the event of British or American troops entering through Abadan they would, after due warning, air burst a small atomic bomb above the main cargo jetty. Anyhow, by allowing for a period of withdrawal from the port to be attacked the Russians could shift part of the responsibility for the use of atomic devices and for the loss of life resulting therefrom on to their opponents. It might fairly be said that such a course of action would be a gamble so tremendous that it is hard to imagine it ever being taken, but a government that had already committed itself to large-scale conventional military action against a neighbouring state would not necessarily be too scared to accept the risks involved in an extension of that policy. Any threat of a selective nuclear strike might be postponed until a trend had become established in the conventional fighting, but it is equally possible that it would be delivered early on before the Western powers had committed large forces to the area in question and whilst they were perhaps still contemplating the wisdom of ever doing so at all.

It is, therefore, apparent there will often be a need for an expeditionary force to diversify its points of entry as much as possible and, for this and all the other reasons listed, a requirement for units equipped to expand the capacity of all ports and beaches up to the limits set by their physical dimensions. Both the British and the American army include specialist port construction formations and the United States also keeps in being ten 'Seabee' naval construction battalions, of which two are equipped primarily with a view to supporting amphibious landings and eight with a view to port improvement.

What is just as necessary is to ensure that such facilities as become available should be utilized to the full as quickly as possible. To some extent this depends on having available ships and mobile equipment that incorporate the improved cargo-handling techniques that have been devised over the last fifteen or twenty years. To just as great an extent, however, it depends upon systematic co-ordination of all the different terminals. In this connection it must be observed that, in the two countries with which we are chiefly concerned, there seems to be little functional co-operation in the formulation of plans or in training between the army port operating units on the one hand and the amphibious forces on the other.

TABLE II

The Dimensions of Certain Characteristic Ships

	Displace-ment[1]	Overall length (ft.)	Maximum draught (ft.)
Essex Class	30,800	888	31
Victory Ship	15,500	455	29
Forrest Sherman destroyer	2,850	418	20
Destroyer Transport	1,400	306	13

Source: *Jane's Fighting Ships 1962–3*
[1] Full load for the *Victory* ship
Standard displacement (i.e. less fuel and water) for the rest

IV—CIVILIAN SHIPPING

All the maritime nations are aware of the historical importance of merchant shipping both as sources of strategic mobility, as the means of sustaining essential imports in time of war, and, indirectly, as providing the national support for naval power. This consciousness has sustained demands for government support of shipping and shipbuilding interests. In Britain this has resulted in a permanent subsidization of the fishing fleets, in the exemption of merchant seamen from peacetime conscription whilst that was in force, and in heavy subsidization of particular construction projects. In the United States the protection has been more continuous and comprehensive. Fifteen or twenty of the sea-going ships built each year are given a construction—differential subsidy to help compensate for the fact that American building costs are about twice those of their competitors.

This subsidy, which only totals about $3,000,000 a year, is given on condition that certain 'defence' features are incorporated. The things chiefly required are booms heavy enough to handle tanks, extra strong mountings for vital pieces of machinery, improved margins of speed, ample damage control arrangements, and enough cranes to enable a dry cargo ship to unload itself and to do so in about a half or one-third the time a *Victory* ship would take. The emphasis on ships handling their own cargo is very possibly a major reason why quay cranes are relatively much less important in the big American ports than they are in the British ones.

It is also felt desirable to offset to some extent the fact that American running costs are about half as much again as general world levels, and this is done by providing operating differential subsidies on about thirty routes felt to be of especial strategic importance. About one-third of the 1,000 ocean-going merchant vessels in active service under the United States flag benefit from this arrangement. That it is positive policy and not inertia that keeps protectionism alive in this sphere is shown by the 1961 legislation that gave the Federal Trade Commission supervisory powers over the award of 'exclusive trading' rate differentials by American shipping companies, thereby acknowledging their basic right to practise something which in any other industry would have exposed them to the anti-trust laws.

In 1949 the Military Sea Transportation Service was founded, partly to keep an organization in being ready to undertake wartime shipping allocation and control, and partly to keep manned and active a number of ships of types which the ordinary market pressures do not favour. The first role was amply fulfilled during the Korean War, when an average daily flow of military supplies to the Far East of over 30,000 tons was maintained by a MSTS fleet that eventually grew to 600 ships. The importance attached to the second role depends on the extent to which one feels that design trends in the merchant fleet favour its employment in war situations.

To some extent, of course, they do. Speeds of most new classes of merchantmen being built in most countries are a few knots higher than was the case before the war. Also, there is a great awareness of the need to get more work out of ships by letting them spend less time in dock. Therefore more and more use is being made of palletized containers, which are square-shaped boxes of standard size that are used in conjunction with roller conveyors and fork-lift trucks. They enable a medium-size cargo liner to get rid of small-item dry cargo in a day rather than a week and are most economical on labour and storage space.

In other respects, however, trends in civilian shipping are

either not enhancing or else are positively reducing their potential military usefulness. For one thing a major increase in
average size has taken place during the last two decades. In the
case of the British Merchant Navy, for example, it has gone up
by 37 per cent in passenger cargo liners and by as much as 82
per cent in the case of tankers.[1] Then again most of the derricks
in a standard cargo vessel still have load capacities of between
3 and 5 tons and even if a larger 'jumbo' derrick is installed it is
unlikely to be able to cope with anything above 20 tons. On the
other hand, there is a considerable military need for vessels
with booms able to take weights in the 40- to 150-ton range and
very wide hatches that can take on board items like heavy tanks,
locomotives, barges, lighters, and large pieces of radar. A number of civilian 'heavy lift' ships are in commission, but the
commercial demand that sustains them is small and only slowly
growing. Likewise, ocean-going 'roll-on, roll-off' vessels are not
popular with private operators because of the wastage of space
involved.

For such reasons MSTS keep in commission about 110
vessels including thirty-four cargo ships, twenty-five tankers,
seventeen transports, four aircraft ferries, eighteen Landing
Ships Tank, and twelve scientific research craft, and all the
members of this fleet except three have civilian crews. The cargo
fleet includes several ships with especially heavy booms and also
the USNS *Comet*, which is the first of five roll-on, roll-off vessels
to be procured between now and 1969, to provide the lift for
an armoured division or its equivalent. They will replace the old
and slow LSTs now in service and would be used particularly
during the follow-up phases of amphibious operations. The
Comet, which was built for $20,000,000, can carry 700 vehicles
and in the course of several hours she can off-load them either
on to a beach, a hardstand, or ramped lighters. The twenty-five
tankers referred to include a score of large oilers fitted out to
replenish at sea, and a few small gasoline carriers that might be
used to run supplies into small ports. The transports have been
held available lest airlifts be rendered impracticable by the
immobilization of the terminal airfields and because ordinary
passenger liners always need extensive refitting before they can
carry a capacity number of troops. Now, however, in accordance

[1] Cmd. 1824; 1962, p. 16

with the principle that the MSTS active fleet should be small and composed of specialized units, the United States government is thinking of putting its troopships into reserve.[1] The great bulk of routine military movements by sea are already being carried out in chartered vessels at a total cost of around $280,000,000 a year.

Some British landing craft are run by the Ministry of Transport, and that department will also be responsible for administering the several Landing Ships Logistic that are to start entering service in 1964. They will each displace 6,000 tons, have two section ramps bow and stern, fore and aft cranes, and pontoons. At one and the same time they will be able to carry 350 troops, about five tanks, a score of wheeled vehicles, and a quantity of mixed stores. A cost of £1,750,000 apiece will make them nearly twice as expensive as commercial cargo liners of a similar size.

Their seventy-man crews will be civilians and will therefore be the first Merchant Navy men to serve in amphibious forces in peacetime. Merchant seamen have, of course, served with success and distinction in armed merchant cruisers, escort carriers, and Royal Fleet Auxiliaries, but their use operationally is always liable to be a cause of friction because their discipline is less formal, their pay is better, and accommodation aboard ship superior to that in the Royal Navy. There need, on the other hand, be little doubt about their dependability under fire. In the spring of 1917, when one in every four of all Merchant Navy vessels leaving British ports was being sunk, there was not a single recorded case of a ship refusing to sail.

Current United States doctrine states that after the first month of any conflict the vast bulk of supplies would arrive by sea under MSTS control, thus preserving the airlift and naval amphibious shipping to deploy other forces elsewhere if so required. It seems clear that by that stage these supplies would include all those needed to support the indigenous Alliance armies as well as the expeditionary ones, since it is most unlikely that any powers outside the North Atlantic and Soviet Bloc areas have stocks of consumable war materials amounting to

[1] The Secretary of Defense, Mr. McNamara, before a Subcommittee of House Committee on the Merchant Marine and Fisheries: April 18, 1962

thirty days' average combat expenditure. It might also soon become necessary to ship considerable quantities of foodstuffs to aid the civilian populations affected. Even during the first month as much sea transport as possible would be brought into service to supplement the airlift and also to keep it supplied with fuel: a C-141 Transport plane, for example, will take on board 80 tons of aviation spirit every time it does a complete refuelling. In view of all the demands for shipping space thus created any Western countries involved in hostilities would inevitably become heavily dependent on their merchant navies to supplement their regular sealifts.

All the same it is possible to recognize the potential importance of segments of the national merchant fleets without subscribing to a lot of the arguments advanced in various countries in favour of subsidy and protection. Marine technology is not the source of prestige it was. Vast reserves of shipping available to compensate for losses by submarine attack are unnecessary, as Battles of the Atlantic are things of the past. Above all, national self-sufficiency in this, as in so many respects, is a less worthy and rational goal than interdependence. All the NATO members have legal powers to mobilize their merchant marines for war service and a NATO shipping pool exists for their co-ordinated employment in the event of an allied emergency. No such plans exist for implementation outside the North Atlantic and Mediterranean areas, but they could no doubt be quickly improvised.

V—THE COMMUNIST NAVAL CHALLENGE

Discussion of the naval threat from the Communist Bloc has been heavily preoccupied with the security of the Atlantic area and of the Pacific seaboard of North America. This preoccupation is hard to understand, bearing in mind that defensive precautions against Soviet ballistic missile submarines in anticipation of general war have only a very moderate value, since the Western powers cannot deny them access to the high seas and would always be bound to concede them the right of first strike. It can be argued that the danger from conventional submarines remains, but it seems unrealistic to prepare for limited war operations against them in such vitally important waters.

The Soviet Union would no more dare to start torpedoing shipping in the North Atlantic as an isolated act than a Western power would to drop high-explosive bombs on the Trans-Siberian railway. The same is and will remain true in respect of the Caribbean, although it is beyond the geographical limits of NATO, and although the Soviet Union has assumed for herself, temporarily at least, the role of protector of Cuba. In 1962 successful Soviet maritime intervention in that theatre would have been physically impossible, but even if that had not been the case the Soviet Union would have felt very inhibited about initiating operations in a sea area regarded as of such importance by the United States.

What is more worthy of consideration is the possibility of Communist sea-power being employed in limited-war situations beyond the fringes of the North Atlantic Ocean. It is conceivable that, when the Soviet strategic deterrent is stronger and Soviet and Chinese naval power greater, one or both of them might declare some rather more peripheral sea area a war zone in order to block or impede a Western mobile operation.

The chief reason why this prospect has never been fully discussed seems to be that Western governments have been fearful of inviting such a challenge by appearing to guarantee that it would not provoke them into strategic retaliation. However, such an attitude militates against adequate precautions being taken in advance and could result in one or both sides making fatal miscalculations in a moment of tension. In any case the public pretensions of indifference appear very hollow in the light of the history of CENTO and SEATO naval exercises. This shows that the possibility of localized conflicts in the Arabian and South China seas respectively play a major part in the contingency planning done by those alliances.

There are three kinds of situation that might precipitate such a clash. The first is one in which allied forces are defending an 'outpost' heavily dependent on maritime logistic support. North Norway, Korea, Quemoy and Matsu, Formosa, Thailand, and South Vietnam are potential examples. The aim of a naval offensive would obviously be to starve the outpost into surrender. Another possibility is that United States naval intervention against a Marxist régime in Latin America might be opposed by Soviet submarines. The expectation here would not be that the United States could be permanently thwarted, but that she might be humiliated by being forced to accept losses heavier and more conspicuous than those the submarine force suffered. Finally, if Western sea-power was being deployed in fulfilment of some alliance or United Nations commitment in the eastern hemisphere of which the Soviet Union strongly disapproved, and if the success of the operations depended on a quick reaction, the Russians might regard it as worthwhile to carry out or threaten a brief blocking action.

Although an effective maritime blockade is a legal method of war according to the signatories of the Treaty of Paris in 1856, it usually causes bitter resentment among non-belligerents. Britain in 1780, 1801 and 1812 and Germany in 1917 brought powerful states into conflict with themselves through trying to enforce it. During the Cuban crisis the United States was careful to use the technique only to prevent the assembly of strategic nuclear weapons systems within the island in question. Likewise, in order to reduce the risk of invoking international hostility, the Soviet Union or China would always seek to avoid seriously disrupting the trade routes of neutral nations. For example, it would always be as well to make any naval action in the Arabian Sea brief and to conduct it in such a way as to ensure that no non-combatant vessels were damaged. That would necessitate firing only on the basis of visual sightings and abstaining from the use of mines. The inhibitions would presumably be rather weaker in an area like the South China Sea. An aggressor nation might feel able to threaten to extend the war zone to embrace the Philippines in the event of the Filipinos affording Western nations any form of military aid. In the same way, although forces blockading Korea would be very ill advised to interrupt the sea-communications of a neutral Japan, a threat that this could happen might serve to keep Japan neutral.

Against this type of threat Mahan's classic solution of dominating 'privateers' by attacking them all the way from their home bases could hardly be applied. Such a remedy would, in many situations, automatically escalate the conflict across thousands of miles. Furthermore a fully submerged submarine is anonymous, and in the process of hunting boats proceeding to limited war zones the anti-submarine forces would probably 'kill' some equipped with IRBMs. By this means the whole operation would be raised to the status of a counter-force strike and thus so might precipitate a thermonuclear exchange. Although no one would be under any compulsion to accept the exact limits set by the opposition on some war zone, broadly speaking a challenge by Communist forces of this kind would have to be met at the time and place of their choosing.

At the present time Russia's largest naval units are the fourteen *Sverdlov* 35-knot cruisers of 15,450 tons standard tonnage. They can do about 5,000 miles at 20 knots. Of her fleet of 130 destroyers about 110 are large and powerful ships, built since 1950, rated at 38 knots, and endowed with good sea-keeping qualities over ranges of several thousand miles. Some of the new-construction destroyers, like some of the cruisers, carry guided missiles. An element in the Soviet Navy that is especially suited to limited war is the 500 or so motor torpedo boats, gunboats, and rocket-craft. It is, however, the submarines that have attracted most foreign comment. Apart from the nuclear-propelled ones, there are estimated to be about 420 altogether of which eighty are large and 150 medium-size ocean-going types. Nearly all of the ocean-going boats and about fifty of the coastal ones have been built since 1950.

This is an impressive order of battle, but its significance in terms of limited war is reduced by the fact that, whether wisely or not, the Soviet Union sees all her fleet, and not just the ballistic submarines within it, as having a general war function, and so is likely always to reserve a good proportion of it against that contingency. Furthermore the traditional weakness of the Russian Navy, that of being divided between several land- or ice-locked seas, is undiminished. Thus one-third of the submarine fleet is based on the northern coast and slightly less in the Far East. The percentage in the Far East could always be substantially increased if so required and is in any case steadily rising in consonance with the very rapid industrialization of the area. The winter freeze is quite a problem, but some naval bases in Sakhalin, Kamchatka, and the Kuriles remain ice-free most years, whilst Vladivostok can be kept continuously open by ice breakers. On the north coast the only sector permanently clear of ice is that around Murmansk and Petsamo. Here, too, port installations are being rapidly expanded. Of course, the strategic mobility of the Soviet Navy within, as well as beyond, the Soviet Union is reduced by the annual freeze-up. The Baltic-to-White Sea Canal is only usable for about half the year and the Northern Sea Route for around fourteen weeks. Nevertheless, the fact that inland deep-water routes capable of taking surface ships of several thousand tons displacement, as well as some of the smaller classes of submarine, are being developed to connect up all the seas peripheral to European Russia, could prove of considerable significance during a period when tension was mounting in some particular theatre.

Soviet naval power would be likely to be employed on active operations in the Pacific in support of Communist China if it were employed at all. There have already been occasional reports of Soviet boats using North Korean and Chinese ports and they might do so more extensively in the event of hostilities. The southward deployment would be facilitated by the movement of depot ships of which the Soviet Union already has about twenty in commission. Meanwhile the only offensive element of any value at present in the inventory of the Chinese Navy is the twenty Soviet-designed W class submarines built in the Wuchang and Shanghai shipyards. About six more are being built a year. It is worth noting that between 1928 and 1940 the Soviet Union built up from scratch a fleet of 170 boats of which perhaps a third were ocean-going. Admittedly the Soviet submarine fleet failed pretty comprehensively in the Second World War owing to its inferior training and equipment, but China may have the backing of Russia to help her get over such teething problems.

The Soviet Union now has her first nuclear submarines in commission and seems to be currently building three different varieties at the rate of several per year. The pace of construction should rise substantially once retooling is complete and adequate design experience has been gained. Her peak annual output of conventional boats was about seventy and her production capacity must be rising steadily as her industry as a whole expands. On the other hand, if American figures can be taken as typical a nuclear ballistic submarine costs about ten times as much as, and a nuclear attack submarine about four times as much as, an ocean-going conventionally powered attack boat. Another critical economic factor, that is not reflected adequately in monetary cost, is that the manufacture of nuclear propulsion units absorbs certain specific and scarce skills. All in all a reasonable assumption is that 75 to 100 nuclear-driven submarines could be flying the Soviet flag by 1970, together with 100 or 200 with diesel-electric propulsion completed since 1956. Then, as now, a substantial fraction of the total would probably be held back against the possibility of general war.

The procurement by the United States of the site at North West Cape, Australia, with a view to establishing a shore-to-submarine communications base, implies that *Polaris* submarines will soon be patrolling in the Indian Ocean. This in itself will tend to attract some Soviet attack U-boats ready to act as counter-force elements if necessary. Also Soviet ballistic submarines are already operating in the Atlantic and Pacific ready to participate in counter-city strikes in the event of a general war and with them are operating some attack and hunter-killer types. The immediate purpose of these supporting units is presumably to give the ballistic submarines protection against physical attack, but their numbers might be so increased that a proportion of them would effectively become a theatre reserve available for localized hostilities.

The limiting factor on the maintenance and operation of such theatre reserves would probably be the human one unless, as is unlikely, they worked from depot ships located in foreign ports. Published estimates of the ranges of Russian submarines tend to be rather misleading, because they are calculated on the assumption that the vessels will proceed at their most economical speeds completely indifferent to the passage of time. This is something that does not happen, because there are limits to the amount of living as submariners that men can stand at one stretch. The United States nuclear submarine *Triton* of 5,500 tons standard displacement has remained totally submerged for eighty-three days, but she has exceptional crewspace and amenities. The longest time any German U-Boat spent on patrol in World War II was about eighty days. Taking into account a certain amount of surface cruising and perhaps one or two visits to a friendly port, we can take ninety days as being the maximum possible patrol period for a typical ocean-going boat. During this time, if dependent on diesel-cum-electric propulsion, it might receive fuel oil from a friendly port or from one of the several members of the Z class that, it is said, have been fitted out as oilers. Without refuelling the fifty combatant members of the F and Z classes would have a surface radius of action of about 13,000 miles at an average speed of 13 knots on a ninety-day patrol. The 236 members of the W class would have a surface radius of action of 11,000 miles at 10 knots. A nuclear submarine with tear-drop fuselage maintaining 30 knots submerged would have a radius of action of 33,000 miles. It is instructive to compare these figures with the distance between Soviet home ports and points central to areas of possible local conflict. Thus the Andaman Islands are 4,500 miles from Vladivostok via Singapore and 13,000 miles on a route circumnavigating Australasia. From Socotra the distances are 7,500 and 14,500 miles respectively. The River Plate is 8,500 miles from Murmansk and from Vladivostok. Since 40 per cent of a fleet would probably always be undergoing training and repairs, to maintain a standing patrol of five F or Z class submarines 8,500 miles from their base would necessitate the commitment of twenty-five boats. For W class boats the number involved would be thirty-two.

Naturally any application of this kind of force would have to be subject to a set of controls intended to minimize the risk of escalation, which we know both sides would be very desirous of avoiding. Submarines would probably proceed to and from a war zone as inconspicuously as possible. This would involve travelling submerged most of the time, which would cut down the range of boats built to an orthodox 'knife-and-prow' hull design. It would involve avoiding natural bottlenecks *en route* like the Straits of Malacca in which it would be tempting to intercept them. In the case of the larger of the nuclear-attack submarines, it might involve proceeding at reduced speed on passage, because at top speeds they produce ultra-sonic emissions detectable hundreds of miles away. By thus revealing their movements they would eliminate the prospects of a surprise concentration and would possibly provoke interdiction against themselves.

A logical conclusion would seem to be that at any time during the next ten years the Soviet Navy together with that of the Chinese People's Republic might, assuming that the overall world situation favoured such a course of action, intervene powerfully in the Western Pacific. Active Communist naval operations elsewhere would hardly seem to be practicable at the moment, but they could very possibly become so with the progressive introduction of nuclear submarines. All the same, the number of boats that could be committed at any one place or time would probably be a very low percentage of the total Soviet submarine fleet. Of course, used passively in support of guerilla operations, even small numbers of submarines could yield rich dividends as long as their movements were not obstructed. A submarine is the ideal vehicle for the illegal shipment of small arms and ammunition.

VI—THE STATUS OF THE SUBMARINE

In any local concentration of Soviet naval forces submarines would play a predominant part and in some they would play an exclusive one. Therefore, in order that we may be able to make an approximate assessment of the significance of such concentrations, it is desirable to attempt an assessment of the technical balance between escort forces and submarines in limited conventional war. This is difficult partly because it is governed by a large number of complex factors, some of which are secret and most of which are always in a state of flux. It is difficult also because the precise balance struck during any conflict would be heavily dependent on the exact situation at the time. Thus small convoys generally suffer a rather higher attrition rate than big ones and, up to the present time at any rate, ships that have not been organized into convoys have experienced a much higher one than those that have. Crowded waters, like the narrow seas around England, prove less congenial to U-boats in both world wars than relatively empty ones. The lack, in any particular sea area, of aerial surveillance would much increase their target location problem. Also, seas less than 1,000 feet deep do not afford the new nuclear submarines the opportunity of taking advantage of their exceptional manoeuvrability and deep-diving capabilities, while those shallower than 300 feet are inadequate for prolonged operations by any ocean-going craft—even those of more conventional design. On the other hand, the opportunities for

lying in wait against the background of an irregular ocean
floor might make coastal waters very suitable for surprise
attack. With all these variables and imponderables no analysis
could even try to predict the results of any attempt to interfere
with Western maritime mobility unless it made a whole host of
very explicit assumptions.

Nevertheless some general observations can be made that
suggest that recent developments have completely reversed the
situation established in the Atlantic in 1943, which was one in
which the anti-submarine forces enjoyed a crushing supremacy.
It is true, of course, that submarines are much more easily
concealed than was the case twenty years ago. A nuclear-driven
boat never has to break surface to recharge batteries, whilst a
diesel-electric one now only has to protrude its schnorkel tube
in order to do so. These advances have much reduced the risks
of visual or radar detection whilst on passage and the importance of this can be gauged from the fact that 49 per cent
of the U-boats destroyed at sea in the Battle of the Atlantic
were sunk by Allied submarines and land-based aircraft, both
of which generally operated away from convoys, and by naval
hunter-killer groups.[1]

One of the biggest changes that has taken place in the last
few years is that the great powers have started building both
nuclear and conventional attack submarines that, even when
submerged, are faster than most supply ships. This has clearly
been a considerable leap forward but it has not been as important a one as some writers suggest. At their present speeds of
25 to 30 knots even nuclear submarines are slower than helicopters and modern escort ships except perhaps in stormy
weather. They are much slower than the anti-submarine hovercraft and hydrofoils that should enter service soon. Their speed
can be assumed to be considerably below the speed in water of
the new anti-submarine rocket-assisted homing torpedoes, for
as early as 1945 torpedoes capable of over 45 knots had become
operational. Furthermore, although the next generation of
atomic submarines will inevitably be faster than the present
one, sensational improvements are not to be expected, because
the power/weight ratios of nuclear engines of any given size

[1] Sir John Slessor, *Strategy for the West* (London, Cassell, 1954),
Chapter IV

will not be substantially reduced even if reactors become much more efficient. The reason for this is that the reactors represent a very modest fraction of the total engine space—in the *George Washington* and *Nautilus* it seems to be about a quarter. Similar considerations make it doubtful whether, in the foreseeable future, it will be worth while to fit smaller submarines with nuclear engines. In the large American nuclear-driven ballistic submarines the overall engine space amounts to about 45 per cent of the internal cube, which is approximately the same proportion as that taken up in ocean-going conventionally powered vessels. Smaller nuclear propulsion units would have much less favourable power/weight ratios, and yet smaller boats would require more power per ton to sustain any given speed. The combined effect would be to raise the percentage of engine space to quite unacceptable limits. Admittedly the United States have produced the *Skate* class of nuclear attack submarines which have a standard displacement of 2,400 tons, but even this is several hundred tons above that of the largest conventionally powered vessels and, in any case, these vessels are reported capable of a submerged speed of only 19 knots.[1]

Even at moderate speeds individual submarines have substantially higher noise levels than individual ships because of their greater external drag, and so are not only more audible but also more liable to create enough noise to ruin their own acoustic reception. This latter effect becomes serious around 15 knots even with modern nuclear submarines, despite their streamlined hulls and well-designed propellers and despite the fact that their engines have relatively few moving parts. It is true that in certain tactical situations a submarine is able to lie in silence waiting for its enemy, but this advantage is in part offset by the fact that most sonar equipment in use today is of the active variety that measures ranges and bearings by timing the reflection from solid objects of sound waves it has manufactured itself. In good conditions such equipment can locate stationary targets at ranges in excess of 10 miles. Once the enemy has been located he can be swiftly annihilated by means of either air-launched homing torpedoes or by the rocket-launched varieties referred to above. The latter are fired through the air to enter the water anything up to 15 miles away.

[1] *Jane's Fighting Ships 1960–1* (London, Sampson Low, 1961)

Bad underwater sound reception severely hampers a submarine's search for targets, although it has got periscope sights and radar as alternative sensors, but once battle has been joined bad reception conditions affect more adversely the ships and helicopters of a defensive screen. Although really serious interference is normally associated with stormy seas, very indistinct, erratic, and misleading echoes can often be received in calm ones through gradual or abrupt changes in salinity, temperature, or oxygen content or through reflection off other solid surfaces which may be animal or mineral in origin. To make the most of sonar sets a thorough knowledge of local oceanography is required. Far too high a proportion of such resources as the West has devoted to that science over the last few years have been expended in the North Atlantic and Eastern Pacific as opposed to the Western Pacific, Indian Ocean, and South Atlantic.

It is widely felt that shipborne sonar is not capable of much further development, but some commentators hold out great hopes of very powerful and effective shore-based sets being produced in the not-too-distant future. A great deal of research is at present being carried out into revolutionary methods of detection through salt-water media. Very low-frequency radar and infra-red and molecular sensors are among the possibilities being investigated. Meanwhile, Magnetic Airborne Detection has made great strides as a means of precisely fixing the position of targets that have already been located approximately. Several reports credit the latest sets with a vertical range extending to about 800 feet below the surface of the sea. Anti-submarine weapons, especially torpedoes and mines, are gradually getting better also. All this research and development together with the anticipated application of hovercraft and hydrofoils to this kind of work make it appear likely that anti-submarine forces will keep the technical advantage they probably enjoy today. However, as implied above, such generalizations afford little guidance as to what might happen in specific situations. The threat of local surprise attacks or blocking actions following prior concentration in selected areas will become an increasingly potent one. The obvious ways of reducing it are by employing high-speed surface ships that remain within combat zones for short periods of time and which are

tactically difficult to intercept, by having adequate escort
forces available, and by having alternative ports and beaches
so as to provide a choice of approach lanes.

VII—TECHNOLOGICAL CHANGE

The most revolutionary change taking place in naval science
today is the introduction of nuclear propulsion. The United
States alone has launched, or is building, one carrier, one
cruiser, two escort vessels, and sixty-one submarines that are so
powered. Nuclear submarine construction has been emphasized because the ordinary diesel-electric boats require cumbersome batteries and even with them cannot run at top speed
fully submerged for more than one or two hours, but the surface
ships also derive important advantages from this new power
source. They include the ability to shut down completely
against fall-out and to generate full engine heat in a matter of
microseconds, but the most important one is that they can
maintain their highest speeds almost indefinitely. Thus a conventional cruiser able to do 10,000 miles at 15 knots would
probably find it could manage about 3,000 at 30, whereas the
Long Beach, for example, can do over 100,000 miles at its
maximum of 30 knots.[1] Unfortunately as of today these gains
are often felt to be outweighed by excessive costs, especially in
the case of small ships which do not reap the large economies of
scale characteristic of atomic energy. Thus, with the pressurized
water-cooled reactors that seem to be the kind universally employed at present, the capital costs per kilowatt of power (that
is per one-third of a shaft horse-power) range from $175 for
a 150,000-kilowatt plant to $1,000 for a 5,000-kilowatt unit.[2]
Since capital payments are pretty consistently around 60 per
cent of total running costs, the spread seems very significant.[3]
However, the extra cost that atomic power incurs even with
large ships must be evaluated in relation to the operational
improvements it is likely to register and in comparison with the

[1] *Jane's Fighting Ships 1962–3* (London, Sampson Low, 1962)
[2] *McGraw-Hill Encyclopedia of Science & Technology* (New York,
McGraw-Hill, 1960), Vol. IX, p. 195
[3] *Ibid.*

total outlay on the vessels in question. Thus, in the high-wage American economy, non-nuclear shipbuilding is about twice as costly as it is in Britain. Also a large and sophisticated warship is so expensive that no propulsion unit affects the final figure by a large percentage. Thus, only $41,000,000 out of the $320,000,000 spent on the guided-missile cruiser *Long Beach* went to provide her reactors.[1] On the other hand, in the case of the 20,000-ton American merchant ship *Savannah*, the reactors contributed $23,000,000 to the final appropriation of $40,000,000. This sum has been estimated to be almost twice what it would have been for a comparable oil-bearing ship.[2]

It is clear that marine reactors will soon get considerably cheaper. Nearly half the price quoted for the model installed in *Savannah* went to cover first-generation research and development and the proportion need not be as high in any subsequent marine unit of similar specification. Also, experience will result in innumerable modifications to pressurized water reactors that will produce higher levels of efficiency. Furthermore, the mass production of artificial fissionable material will gradually make the nuclear cores cheaper and they will eventually be more fully utilized than at present. Additionally for some years work has been in progress in the United States on the first gas-cooled reactor intended for marine propulsion, and the experts feel this presages power plants substantially cheaper and more compact than comparable pressurized water ones could be.

Unfortunately even when seaborne nuclear fission becomes very cheap and compact it will still be difficult to get much higher top speeds out of ships of orthodox design. This is partly because ordinary frictional drag increases with speed, but more particularly because the amount of energy uselessly absorbed in wave-making grows ever more quickly. The proportion of the external resistance of a typical fleet destroyer that is due to wave motion rises from 30 per cent at 16 knots to 80 per cent at 27 knots. The total drag encountered at 24 knots is nearly four times what it is at 16 knots and at 27 knots about twenty times.[3] This trend is the basic explanation of why about 35 per cent of the internal cube of a modern destroyer is given over to

[1] *Sunday Times*, January 28, 1962
[2] *New Scientist*, July 16, 1959
[3] D. Phillips-Birt in *New Scientist*, November 13, 1958

engines and boilers. In smaller ships the problem becomes acute earlier than in big ones, thus complicating the task of keeping station in a balanced force. For example, to maintain a speed of 33 knots in a calm sea normally requires the application of about 5 shaft horse-power per ton in a 60,000-ton carrier, 10 in a 10,000-ton cruiser, and 60 in a 100-ton torpedo boat.[1] With craft displacing less than 1,000 tons the problem is aggravated by structural and engine installation requirements necessitating their being unduly short and stubby, thereby increasing wave production. The corollary of this is, however, that we could always damp down the wave resistance of larger ships by making them more slender than now. A 750-foot vessel with a 40-foot beam would offer the same resistance at 37 knots as a 500-foot one of similar displacement and 60 feet beam would at 30. The snags are principally that inshore navigation and docking would be made that much harder and that pitching strains would become greater—a serious matter, since, at present, stabilizers are only useful against rolling.

It does therefore seem that the advent of nuclear propulsion is not going to result in much faster ships. The great gain, as we have seen, is that optimum cruising speed and maximum speed will become, to all intents and purposes, synonymous. Since there may often be a critical difference between 30 knots and 20 knots both in respect of the time involved in strategic movement and in respect of minimizing the danger from submarines, this could constitute a very significant advance.

With regard to smaller size ranges, interest is focusing more and more on the possibility of breaking through or pushing back the resistance barrier by the adoption of revolutionary design techniques. Thus 'air-cushion vehicles'—which are still usually referred to by their more colloquial title of 'hovercraft' —are widely recognized as having potential applications in defence as supply vehicles for use on shallow and unobstructed jungle waterways, armoured fighting vehicles for assault across marshland, streams, or minefields, and as anti-submarine vessels, lighters, and assault landing-craft. It is because their prospective utility seems greatest in these maritime roles that they are considered here as essentially marine craft.

[1] Based on various figures in *Jane's Fighting Ships 1961–2* (London, Sampson Low, 1961)

All the indications are that hovercraft are on the verge of a development boom, though its extent and pattern are hard to predict: this is partly because laboratory tests cannot provide any conclusive evidence about the performance of vehicles intended to operate close to extremely heterogeneous surfaces, and partly because we lack experience of the mass production of these craft. Research on them began in Britain in 1953 and design work on the first operational model—the SRN-1— began in October 1958. Eight months later it made its first flight and it has been followed by the SRN-2, which, in August 1962, maintained block speeds of 50 knots in the crowded *Solent* during a four-day experimental service. Meanwhile, the Russians have done trials on a 12-ton model and the British firm of Vickers Armstrong have begun design studies on a 110-ton machine.[1] Certain advantages accrue from increasing scale and it has been estimated that a vehicle of 300 tons all-up weight could maintain a competitive passenger-and-car service across the English Channel and that one of 1,000 tons a.u.w. could achieve an airspeed of 100 knots, carry a 400-ton payload, and negotiate 12-foot waves.[2] The Mark II version of the SRN-2 is to be of 27½ tons a.u.w. and, cruising at 74 knots, it will carry 12 tons or 150 passengers for 230 nautical miles or 5 tons and 60 passengers for 700 miles. At 40 knots it will be able to negotiate 4-foot waves riding on its cushion, but at higher speeds it will have to lower itself on to the water in order to be able to do so, unless, of course, the distances between successive waves are great as they will be in the deep open sea. Since even in the relatively storm-bound English Channel wave amplitudes are below 5 feet 81 per cent of the time and below 10 feet 98.5 per cent of it, wind and sea should rarely curtail operations, though no doubt, as with standard landing craft, plunging surf could on occasions prove an obstacle to beaching.[3] One characteristic of hovercraft that will be valuable for submarine evasion and submarine hunting is that they induce relatively little sea turbulence and so their sonar echoes are weak. As admitted above, no concrete knowledge has yet been acquired of production costs, but tentative

[1] *Jane's All the World's Aircraft 1961–2, op. cit.*, p. 365
[2] *Interavia*, 6/1963, p. 703
[3] *Ibid.*, p. 692

estimates suggest that 70-ton machines would cost £750,000 apiece and 1,000-ton ones £4,000,000.[1,2]

On this basis a 1,000-ton hovercraft would be over twice as expensive to build as a Landing Ship Logistic and because of its high fuel consumption it would have perhaps a tenth of the payload on long-distance voyages. At the same time high fuel consumption would combine with heavy maintenance requirements to produce high running costs. From the standpoint of being able to move supplies as cheaply as possible these limitations are by no means completely offset by the higher speeds available. It does seem, therefore, that hovercraft are unlikely ever to become the standard media of sea transport during the resupply and reinforcement stage of operations, except, perhaps, when submarines are barring the passage of ships of orthodox design.

Hydrofoil craft are ones whose hulls are supported above the water surface on stilts that extend up from submerged inclined planes—known as 'foils'. They share with hovercraft the high speeds and accelerations derivative from low frictional drag and little wave disturbance, but unlike them they suffer from severe diseconomies of scale, because the lift from the planing surfaces, at each particular angle of incidence, varies as the square of their linear dimensions, whereas the weight to be supported changes in an approximately cubic relationship. Another, but presumably less intractable, problem is the supercavitation effect that increases drag above 60 knots or so. The largest vessels extant can proceed on their foils through moderate seas, but can settle on the water to ride out rough seas or to lower their sonars. The *H. S. Denison*, which weighs 90 tons, has recently been built for $5,000,000 for experimental operation on the Miami–Bermuda route. It reaches 50 knots in low seas and at 30 knots is said to be able to negotiate 12-foot waves. If this claim is consistently borne out by experience, then its sea-keeping qualities will be superior to those of hovercraft of comparable size, but it must be noted that so far the behaviour of hydrofoils at sea has been notoriously unpredictable. Nevertheless they seem to have a future as submarine chasers, and the United States Navy is at present designing a 500-ton model for

[1] *Interavia*, 6/1963, p. 703
[2] *Economist*, June 23, 1962

this purpose. Their speed and moderate degree of immunity from underwater obstacles also guarantees them a role as assault-landing craft, but, since 1,000 tons seems to be a theoretical upper limit for their displacement, they will probably have few other military applications.[1]

Russia has a long tradition of mine warfare and this fact renders all the more significant the major advances that have taken place in it over the last two decades. Modern aircraft can lay mines with acceptable precision from 15,000 feet and the Soviet naval flying-boats in particular seem well adapted to this purpose. Also, the cruiser, destroyer, and minelayer surface fleet, to say nothing of the light coastal forces, can carry 19,000 mines in one lift, which is about one-sixth of the total number of sea mines laid by the Germans off North West Europe during the last world war.[2,3] All the same, the mine-laying capacity of the Russian submarine fleet, though only half that of the ships, is of more importance tactically.

The great sophistication of the latest mines has made the sweeping of fields composed of well-assorted acoustic, magnetic, and pressure types a very difficult task. Fifty thousand men in 250 ships had to stand off for eight days during the tactical landing at Wonsan in 1950 whilst 3,000 mines were cleared from that harbour. A new and very serious threat to inshore operations is posed by the pressure mine. This is a device that was first brought into use by the defenders of the Atlantic Wall one week after D-Day. It is activated by the change in hydro-static pressure due to a ship passing overhead. It has its weaknesses, the chief ones being that it can be permanently incapacitated by heavy seas and that it is only effective in shallow waters which, among other things, virtually precludes its being laid by submarines. The relevant Admiralty instructions in 1944 ordered destroyers to proceed at 8 knots in less than 10 fathoms of uncleared waters and larger ships to stay below 4 knots, but permitted even the largest ships to steam at moderate speeds

[1] Report on Hydrofoil Development of House of Representatives Committee on Science and Astronautics: 27.6.60 (Washington, Government Printing Office, 1960)

[2] Based on data in *Jane's Fighting Ships 1960–1* (London, Sampson Low, 1960)

[3] Captain J. S. Gowie, *Mines and Minelaying* (Oxford University Press, 1949), Chapter VIII

above 25 fathoms or more of water. On the other hand, in those waters in which it can be used the lethality of the pressure mine is much enhanced by it being so difficult to destroy. It has to be neutralized by frogmen and divers who descend after the mine has been located, assuming it lies on the sea floor and is not embedded in it, by very short-range oblique sonar. Unfortunately the inshore detection vessels and minesweepers appropriate for such work, and for that matter the rather larger coastal minesweepers, too, are strategically very immobile because of their low speed, short range, and poor sea-keeping characteristics.

The menace that mines might constitute during the opening stage of a seaborne landing is enhanced by their passive qualities. A country using them would be able to warn its opponents that a certain stretch of water had been mined and so make them the ones immediately responsible for deciding whether or not any of those mines kill people. They might be faced with the choice between calling off any proposed seaborne operations, sailing over an unswept minefield, or waiting days whilst minesweeping forces assembled and performed their labours. It is clearly desirable to reduce the risk of having to make that kind of choice by configuring seaborne forces to be as invulnerable to mines as practicable. This is an additional argument in favour of making them able to use a wide range of ports and beaches and, more specifically, it is one in favour of using heavy-cargo helicopters and hovercraft for ship-to-shore movement. Hovercraft are immune from contact mines and helicopters, obviously, from mines of all kinds.

It is still occasionally asserted that the dramatic eclipse of the flying-boat transport just after 1945 was an accident resulting from inter-service rivalries, subsidization of airport facilities concealing real operating costs for civil landplanes, and a series of abortive development projects. Enthusiasts have claimed that such machines could still have a future and cite the American R3Y *Tradewind* and the British *Princess* as being the kind of thing required. Eleven *Tradewinds* were built for the United States Navy. Each weighed 175,000 lb. and had performance ratings closely comparable to those of landplanes of similar size, type, and vintage. The R3Y-2 variants had lifting noses enabling them to off-load items as large as $2\frac{1}{2}$-ton trucks. The three *Princesses* built were each of 345,000 lb. all-up weight and each had a maximum speed, payload, and range of 360 m.p.h., 50,000 lb., and 6,000 miles respectively. The argument in favour of giant boats has rested on the proposition that as size increases the extra drag consequent on the poor aerodynamic shape of any flying-boat is compensated to an even greater extent by the weight reduction resulting from the absence of undercarriage. A paper written in 1949 put the crossover point at 500,000 lb. and contended that anywhere above 300,000 lb. the efficiency differences between flying-boat and landplane were small.[1] For cruising speeds of less than, say, 450 m.p.h. this is probably true today, but at higher speeds the importance of the drag effect is much enhanced. Both the Soviet M-10 and the American P6M *Seamaster* only attained speeds of about 600 m.p.h. through having exceptionally powerful engines and such would undoubtedly be the case with larger machines. More general operational objections to military transport flying-boats are their vulnerability to ocean swell and floating debris, the great maintenance problems presented especially by high-mounted engine nacelles, long loading and unloading times, and the lack of any civil seaplane bases in the world today. There would be, moreover, high capital costs, for it is practically certain that there would be no civil version built to help spread development changes. Civilians have always had a pronounced antipathy to aircraft that have to be boarded from small boats and are unlikely to revert to using them. They would have the advantage of independence from vulnerable runways, but the dividends gained from this would be diminished in any place where large fixed ground facilities were installed, and where no adequate facilities existed for refuelling and maintenance parachute delivery by landplanes would be at least as convenient.

Non-nuclear mine technology is probably now close to its developmental limits, though it has recently made some formidable advances the full significance of which has yet to be fully recognized. Flying-boats seem to be unsuitable for revival and so that leaves us with three basic techniques that are likely to

[1] Paper given by D. Keith-Lucas, Esq., to R.Ae.S./I.Ae.S. Conference in New York, 1949

be more widely applied in marine engineering in, say, ten years' time than they are today. They are those of the hover-craft, the hydrofoil, and the nuclear reactor. All of them, but more particularly the last, should have a significant effect on the mobility, flexibility, and strength of sea-power.

Chapter 6

Mobility by Air

I—THE GLOBAL MOBILITY OF AIR SQUADRONS

THE form of military strength that can be most readily applied across thousands of miles is strategic air power. The final production version of the first British V-Bomber—the *Valiant*—could deliver a warload of 10,000 lb. 1,600 miles, or one of 21,000 lb. 1,300 miles, from base. It can be assumed that the more modern medium bombers—the British *Vulcan* and the American B-58 *Hustler*—have significantly better capabilities in these respects. A particular virtue of the B-58's, of course, is its low-level performance, enabling it to slip under any but an intense and sophisticated radar screen. This was demonstrated by a 1,400-mile flight from Texas to California in which the plane concerned averaged 700 m.p.h. and was never more than 500 feet above the ground. Furthermore, nearly all the intercontinental B-52s can carry some non-nuclear weapons in internal bomb-bays. Any of these aircraft could bomb area or pin-point targets from low or high altitude under any weather conditions, and it would be reasonably certain that a majority of the projectiles would fall within a very few hundred feet of the aiming-point. This is not to say that they could be employed in non-nuclear strikes against first-class powers without experiencing quite disproportionate losses.

General Power, Commander-in-Chief of SAC, has acknowledged, albeit reluctantly, that his planes could make a contribution to non-nuclear war given a period of several hours to effect the necessary redeployments and technical conversions.[1] Likewise, a Senate subcommittee reporting on the cancelled B-70 stressed its limited war utility at least against fixed

[1] General T. S. Power before United States House of Representatives Subcommittee on Defense Appropriations, April 13, 1959 (Washington, US Government Printing Office, 1959)

targets.[1] RAF Bomber Command has always had a limited-war role. Units of Bomber Command are frequently deployed overseas, particularly to Malta, Cyprus, Aden and Singapore, and although these movements are partly to show the flag and partly to practise dispersion for general war, they also imply a local war doctrine and capability. Of course, a major obstacle against the employment of strategic bombers in this way is the fact that any local crisis is liable to produce a marked rise in world tension and hence create a need for full preparedness against the possibility of general war. This conflict has recently been sharpened, as far as Britain is concerned, by her decision to assign Bomber Command to NATO. The Minister of Defence has indicated that the British Government would feel free to withdraw it to defend special British interests, but the inhibitions against so doing would always be considerable. On the other hand, it does not seem justifiable to create or keep in being extra long-range bomber forces solely for local war purposes. A V-Bomber costs around £1,000,000 to build and about half as much again in annual maintenance, and it has been said that to equip a wing containing about forty-five B-52s and keep it operational for five years costs over $1,000,000,000.[2]

At the time of the Korean War the virtual American nuclear monopoly made the conflict of priorities less acute and B-29 *Superfortresses* were freely diverted to the combat theatre and frequently employed on very tactical missions. The invasion began on June 25th, and, on the afternoon of the 28th, B-29s, which had just arrived in Okinawa from Guam, were bombing Communist-controlled roads leading into Seoul. The following day more of them attacked Kimpo airfield. Subsequently they intervened against tactical targets on various occasions often using 500-lb. fragmentation bombs proximity fused to explode 50 to 100 feet above the surface. Thus in mid-August 1950 B-29s dropped a 'carpet' pattern of about 6,000 500-lb. bombs

[1] Report of the Preparedness Investigating Subcommittee of the United States Senate Committee on Armed Services (Washington, U.S. Government Printing Office, 1960), p. 13

[2] US Department of Defense Appropriations 1963. Statement by Secretary of Defense before the House of Representatives Committee on Armed Services, January 24, 1962 (Washington, US Government Printing Office, 1962), Part 2, p. 15

over a 24-mile square area against an estimated 40,000 troops massing for assault in the Waegwan sector. Against such a diffuse target dispersed very irregularly with an average density of one man every 200 yards this was clearly a much less economic method of attack than, say, close-range, small calibre aimed fire by fighter bombers, but it seems to have achieved the desired results, for the attack was not launched. Many of the B-29 strikes on bridges and the like in rear areas must also have had a direct effect on the battlefield situation. As seasoned combat crews refined their techniques mean circular errors of probability fell to 500 feet or less, although bombing runs were generally conducted at over 20,000 feet. With radio-controlled bombs average CEPs of 200 to 300 feet were achieved.[1,2]

RAF Fighter Command is now quite experienced at moving *Hunter*, *Javelin*, and *Lightning* fighter and close-support squadrons overseas using in-flight refuelling techniques, but it is the USAF Tactical Air Command that has most fully developed this art. TAC has evolved the concept of the Composite Air Strike Force—that is, of a task force tailored to deal with a particular contingency and able to deploy abroad at short notice. The ground echelon and all the spare parts and light equipment required to keep the CASF in question fully operational for thirty days are assembled in Fly Away Kits and dispatched by air transport. It would not be practicable to airlift the fuel and ammunition required by modern combat planes— a F-104 *Starfighter*, for example, would probably consume about 30 tons a day on active service—and so this is stockpiled in advance or else moved in by sea. The heavier items of equipment like starter units, cranes to change engines, trucks and crew-stands are also normally prepositioned. The Fly Away Kits with their tyres, aero-engines, gaskets, ground power units, and the like can be shipped aboard their transport aircraft in a couple of days. When TAC receives its quota of KC-135 serial tankers this reaction time will be cut by a further twelve hours or more because their use will eliminate the initial delay now

[1] James T. Stewart, *Air Power—The Decisive Force in Korea* (Princeton, Van Nostrand, 1957), Chapter VII
[2] A Circular Error of Probability is that circle centred at an aiming point within which half the projectiles can be expected to land. Its size is expressed in terms of its radius

created by the need to dispatch piston-driven KB-50 tankers to stations *en route* ahead of the tactical jets. Global communications are maintained during CASF movements resulting in a mean accident-rate of only 0.002 per cent. The great disadvantage of this way of providing air support is that up to ten hours' solo flying in a cramped cockpit whilst trying to keep formation and carry out refuellings is very fatiguing.

Various other techniques have been adopted at least experimentally. In 1958 a F-104 squadron was dispatched to Formosa from California in *Globemasters*. One *Starfighter* was stowed in each transport. They left on the Monday, arrived on the Wednesday, and became operational on the Friday. Likewise, HC-1B *Chinook* helicopters (all-up weight 16,000 lb.) have been packed into the cargo envelopes of C-133 *Cargomasters* after their rotors and pylons have been removed. The *Chinooks* have also been used for a series of experimental transoceanic helicopter movements using Narsarssuak, Keflavik, Attu, Midway, Guam, and Ascension as staging posts. A 1,500-mile ferrying range has been obtained through the fitting of auxiliary fuel tanks inside the cargo compartment, but even so it is not easy to imagine this technique proving satisfactory during an emergency.

II—STRATEGIC AIRLIFT

One of the important extensions of airpower in recent years has been the build-up of strategic lift. Though several hundred medium- and long-range transports, including well over 200 C-130 *Hercules*, are in service in other branches of the American air force, navy and marine corps, the only command that reserves planes for the explicit purpose of providing a military airlift is the Military Air Transportation Service. Of the 79,000 men and 854 planes in MATS, at the beginning of 1961, 48,000 men and 471 planes belonged to this force of four-engined transports. By the middle of 1963 it is expected to include 620 planes of which 110 will probably be *C-118*s, 60 *C-121*s, 325 *C-124*s and 50 *C-130E*s, *C-133*s and *C-135*s respectively. This fleet will have the nominal capacity to carry 12,000 tons for 1,500 miles or 8,500 tons for 4,000 miles. The word 'nominal' is used because of the fact that the volume and shape of their cargo envelopes can still be such as to prevent planes carrying

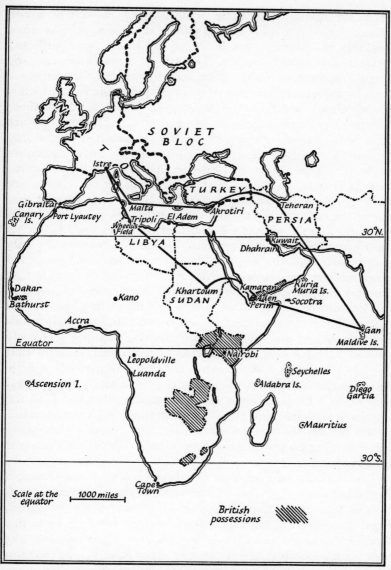

Air routes across Africa and the Middle East

as much material as their weight-lifting capacities would permit despite an effort on the part of designers, at least when working to military specifications, to bring these different factors more into harmony. The problem arises because the cargo densities of cubes occupied by loaded 'soft-skinned' vehicles are generally some 10 or 12 lb. per cubic foot, which is round about one-fifth the density of water, and of those occupied by armour between 20 and 30 lb. These values are quite high in comparison with the figures obtained by dividing the cargo envelope of transport aircraft by their maximum payload. These nearly all lie between 5 and 10 lb. per cubic foot. It is true, of course, that the dimensions of vehicles are such as to leave normally a great deal of space around and above them. Some light trucks are less than 8 feet wide, whilst even the M-41 tank has a breadth of only 10½ feet. Likewise, most armoured cars and armoured personnel-carriers are only 7 feet high and the airportable 155-millimetre self-propelled howitzer just over 10 feet. What is also true, however, is that men take up a relatively large amount of space and planes that can be configured for either troops or cargo can in most cases carry a body of men equal to about two-thirds of their maximum payload. Since an infantry division equipped entirely with airportable tanks weighs about 21,000 tons, it seems that the MATS military airlift could move simultaneously a little less than one-half of a division complete with all equipment and stores over a range of 1,500 miles. If, on the other hand, all the required vehicles had been prepositioned, they could move nearly two divisions over the same distance. Another alternative lift, assuming no prestocking, would be to lift fifteen Pentomic infantry battle-groups.

Royal Air Force Transport Command has been considerably expanded since 1957 and in late 1962 its four-engined aircraft included ten *Comets*, twenty *Argosies*, twenty-three *Britannias*, thirty-two *Beverlies*, and forty-eight *Hastings*. Between them this force could nominally carry 1,600 tons for 1,500 miles or 425 tons for 4,000 miles. About the only other RAF planes that can be used for strategic movement are the maritime reconnaissance *Shackletons*. These can be made to provide noisy and uncomfortable accommodation for up to thirty troops apiece. Among the smaller Transport Command aircraft are the two squadrons of *Belvedere* helicopters and two squadrons of *Hunter* strike fighters that make up No. 38 Group RAF which is intended to act as a spearhead formation. It is said that about two-thirds of the Command's activity is on the Army's behalf in peacetime and practically the whole of it could become available at one or two days' notice to move troops and their equipment in the event of a crisis.[1] The French strategic lift, which consists of 200 *Noratlases*, has been designed to operate across the Western Mediterranean and between the major airfields of the Community nations in Africa. It can carry 1,000 tons over a 1,500-mile stage which is a distance close to the maximum range of any mark of *Noratlas*. The transport fleet of the Soviet Union is usually said to be able to lift simultaneously two of her nine airborne divisions. Whilst most other air forces include some transport squadrons, in only a few cases are they conceived of as a means of strategic reinforcement.

Substantial improvements are taking place in the general quality of transport aircraft. Roller conveyors, which much facilitate the manoeuvring of cargo contained in standardized pallets, have been the chief means of reducing characteristic turn-round times for loading or unloading and refuelling from two or three hours to half an hour.[2] The military version of the *Argosy* has an 18-kilowatt auxiliary-power unit to make it independent of ground sources, and it also has a complete range of electronic equipment including a blind landing system.

The generation of aircraft due to come into service around 1965 will represent no fundamental revolution in terms of basic engineering, but will nevertheless constitute a considerable leap forward in size, power, and efficiency. Whereas the Lockheed C-130E *Hercules* can only carry 16 tons 3,000 miles and must use 22 tons of fuel in the process, the C-141 *Starlifter* will be able to lift a 42-ton payload over the same distance and will only require 45 tons of fuel to do so despite a 500 m.p.h. sustained cruising speed. The direct operating costs are expected to be about half those of the *Hercules*. This is largely because the turbofan propulsion units will enable it to operate in the rarefied air of the substratosphere. Later versions of the C-141 will probably reduce costs further by incorporating laminar flow

[1] E. Colston Shepherd in *Brassey's Annual*, 1961
[2] G. W. Williamson in *Brassey's Annual*, 1961

control. It is claimed that this technique, which is well suited for use in high-flying transports, can often double the range of aircraft incorporating it and at the same time cut down take-off distances substantially.[1] This is because it reduces drag by checking the turbulence in the boundary layer of air around the mainplane. It does this by fitting in the wings a series of suction holes that help to hold the layer against the mainplane surfaces. Of course, one problem, that is likely to be accentuated by the powerful engines that aircraft of the C-141 vintage and later will require, is the human fatigue induced by high noise levels, but fast and high flying, and the use of turbofans mounted on pods will help make the effect less than would otherwise be the case for the same amount of engine power.

The generation of transports that will come into service around 1970 is likely to include supersonic machines. It is a little uncertain what their military value will be, as they will have to be built with long and slender fuselages that may be unable to accommodate bulky vehicles. Another possibility is that some really giant aircraft will appear around that time. The USAF have recently issued an Operational Requirement for a global logistics aircraft of 250 tons all-up weight and a hold with an 18 feet by 16 feet cross-section.[2]

I have already pointed out that in recent years a much wider variety of equipment has been designed with a view to being transportable in some aircraft or other. A striking example is the American 30-ton and 10-kilowatt AN/TSC 16-wireless transceiver. With two-voice and sixteen teletype channels, that can be operated across 1,000 to 2,000 miles, it has a capability previously only associated with large fixed installations.[3] Mounted in two vans it can be moved, together with fifty operating personnel, in three C-124s, It can be ready for interim operation in four hours and full-scale operation in two days. Apart from large radar and engineering items about the only movable objects of military value that are not airportable are battle-tanks and their transporter lorries. As implied above, American armoured units take with them when travelling by air 25-ton *M-41* reconnaissance tanks rather than 45-ton

[1] W. E. Gasich in *New Scientist*, November 1, 1962
[2] *Flight International*, November 1, 1962
[3] *Military Review*, October 1959

*M-48*s and *M-60*s. In fact, a *M-41* compares favourably in many respects with, say, the *M-48 A2*. Its road-speed is greater and its range, ground pressure, and gradient climbing ability is about the same. Its big drawbacks are that the 76-millimetre gun can only penetrate up to 150 millimetres of standard armour, whereas the 90-millimetre one of the larger model can go through up to 200 millimetres, and that its strongest armour is 30 millimetres thick as against 110 millimetres on the *M-48*.

The Berlin airlift was handicapped by never having more than three airfields available for off-loading. Nevertheless, in good weather planes were touching down somewhere in the Western sector of the city once every three minutes and eventually the average daily cargo consignment, delivered principally by *C-54 Skymasters*, reached some 6,000 tons, of which over half was coal.[1] The difficulty was that high rates of usage for many months inflicted severe wear and tear on the runways of the aerodromes in question. This experience could easily be repeated, and probably within a much shorter time span, in the course of any future strategic movements to places outside the Atlantic borderlands. Within a fortnight of the beginning of the United Nations intervention in Korea the concrete runways of the main air terminus had been pounded into uselessness by the incessant Skymaster landings.[2] American government spokesmen have recently testified to the inadequacy of South East Asian airfields. They have revealed that monsoon rains have produced dangerous buckling and heaving of the concrete surfaces of the 6,500-foot main runway at Saigon, and have stated that, in their opinion, only two airfields in Thailand are at present fit to take modern aircraft.[3] Many of the airfields in newly developing countries that do have runways of adequate length are deficient in other respects, such as runway strength, fuel reserves, air traffic control installations, lighting, and electronic landing aids.[4] It is argued below, in connection with an examination of intra-theatre air support, that the frequency

[1] *A History of the United States Air Force* edited by Alfred Goldberg (Princeton, Van Nostrand, 1957), p. 240
[2] C. Gavin in *Military Review*, April 1962
[3] Department of Defense Appropriations 1963. Hearings before a Subcommittee of the House Committee on Appropriations (US Government Printing Office, 1962)
[4] See Appendix A

of routine scheduled landings at a civil airfield is some guide, however rough and impressionistic, to the traffic it could cope with during a military emergency.[1] Using this indicator to assess the distribution of large-capacity airports suitable to serve as termini for major force deployments we find that, for example, in 1957 in an area embracing Morocco, Equatorial Africa, Persia and Sardinia only thirteen places normally accepted more than fifty airliners a week.[2] It is true that in many of the emergent nations percentage increases in international and internal air traffic are much higher than they are across the world as a whole, but for some years to come inadequate airfield capacity is likely to remain a potential bottleneck in many Afro-Asian areas, especially those that have exceptionally low living standards or population densities, that have subsistence rather than market economies, or which were not subject to military airfield development in World War Two. A high proportion of the nation states of the world have at least one airfield that is being used as a port of call by one of the Boeing 707 liner services, but in many cases it is only one. Furthermore on any such airfield there will normally be only one runway capable of accepting civil or military planes as large as that, and such runways can very easily be immobilized. A few oil drums placed on it or a group of demonstrators standing on it could render one of them unusable for as long as they remained and a well-placed high-explosive bomb could easily put it out of action for several hours. It would always be possible to wreck an airfield terminal with far less explosive and with far less risk of taking life than would be the case with, say, port or beach installations.

Of course, the fear of interdiction can be to some extent removed by the employment of short take-off techniques to increase the number of runways eligible for use. A STOL variant of the *Hercules* has been designed, but since this gets the required performance by using more powerful engines, heavier controls, and a parachute brake it has to sacrifice quite a bit in terms of range and payload. The proposed STOL development of the SC 5/20 *Belfast* will, if proceeded with, utilize a boundary

[1] Chapter 7, Section III
[2] *Oxford Regional Economic Atlas of the Middle East & North Africa* (Oxford, Clarendon Press, 1960), pp. 56–57

layer control-system powered by three detachable turbine air compressors. It will have a long-range performance about as good as that of either of the first two marks of the aircraft, but much inferior to that of the projected SC 5/31. A similar conflict between range and weight on the one hand and adaptation to terminal facilities on the other will appear in connection with the global logistics aircraft the USAF wishes to acquire. It appears quite probable that only about six European airfields and approximately the same number in Africa and Asia will have runways strong enough to bear it.

Even when very long-range aircraft are being employed it is essential for economic operation to have staging posts at intervals well below their maximum ranges. Thus a C-130A could carry a 16-ton useful load from New York to Paris if it staged through the Azores, but only a 12-ton one if it flew direct. Some transports, such as the *Argosy*, can be refuelled in flight, but although this is obviously a means of achieving higher absolute ranges it is not an *aid* to economic operation because of the demands made on tanker aircraft. In order that staging posts can be given all the requisite facilities and aircrews given a fund of experience to draw on, it is also most desirable that the flying should take place over routes that have been much used for routine operations. The grid of such routes employed by the eastern wing of MATS includes such staging posts and terminals as Keflavik, Prestwick, the Azores, Frankfurt, Tripoli, Cairo, Dhahran, Recife and Ascension. Among the more important Western military ports of calls are Shemya, Midway, Hickham in the Hawaiis, Johnston Island, Kwajalein, Guam, Tokyo, Clark Field in Luzon, New Delhi, Karachi and Dhahran. Transport Command also have a wide network of staging posts, the principal ones being El Adem, Bathurst, Ascension, Luanda, Nairobi, Mauritius, and the Cocos Islands. As a result of the rescinding of the Anglo-Nigerian Defence Agreement of 1960 facilities at Kano, which included fuel reserves built up in collaboration with the local oil company, have been lost.

This latest consequence of Afro-Asian pressure towards non-alignment reminds us of the political vulnerability of the remaining 'east-about' routes between Britain and the Orient. The Turkey-Persia corridor is, moreover, extremely unsatisfactory in certain practical respects. The mountains along the common frontier of the two countries range between 7,000 and 17,000 feet and are not safe to cross in unpressurized aircraft. All modern strategic transports are now completely pressurized, but the cargo envelopes of tactical aircraft are often not. What is more, the frontal cloud and precipitation that invades the district in winter is much intensified on windward slopes and the frequently heavy rain and snow is often associated with severe icing up to 20,000 feet. These natural hazards are accentuated by poor air traffic control and meteorological services and consequently several crashes have occurred in the area in recent years. Ground-based flying aids are being improved, but the risk of their being jammed by the Soviets must always remain, since no point on the border is more than 120 miles from Russian territory and we cannot rule out indefinitely the possibility of physical interdiction in so narrow a fairway.

The alternative routes across Africa are also unsatisfactory. The Libya-Sudan one depends upon Anglo-American agreements with the aging King of Libya and upon good relations with the Sudan, which is currently under military rule and whose political future is indeterminate. As far as Britain is concerned the viability of the other ones depend upon her being able to continue to use Bathurst, which might be ruled out when Gambia becomes independent. From the physical standpoint alone Bathurst is far from satisfactory, for it is 2,800 miles from London, has a main runway only 6,000 feet long, and a normal scheduled landing-rate of only three or four a day. Ascension lies 1,500 miles farther south and so would be an unsatisfactory first port of call for anything smaller than a SC5/31 *Belfast*. In any case the prospects of British and American military aircraft flying across southern Africa are henceforward going to be very uncertain. Newly independent African states are already proving reluctant enough to grant over-flight permission and this reluctance is likely to grow. Meanwhile, Portugal, Southern Rhodesia and South Africa can be expected to relate their policy towards aerial transits to the attitude displayed by Anglo-American spokesmen in the United Nations towards their racial policies. The problem is intensified by the fact that the states concerned are never prepared to grant others general and unconditional over-flight permission. Separate applications have to be made for each specific occasion.

For these reasons some interest is now being shown in Britain in the 'west-about' route to Singapore or Australia. If Singapore is the destination, westbound flights are, unfortunately, pretty uneconomical. It is approximately 11,400 miles from London via Anchorage in Alaska and 12,600 miles via Montreal, Vancouver, and Tokyo as compared with 7,500 through Malta, Tabriz, and Karachi. The longest stage-length flying east would probably be the one of 2,500 miles between Gan and Singapore. To bring the maximum distance between stops on the Polar crossing down to such a figure would involve stopping in Greenland or in nearby Arctic Canada. Some air bases do exist in this region, but they mostly have poor weather factors. Thule, for example, which has a 10,000-foot runway, is prone to blizzards that sometimes last for days on end. To get stage-lengths little in excess of 2,000 miles on the other west-about route one would have to reorientate it so as to include either Attu or Hawaii, thereby incurring a substantial increase in total distance. The Polar route has the advantage of making possible sustained flight through the clear still air of the low polar stratosphere and so the partial avoidance of the westerly headwinds which, as Table III shows, bedevil flying with the sun at high altitude in temperate zones, but, as a corollary, facilitate flying against it. Their most marked manifestations are the jet streams associated with fronts in the upper troposphere. They are often surrounded by zones of dangerous turbulence, but can sometimes be used as flight paths if their axes are aimed in the right general direction.

Jet streams near Japan have been known to reach 400 miles an hour during the winter. Adverse winds are much less of a problem for planes west-bound for Australia, because they fly well south of west and also because upper winds in the inter-tropical zone are much lighter and more variable. Also if Australia is the destination the differentials in distance and so in time and payloads between the two approaches is less. Sydney is 12,000 miles from London over the Panama Canal, whereas Perth is 8,000 miles out via Malta, Teheran, and the Maldives or 11,500 miles via London, Bathurst, and Salisbury. Among the coral atolls of the South West Pacific numerous actual and potential large airstrips and seaplane bases exist. If the excellent landing-grounds of the Azores and Bermuda were used on the

TABLE III

*The average Westerly wind component in m.p.h. at various
pressure levels and latitudes*

Milli-bars	January				July			
	50°N.	35°N.	20°N.	0°N.	50°N.	35°N.	20°N.	0°N.
500	40	40	24	−7	24	11	−8	− 9
300	51	68	43	−1	38	23	−7	−11
200	47	84	55	−2	47	25	−7	−12

Notes: (1) Those sectors of parallels of latitude lying within the Sino-Soviet bloc have been ignored

(2) The 500 mb average pressure level lies between 17,000 and 19,000' in the cases taken. The 300 mb one lies between 28,000 and 32,000' and the 200 mb one between 36,000 and 41,000'. In each case the lower values are associated with lower mean temperatures in the air below

(3) The figures are calculated from the relevant charts in Geophysical Memoirs No. 103, H.M.S.O., London, 1960

Atlantic crossing the biggest difficulty would be the 4,000-mile leg from the Canal Zone to the predominantly French islands of the Marquesas and Tuamotu groups. Despite this hurdle a modified version of this route which involved stops at Curaçao was used by Dutch air transports reinforcing West Irian during the recent dispute, after permission to over-fly the United States had been refused.

MATS and Transport Command planes are in constant use for routine logistic support, a practice which is favoured by the growing number and variety of high-value items and by the introduction of integrated high-speed data processing systems for improved stock control. The American services are currently using about a billion ton miles of capacity a year, including, of course, that of chartered civilian freight aircraft. In addition to cargo movement there is much trooping and aeromedical evacuation to be done and mobility exercises to be carried out. Since it provides a *rationale* for continual flying experience, such regular work is an essential means of maintaining efficiency. The Chief of Staff of the USAF has testified that a peacetime utilization rate of the planes of the MATS military lift of at least four hours a day is desirable, given a requirement for a

wartime surge rate of eight hours.¹ This is yet another instance
of the way in which strategic reserves and forces overseas are
in a complementary relationship.

A general war function is envisaged for British and American
strategic transports and consists of helping the bombers to disperse and, in the American case, in missile resupply. In the
Soviet Union they may also come to be regarded as air-
launched missile-delivery vehicles, since she appears to be
continuing with the development and use of that class of
weapons system. However, the chief relevance of military airlift
is obviously to actual or potential limited wars or internal
security operations. There is naturally great emphasis on speed
of reaction and, through rotation, Strike Command ensures that
a company of 200 men is always ready to move within one hour
and a battle-group within three.² To move several battle-groups
at one go would necessitate about a day's troop preparation,
because of the need to plan and brief in detail, which would not
be possible until the nature of the proposed operation, the kind
and amount of airlift to hand and the particular air routes
available were known. If a movement was to take place over a
route 5,000 or 10,000 miles long that was not currently being
used by Western military aircraft, it would probably take a
couple of days to bring it to a state at which it could bear a
heavy traffic. This time would be needed to fly out slip crews,
maintenance men, equipment, and stores. Current American
doctrine states that airlift will normally be required to serve as
the chief means of supply during the first thirty days of any
operation. This is about the length of time that most planes can
operate without an overhaul in a main depot.

Parachute-dropping operations of men and supplies is only
practicable if a dropping zone about 1,000 yards long is available, a wind not in excess of 30 knots is blowing, and the cloud
base is not below 600 feet. Also, since aircraft must fly up their
dropping zones straight and level at steady airspeeds of around
100 knots, it is essential that the dropping zones should not be
covered by significant enemy anti-aircraft defences. Another

¹ Report on National Military Airlift by a Special Subcommittee
of the House of Representatives Committee on Armed Services,
1960 (Washington, US Government Printing Office, 1960), p. 4040
² Richard Brett-Smith in *Daily Telegraph*, October 4, 1960

limitation is that if an airdrop is intended a plane usually has to reduce its useful load by about a third. Nevertheless, operational parachute drops are still envisaged as a means of tactical assault to secure airheads and other key objectives and as a means of resupply in the absence of landing strips. Therefore, the development of techniques continues. Unit loads in excess of 20 tons can now be safely dropped by means of groups of parachutes each with canopies of up to 100 feet in diameter and by the use of light paper honeycombs and other materials to cushion the impact with the earth, whilst loads to which a hooked line has been attached can be snatched by means of arrester wires from planes that touch down only momentarily. Yet another idea being experimented with is the Ragallo parachute that on opening remains attached to the rear of the fuselage by means of a long line so that its load, which is suspended on another long line, falls backwards to earth with a pendulum motion. The intention is that at the moment of impact this motion should balance the forward speed of the aircraft, thereby producing an absolute horizontal velocity of zero. Then again loads like partially filled oil drums or bags of bread can be free-dropped from moderate heights without ill effects. Although such delivery of men and supplies by air is normally conceived as being a tactical deployment, it can be the culmination of a strategic one. Several years ago, during exercise 'Banyan Tree', men of the 82nd Airborne Division flew 1,600 miles to their dropping zone.[1] This method of transport could presumably be given substantially greater radii of action by the use of in-flight refuelling, although that technique does not seem to have been experimented with in that particular context.

The British and American airlifts are still of light capacity in proportion to the tonnages that would be involved in moving their respective strategic reserves into any regions in which there were no prepositioned stockpiles. Also they are as yet relatively slow, which would be a serious matter if several return trips proved necessary to complete an initial build-up. Thus over half the American long-distance capacity is made up of planes that cruise below 300 m.p.h. The British are more strongly placed in this respect in that most members of their *Britannia* fleet can cruise long distances at around 350 m.p.h.,

[1] F. C. Krause in the *Military Review*, November 1959

but that fleet is small and would be unsuitable for the transportation of much except light forces intended for internal
security operations. On the other hand, the average speeds and
aggregate payloads of both airlifts are being increased. In 1964
Transport Command will probably receive the first of the slow
but powerful *Belfasts* and the fast and powerful VC-10s, while
at the same time MATS will be beginning a phase of rapid
expansion. More C-130E *Hercules* turboprops will be coming
into service to replace the C-124 *Globemasters*, some of which will
be fifteen years old by then. The following year the first of the
132 C-141 *Starlifters* that have been provisionally ordered are
due to enter service. They will be able to carry at one go nearly
4,000 tons over as many miles, and, used in conjunction with the
C-135 *Stratolifters* already in service, will constitute a formidable
armada of turbofan transports capable of cruising to objectives
almost twice as fast as the *Globemasters* can.

III—CIVIL AIR FLEETS AS RESERVE LIFT FORCES

Most states have a significant auxiliary lift available for use in
a national, or perhaps a United Nations, emergency in the form
of their civil airlines. Almost all of them, apart from the Soviet
Union and China, are members of the International Civil
Aviation Organization, and about 85 per cent of their aggregate
capacity is controlled by companies who are members of the
International Air Transport Association. The IATA members
reported in 1960 having approximately 2,000 four-engined
aircraft, which is about four times the number in MATS and
fifteen times the number in RAF Transport Command, and
which included nearly 800 turbojets or turboprops.[1] ICAO
operating statistics for the same year indicate that its members
flew 180,000,000 passenger miles a day and conducted freight
and mail traffic of 3,400,000 ton miles a day.[1] If we combine
these figures we get a total of 27,500,000 ton miles which would
rise to about 50,000,000 if all the aircraft concerned suddenly
started working at full capacity.[2] This latter figure is about a

[1] ICAO Digest of Statistics No. 85
[2] Calculated assuming that eight passengers are an equivalent
load to one ton of freight

quarter as much again as, say, the MATS military airlift could manage if it were working at full stretch, though that comparison is not very meaningful, as MATS is far better adapted for the transportation of military equipment and warlike stores. On the other hand, civil aviation is bound to rise rapidly in volume and range and to emphasize freight traffic more and more. According to the Report to the United States President by the 1961 Task Force on Aviation Goals, world passenger traffic should almost double during this decade. Meanwhile cargo movements are expected to expand four or five times as freight charges are cut by half.[1]

In 1960 as much as 56 per cent of the traffic of the ICAO countries was carried by American companies, 5.5 per cent by the two British nationalized corporations, 2.5 per cent by the airlines of Canada, Australia and New Zealand, and 3.7 per cent by Air France. The Indian and Pakistani companies together contributed 1.5 per cent between them, but Egypt, which has a larger civil air fleet than any other of the independent African states, apart from the Republic of South Africa, handled only 0.2 per cent of the world's traffic. All the independent African states, excluding again South Africa, had in their civil airlines in 1962 just over 100 medium and long transports of which twelve were modern turbojets and turboprops and the majority Skymasters and Dakotas.[2] The total number of four-engined aircraft owned by the members of IATA in 1960 was 2,000 of which nearly 800 were turbojets or turboprops.[3]

The proportion of the annual passenger movement in the Soviet Union that was undertaken by air in 1956 was about half what it was in the United States, but a sixfold increase in Aeroflot passenger mileage is planned between 1959 and 1966 and nearly all the new planes to be provided will be either pure jets or prop jets.[4] It is claimed that by 1980 some 200,000,000 people will be travelling by Soviet aircraft each year.[5]

[1] Published by the Federal Aviation Agency, September 1961
[2] Interavia, No. 3/1962
[3] ICAO Digest of Statistics No. 85.
[4] J. P. Cole and F. C. German, Soviet Geography (Butterworths), 1961
[5] Col. Gen. Y. F. Loginov, The Soviet Civil Aviation Chief, quoted in Interavia, 2/1962

In general, civil aircraft are rather unsuitable for military purposes. They are normally designed for operation on routes with plenty of ground-based navigational aids and large and well-appointed airfields. Also the cargo carriers are badly designed from the soldiers' standpoint. Commercial aircraft are often equipped with side cargo doors which almost or completely preclude the loading of vehicles. If there is a large door at one end, it is usually in the nose, because this is aerodynamically preferable and because it simplifies manoeuvrings at freight terminals and affords any passengers on board extra protection. A nose door cannot be used for supply drops by parachute. To all these difficulties is added the fact that the sizes and shapes of cargo envelopes in some civil aircraft are designed on the assumption that their cargoes will be of high density.[1]

Then again wheeled vehicles produce heavy point loads on the floor and tracked vehicles heavy area ones. Thus at the base of each wheel of a *Saladin* armoured car is a point load of about 3,500 lb. and the pressure under the tracks of a M-41 tank is about 1,900 lb. a square foot. Such loads can be distributed to some extent by resting the items concerned on cargo spreaders. Thus, if the weight of a *Saladin* were spread evenly over the whole floor area beneath it, the resultant mean pressure would be 160 lb. a square foot. The corresponding figure for a M-41 would be 280 and for a 155-millimetre self-propelled howitzer 300. The difficulty is that any load spreader capable of producing a high degree of weight dispersion would itself be rather thick and heavy, whilst the problem of moving equipment in and out of the plane would remain. For these reasons, military aircraft are often given stronger floors than their civilian counterparts. For example, the military version of the *Argosy* has a floor area strength of up to 650 lb. a square foot as compared with a civilian maximum of 380. Similarly the military version of the *Britannia* has a strengthened floor.

It is, of course, inevitable that any military mobilization of civil aircraft would lead to disruption of commerce. But one can argue that the companies could adjust easily enough, because on the average flight under normal conditions only 55 to 60 per

[1] See Chapter 6, Section II

cent of load-carrying capacity is utilized. Admittedly the burden would fall much more heavily on cargo-carrying capacity than on that for passengers, but even in this sector it is easy to overestimate the inconvenience caused by anything short of a complete takeover. In most situations that can be envisaged the government concerned would not need the aircraft in question for more than a week or two, and only a minor portion of the cargo moved under normal conditions is urgent in the sense of consisting of mail or perishable commodities; if the United States 1952 figures are at all typical, the proportion is about one-third. Perhaps the most valid argument against depending on civilian aid in this connection is that it gives the firms concerned a *prima facie* case for claiming subsidy and protection. It is to be hoped that we may avoid a sordid repetition of the way in which shipping interests continue to extract favours by using very largely obsolete arguments about a merchant marine of the maximum possible size being a strategic necessity.

Despite all the objections, many governments have been, and are, prepared to charter or requisition civil aeroplanes to serve in a military logistic role. The British Civil Aviation Act of 1949 allows the Secretary of State for Air to commandeer, during times of national emergency, any aircraft or ground facilities he wishes as long as compensation is subsequently paid. In the United States, the President has long had a general authority to take over any transport facilities in time of war, but in 1952 such general government powers were given greater substance and precision by the formal establishment of the Civil Reserve Air Fleet under the auspices of MATS. About twenty-two airlines are now members of the scheme and all MATS routine airlift contractual work is given to them. Each contract contains a MATS expansion clause requiring the firm concerned to designate a number of planes to a first-line reserve which currently amounts to some seventy aircraft. In 1962 the total CRAF force was made up of just over seventy passenger aircraft, of which half were Boeing 707s and the rest DC-8s, and about 170 four-engined cargo transports including twelve CL-44s. Many of the machines had been wired and bracketed so as to facilitate quick conversion for active service. One great weakness was the fact that only a dozen turbine-powered cargo or convertible aircraft were available and pressure is being put on companies through contract awards to remedy this situation.[1]

The United States Secretary of Defense does not require a Presidential declaration of national emergency to activate CRAF, but he cannot call it up selectively. He must mobilize either all of CRAF, or all the first-line reserve, or none of CRAF. Though the fleet responded very well in, for example, the Lebanon and Formosan crises in 1958, the American armed forces are reluctant to rely on it too heavily. This is partly because of the manning problems that might arise in the course of a crisis. Many company pilots would be called to active duty in the entirely separate Air Force Reserve. The rest would retain full civilian status, and so it is doubtful whether they could be legally compelled to carry out operations in combat zones and certain that if they did they would not enjoy the protection of the Geneva Convention. Labour unrest is another hazard. Eventually new legislation may get round some of these difficulties. Meanwhile, contingency plans assume that CRAF can become available at forty-eight hours' notice to participate in the follow-up phase of any major deployment. During that phase there would be a need for large numbers of rear echelon troops and many high density resupply items, but there might also be one for great numbers of lorries to operate long lines of communication. The CRAF fleet would be suitable for moving the men and the more compact stores, but very ill adapted to carrying lorries.

The nominal lift of the CRAF fleet was, in 1962, only 1,600 tons over 4,000 miles, which is less than 20 per cent of that provided by the MATS military airlift at the beginning of the following year. Also the average MATS aircraft is faster than the average CRAF one. The business that the CRAF companies get for holding this capacity ready is about $145,000,000 a year, which amounts to about one-third of the trade carried on by the 'industrial' section of MATS.[2] There is no doubt that if this

[1] Department of Defense Appropriations, 1963. Hearings before a Subcommittee of the US House of Representatives Committee on Appropriations (Washington, US Government Printing Office, 1962), Part 3, p. 579

[2] US Department of Defense Appropriations, 1963. Hearings before the House of Representatives Committee on Armed Services (Washington, US Government Printing Office, 1962), Part 2, pp. 575, 587

contracting stopped MATS could cope with much if not all of the excess demand thereby created and that it could do so at substantially less expense to the American taxpayer. The 1962 planned cost of operating the MATS military airlift was only $480,000,000.[1] The Civil Reserve Air Fleet seems to be an only moderately cheap and moderately efficient means of providing a marginal increment to the airlift forces in being.

[1] Taking pay, maintenance, and direct operating costs into account

Chapter 7

Airpower in Limited War

I—CLOSE AIR SUPPORT BY FIXED WING AIRCRAFT

IN nearly all of the more formal campaigns of the last twenty-five years air superiority has been a condition of success. Aerial reconnaissance has been invaluable and interdiction of supply routes has, on occasion, resulted in the near isolation of front-line troops from their rear bases. Also many close-support strikes have been carried out as little as 100 or 200 yards ahead of friendly troops, often at immediate request. In strict economic terms this means of delivering a given weight of munitions is far less efficient than artillery bombardment, but it probably has a greater psychological impact. Furthermore, the great tactical mobility of aircraft is an advantage in supporting an advancing spearhead or checking an impending breakthrough.

Enthusiasts often cite Korea as the supreme demonstration of the successful application of airpower to limited war, but it is unwise to draw any general conclusions from that body of experience, because the extent of the achievement was largely governed by the quality of the weapons employed by the respective sides. The North Koreans began the war with about thirty-five anti-aircraft guns, chiefly grouped around Pyongyang, but after the Chinese intervention the Communist anti-aircraft deployment steadily increased to include eventually about 750 guns supported by about 200 searchlights, about half the guns and most of the searchlights being radar controlled. They had as well some ground-to-air rockets which were put into service on a few occasions. The artillery was grouped for point defence around eighty key targets. It inflicted little material damage, only destroying, for example, four B-29 *Superfortress* bombers during the 21,000 sorties these aircraft made. It did, on the other hand, force the *Superfortresses* to maintain altitudes that were generally above 20,000 feet over the targets in question.[1]

[1] J. T. Stewart, *Air Power—The Decisive Force in Korea* (Princeton, Van Nostrand, 1957), Chapter VII

In the forward areas and along supply routes Communist light automatic weapons, used without any inhibitions in the virtual absence of planes friendly to themselves, shot down over 800 USAF planes (about half of which were fighter bombers), and about as many aircraft again belonging to other elements in the United Nations Command. This was a low attrition rate, since the USAF fighter bombers alone flew 350,000 combat missions, but the rate was kept down by the general rule made by the Far East Air Force in 1951 to the effect that attacks should not be pressed below 3,000 feet, and that only one pass should be made at each target. This much reduced the effectiveness of such ground defences as machine-guns with crude computer sights, but conversely it lessened the power and accuracy of the offensive. In particular it meant that the United Nations Command was never able to induce a complete breakdown of supplies to the Communist front line.

In the last several years some very advanced attack planes have been produced. The best example is the F4H *Phantom II*, which can, for example, sustain supersonic flight below 300 feet, thereby making active defence from the ground very difficult because of the silence and high angular velocity of its approach. Unfortunately, except over the open sea and over parts of the North German plain, there are few areas on or near the Iron Curtain where such flying is possible, and always it involves substantial metal fatigue and structural strain. In any case, acquisition of targets of opportunity is quite impossible at such heights and speeds. In order to deliver precision tactical attacks at high speeds and safe distances both the United States and the Soviet Union have developed supersonic air-to-ground guided missiles. The American *Bullpup* is reported to be able to deliver a 250-lb. warhead over a slant range of 10,000 yards with a standard accuracy of 40 feet.[1] This claim gains plausibility from the fact that as early as 1945 the Henschel 293 airborne subsonic flying bomb was achieving a similar degree of accuracy.[2] Three *Bullpups* can be carried by an A4D *Skyhawk* and five by a FJ-4B *Fury*.

Several other improvements in technology have occurred to

[1] *Interavia*, No. 11/1961
[2] Rudolph Lusar, *German Secret Weapons of World War II* (London, Neville Spearman, 1959), p. 292

help strike aircraft complete their missions safely. The 84,000-lb. *Skywarrior* can press home attacks in all weathers (as long as it does not fly into cumulonimbus cells), and can help the 17,000-lb. A4D to do likewise. Side radar, which is very difficult to jam, is available for all weather reconnaissance and very high-speed and good-quality optical or infra-red photography is now possible. Speeds of around Mach 2.5 are being achieved at altitude by the *Phantom II* and the B-58 *Hustler*, whilst the Russians now have a supersonic heavy bomber in the *Bounder*. Considerable strides have been made with electronic counter measures to jam or deceive ground-to-air missiles.

Against this must be set the fact that few armies in the future are likely to be saddled with anti-aircraft defences as amateurish as those employed in Korea. Indeed, more adequate equipment was in existence at the end of the last war and was getting much more impressive results. Records kept by the United States Army 14th AA Command in the Pacific during 1944 state that 1,350 Japanese aircraft launched 650 raids.[1] In nearly 600 of these the enemy was engaged by gunfire and the average proportion of probable 'kills' was 37 per cent. Similarly, the 1st Army in Europe claimed that, after the launching of the Second Front, it probably destroyed 904 out of 3,888 planes employed in 1,701 raids.[2] Furthermore, since 1945 anti-aircraft artillery has much improved and much smaller-calibre pieces can now be radar laid, power operated, and electronically directed, whilst rates of fire for each particular calibre have substantially risen. Nevertheless because their shells are necessarily unguided and because they are virtually ineffective above 35,000 feet, guns have been very largely replaced by rockets in this field. The American Nike *Ajax* and *Hawk* missiles have been operational since 1953 and 1959 respectively. They both have burn-out speeds of about Mach 2.5 to 3.0 and are effective to 40,000 to 50,000 feet. The *Hawk* has the advantage of having all solid propellants and very refined electronic systems. Consequently it can engage fast-moving targets down as low as 50 feet at short notice. Also, it is relatively easily transportable by means of fixed wing aircraft, helicopters, or land vehicles.

[1] G. M. Barnes, *Weapons of World War II* (New York, Van Nostrand, 1947), p. 158
[2] *Ibid.*

However, when operational a Hawk battery is a static unit extending over at least 40 acres. The British equivalent of *Hawk* is *Thunderbird I,* which may be transported by air or in standard army vehicles complete with its power generators and workshops. Each regiment has an establishment of about 700 men in two batteries, each with four missile launchers and forty-four vehicles and trailers. Another American missile that has been in service since 1958 is Nike *Hercules.* This missile has an all-solid propellant, but is heavily built in order to achieve an altitude of over 100,000 feet. Despite this it has proved possible to fire it experimentally from a mobile battlefield transporter/launcher.

The *Mauler* is a United States system currently being developed to give protection to advancing forces and supply columns. It is hoped that production will start round about 1965. Each *Mauler* battery of about twelve missiles will be contained entirely within a single-tracked vehicle of standard design, which will be capable of delivering accurate fire, even when moving. Its missiles are guided by a combination of radar and infra-red controls and are said to be effective against, for example, short-range ballistic missiles and very low-flying subsonic aircraft. A complete unit of this type should weigh about 25,000 lb. and be compact enough to be carried aboard transport aircraft and to be dropped by parachute in combat areas. Also for small-unit protection in forward areas the one-man rocket *Redeye* should become available in 1964. This is completely dependent on infra-red guidance and so its projectile will always be travelling directly towards the target rather than adopting a more economical and reliable interception course. Even a rough and ready comparison with other rockets of comparable dimensions for which some performance data has become available suggests that the original claim that *Redeye* would be effective up to 12,000 feet was quite unrealistic. The rather smaller-calibre *Bazooka* of the last war would have had a ceiling of about 1,500 feet if fired vertically, and the Henschel 217—a developmental anti-aircraft rocket a little larger than *Redeye*—had one of 3,700 feet.[1] Moreover, these rockets only maintained velocities that would have enabled them to catch a supersonic fighter during a quite small fraction of their upward trajectory and we can take it for granted that the same

[1] Lusar, *op. cit.,* p. 181

observation will be true of *Redeye*. An infra-red system is, in any case, useless against targets concealed by mist or cloud and is always liable to home on false echoes such as the sun. The latest information is that the *Redeye* production programme is being reduced and this may well be due to a disappointing performance during trials.

Of course, anti-aircraft defences can be conducted by manned fighters operating as alternatives to or complements of the larger anti-aircraft missiles. Against planes making deep-low altitude sorties manned fighters can be more economical in so far as high altitude gives them much wider horizons. On the other hand, their speeds of reaction, speeds of flight, and manoeuvrabilities are now dropping behind those characteristic of the missiles, their capital and operating costs are greater, and they are more exposed to destruction on site. Above all they can only be used effectively against intruders if they have first of all secured a general command of the skies over the combat zone. It is possible to imagine certain allied mobile operations which would have to be conducted initially beneath skies controlled by the airpower of a first-class hostile power. Until *Mauler* is available to augment *Hawk* the defence of forward areas and nodal communications points will be difficult during the initial phases of any deployments because *Hawk* is tactically immobile. Conversely, in any situations in which the West and its allies have air superiority, advancing Sino-Soviet troops would be exposed to attack, though they would only be markedly vulnerable if travelling in columns of soft-skinned vehicles. Armoured vehicles afford their occupants considerable protection against cannon and machine-gun fire, napalm, and against near misses by bombs and rockets, and, if travelling in open formation, they are difficult to hit with rockets. In any case, if and when the front line had become slow moving and a dense and sophisticated network of anti-aircraft defences established, 'tactical air' would not be able to influence the course of the land battle in the way it sometimes did in World War II without incurring quite unacceptable losses. Another factor that has to be borne in mind is that the usefulness of airpower against an enemy conducting a fluid defence of a jungle area, and drawing his supplies from chains of human porters using primitive tracks, has always been very limited and is likely to remain so. The French had built up a force of over 200 tactical aircraft by the end of the Indo-China campaign, but these planes rarely had a direct effect on the fighting, and the claim that, for a time at least, they kept the tonnage of supplies from China down is hard to accept. The actual volume rose rapidly as the interdiction campaign was stepped up and there are no grounds for thinking that it would have risen much faster if aerial interference had been removed.[1] Furthermore, when the possibility of United States naval air intervention at Dien Bien Phu was being considered it was recognized that any such action could only be rendered effective by the employment of nuclear warheads.

It must be pointed out, in conclusion, that any overall assessment of the technical balance between the most advanced kinds of tactical aircraft and the most advanced kinds of anti-aircraft defences does not, even if correct, provide us with a general prognosis of the role the former would play in particular situations. The rate of innovation in this department of weapons technology is now such as to create the possibility of wide qualitative gaps existing between the equipment available in different countries: and ultra-modern aircraft operating against concentrated but obsolescent fixed defences would enjoy considerable immunity. This does not mean, however, that the rich and powerful countries will always have the edge on the poorer or smaller ones in these categories, because some of the latter will get up-to-date weapons and technical assistance from some of the former.

There is, moreover, the underlying political difficulty that it may on occasions be escalatory to initiate the use of tactical aircraft. This is because the warplanes of today are sophisticated systems, usually able to carry nuclear weapons, always capable of deep penetrations into their opponents' rear areas, and based on airfields well behind their own lines, which thus become tempting targets for counter-strikes. Even attacks on front-line targets usually involve them in intrusions of several miles, because the characteristic turning circles of modern warplanes is so large even at low altitude. Because of this, the idea that extra tactical air support can be used to compensate for de-

[1] G. J. Tanham, *Communist Revolutionary Warfare in Indo-China* (New York, Praeger, 1961), Chapters III and V

ficiencies in armour and anti-tank weapons on the part of light
mobile forces is unsatisfactory from the political standpoint as
well as from the technical one.

II—HELICOPTERS

Although helicopters are hardly instruments of strategic mobility, they are relevant to any discussion of it. This is partly
because they are an essential part of the commando ship system,
and partly because they are now generally regarded as necessary
components of all major conventional war formations, particularly those adapted to anti-guerilla operations and to fighting in
jungle terrain. Their utility derives chiefly, of course, from their
ability to land and take-off vertically and to hover, but in part
it is a consequence of the great operational versatility many of
the machines have, because of the ease with which they can
change at short notice the nature of their useful load. But their
value is decreased by shortcomings in certain other aspects of
performance. Although these shortcomings are being rendered
less serious by technological advance, and in particular by the
progressive introduction of turbine engines that are lighter,
simpler, and less productive of noise and vibration than piston
ones, they remain significant.

For one thing the disposable load of few helicopters flying
today is more than 40 per cent of their all-up weight: of this
about 400 lb. is normally taken up by the weight of the crew,
and, if all-weather operation is intended, as much again by
extra electronic equipment. Therefore the fact that the rate of
fuel consumption is normally two or three times that of a comparable fixed-wing aircraft sets severe limits on payload or
range or both. Thus the largest British military helicopter so
far produced, the Mk. I *Belvedere* of 19,000 lb., can carry only a
2,600-lb. payload 430 miles or a 6,000-lb. one 75 miles. An
inevitable corollary of this is that rotorcraft are expensive to run
and this is reflected in the statistics provided by civilian
operators. A typical direct cost up to the present time, including
depreciation, and maintenance, and crew pay, has been about
10*d*. per passenger mile. Initial costs are also high and a German
survey of the problem in 1959 concluded that even helicopters
with take-off weights as high as 60,000 lb., which would enjoy

the benefit of appreciable economies of scale, would still, at the current level of technology, incur overall costs double those of comparable fixed-wing aircraft. On the other hand, helicopters are expected to become gradually less expensive as their power plants become more efficient, aggregate flying times per year greater, and average size larger. Already various design studies have been made to specifications for gross weights over three times as large as even the Soviet MI-6 (71,000 lb.). For example, the largest projected model in the Sikorsky *Flying Crane* series will have an all-up weight of 230,000 lb. In fact, however, it will not be easy to produce such large aircraft without departing from the pure helicopter concept, as the MI-6 with its pair of stub wings does. The characteristic weight loadings of 'rotor-discs' (the circles within which blades revolve) is already very high and the extent to which they can be increased, even with the provision of extra blades, is debatable. Conversely any attempt to raise the upper limit on the areas of discs will push the speed of advancing blade-tips very close to the sonic barrier, thereby setting up dangerous vibration stresses. The same problem is being encountered in the course of endeavours to improve forward airspeeds above the present general limits of 160 to 170 m.p.h. In this case there is the added complication that the absolute speed of retreating blades is being brought close to the stalling value, though this difficulty may be obviated by markedly reducing each blade's angle of incidence during the retreating phase of a revolution. That progress is possible in this respect is being shown by the Sikorsky HSS-2 operated by the United States Navy. A stripped-down version of this machine has already reached 192 m.p.h. and the United States Army is developing a standard variant of it with an intended maximum speed of 224 m.p.h. Meanwhile trials are being carried out on the Derschmidt rotor, which is designed to extend aerodynamic limits through the use of mid-span hinges. Its inventor claims that it will make speeds of 300 m.p.h. possible.

Over the last ten years much research has been carried out in order to develop methods of automatic control. Although a very elementary auto-pilot merely capable of keeping a helicopter approximately on a prescribed linear course may only weigh 20 lb. or so, a full set of automatic equipment (including gyros, radio and sonic altimeters, doppler registers, and computers) is heavy, intricate and costly. Nevertheless, once installed it can render a pilot more free to attend to other things whilst giving his aircraft more of a 'round-the-clock' performance than helicopters had during the Korean War and Malayan Emergency, when flying in bad weather was unusual and night flying almost unknown.

In other respects, too, helicopters have become less susceptible to the vagaries of the natural environment. Thus the British experience in Malaya that warloads were often reduced by half by the effects of tropical temperatures and humidities, and might be reduced as much again when operating at several thousand feet, is unlikely to be repeated. This is partly because turbines are more tolerant of climatic extremes than piston engines. It is more particularly because helicopters have been designed with much greater reserves of power. The little Westland *Wasps* can operate up to 7,000 feet under tropical conditions. Likewise the large *Belvederes* have engines with a combined continuous power rating of 2,400 h.p., of which only 1,900 h.p. would ever be needed in a temperate régime. In higher latitudes rime, wet snow, and freezing rain remain major hazards despite the introduction of rotor de-icing systems. This is because the revolving blades are very thin, so that 'wing loadings' are high at the best of times.

Too much has been made of the fact that helicopters are harder to maintain than either ground vehicles or fixed-wing aircraft, for, although some disparity exists because a helicopter includes many components and in particular a number of large masses rotating at different frequencies, it is becoming less significant as more design and servicing experience is accumulated. An availability rate of 85 per cent and intervals of 1,000 hours between major overhauls are now normal. Furthermore, the spare parts required are these days very generally heliportable, whilst built-in maintenance platforms and easy access to all moving parts make the servicing crews largely independent of fixed ground systems.

Assuming that ample supplies of fuel are available within the divisional or brigade rear echelons the flexibility of these vehicles can be exploited to the full in supply and movement within the battle zone. A test in a German mountain infantry school in 1944 suggested that two helicopters could do the work of a pack-horse battalion. Whether or not they are the best means of logistic support will depend upon circumstances, but even when these favour the predominant use of lorries or fixed-wing aircraft, helicopters may still fulfil a valuable auxiliary role. This is partly because of their ability to travel much faster than lorries and to operate from much more confined spaces than any fixed-wing aircraft. It is also because they can carry loads that are bulky and awkwardly shaped. They are emancipated by their own inherent slowness from the necessity to streamline their fuselage. Thus the *Yak-24* (32,000 lb. gross weight) can carry internally two field guns and their crews. Also payloads can be carried externally, and Sikorsky are designing a series specifically as 'flying cranes'. The largest now under development is the *S-64*, which will have a useful load of 21,000 lb. The *S-64* will have attachments for interchangeable pods to enable it to serve as a sixty-seat troop transport, air ambulance, submarine destroyer, or minesweeper if so required.

Helicopters can also be of immense use tactically, especially over battle areas in which the front line is thinly held and discontinuous. Their unique value in the combat zone lies in the application of the old military principle that inferiority in overall numbers can often be more than compensated by the ability to send small bodies of men to precisely the right place at precisely the right time. They rarely need any kind of prepared landing zone and when they do their requirements can easily be met. Experience in Panama has shown that, as long as a stream runs nearby into which debris can be jettisoned, eleven men using light implements including a small power saw, can in five hours clear a space in primary jungle large enough to accept a 7,500 lb. *HU-1*. To cover tactical movements and to carry out aggressive reconnaissance many helicopters can now be, and are, well armed. For example, the United States Army *H-13 Sioux* (one of the *Bell-47* models with a gross weight of 2,600 lb.) can carry two *SS-10* anti-tank missiles or alternatively two machine-guns, whilst an *HU-1* can be equipped with six of the much faster and more potent *SS-11* missiles. One factor which can, of course, reduce tactical radii as much as fuel consumption is the stress imposed by high noise levels.

Vulnerability is another problem, because a helicopter can
never be very adequately armoured, but if they contour fly,
make full use of cover, avoid prolonged exchanges of fire, and
do not attempt to cross strongly held enemy areas, they should
normally be able to avoid unduly heavy losses. During the
Algerian War, the French had only 110 craft hit in the course
of 35,000 operational sorties and of these only six were forced
down.

Since Korea the American forces have used helicopters more
and more. The Marine Air Wings planned for the new Marine
Divisions will have about 130 helicopters each. In 1961 there
were about 2,000 service and 700 civilian helicopters in operation in the United States, and these totals are expected to reach
4,000 and 2,500 respectively by 1970. Correspondingly, the
RAF has several squadrons in service and the Army Air Corps
several flights, whilst each Royal Naval commando ship will
have a squadron. There are also a fair number on general naval
duties. Likewise we can assume that several thousand are
flying in the Soviet Union, including a considerable number in
A-VDV—the Aviation for Airborne Forces Command.

However, the simple antithesis between machines that climb
vertically, and those that have the high speed and duration
associated with the fixed mainplane, is becoming false. Increasingly specifications will come to represent compromises
between a pure concentration on either ideal and they will be
met by a variety of different techniques. Whilst the employment
of helicopters will continue to grow, especially in roles in which
a hovering capability is of prime importance, they will gradually relinquish their monopolistic position and become merely
one of a number of different kinds of vertical or short take-off
and landing aircraft. This prospect must now be examined
against the background of the general problem of the operation of tactical planes and light transports in underdeveloped
areas.

III—THE PRESSURE ON AIRFIELD SPACE

The dilemma of how to deploy airpower in underdeveloped
areas has been aggravated by the fact that for a long time past
the sizes and operating speeds of most kinds of aircraft have

stronger runways. For planes like fighters which have a high
lift/drag ratio the critical factor is landing distance. With
loaded transport aircraft take-off requirements are the decisive
ones. At sea-level a runway usually has to be some 3,000 feet
in excess of the designed landing distance of fighters, which
means over 10,000 feet for planes like the F-105D *Thunderchief*
and the *Lightning*, and 2,000 feet or so greater than the take-off
distance of large transports. An added complication is that low
air density due to high temperature or altitude lengthens take-
off because of the effect it has on engine-power and also on lift.
A rise in altitude of 1,500 feet generally increases the length
required by 10 per cent.

Fortunately the trend towards increased take-off runs is now
being arrested, even in machines of standard specifications, by
the employment of much more powerful engines which are
needed to combat the marked drag increases encountered at
high subsonic speeds: but, in spite of this, the problem is still
serious. Long and wide concrete runways are vulnerable, are
difficult to repair, and are, in any case, often scarce. Hence great
interest is being shown in producing fixed-wing aircraft that
either take-off and land vertically or else require relatively small
landing grounds, of a kind that would be available in adequate
numbers in most potential theatres of operations, or could
quickly be improvised. Some of the solutions discussed have
applications, either now or ultimately, in the sphere of long-
range strategic airlift, but most of them are only relevant to the
deployment of airpower for strike, reconnaissance, and transport duties within actual or prospective battle zones.

There are a variety of techniques in use for reducing take-off
and landing areas that do not involve basic modifications of the
aircraft in which they are employed. Naval and marine aviators
using shore stations frequently make use of arrester gear: in
Korea the United States Air Force introduced a nylon and cable
crash barrier that they claimed absorbed an incoming plane's
kinetic energy even more gently than arrester wires did.[1] The
RAF now uses this system also. Parachute brakes, which cut
down landing distances by half a mile or more, are fitted on

[1] D. M. Desoulter, *Aircraft and Missiles* (London, Faber and
Faber, 1959), Chapter X

some fighters and bombers and certain planes can reverse their jet engine thrust on touchdown. A few of the F-100 *Super Sabre* fighters were fitted with 130,000-lb. thrust rocket bottles that enabled them to rise from a standing start, and some F-104G *Starfighters* are to be fitted with modified versions of the same thing. Pairs of JATO units with a 45,000-lb. combined thrust are sometimes attached to A4D *Skyhawks*, but they are too bulky and costly for regular use.[1]

More fundamental modifications in design can be incorporated to produce extra lift for a given speed. The *Scimitar* and *Starfighter* strike aircraft incorporate the 'blown flaps' device. This is a mechanism that feeds compressed air through the mainplane to jets above its trailing-edge flaps. Likewise boundary layer control should decrease drag in proportion to lift and so make possible shorter take-offs.[2] Humble tactical transports like the *Caribou* use a range of slats, slots, and ordinary mechanical flaps to produce the required results and they have especially strengthened undercarriages to help them land crosswind on rugged surfaces. A much more ambitious approach is that of the 'variable-sweep wing' which has been advocated for many years by the British designer Dr. Barnes Wallis as a means of securing a much more versatile performance in exchange for a modest weight penalty. In the 'spread position' lift is high in proportion to drag and this considerably shortens take-off and improves range at high altitude. For maximum speed the wings are swivelled into the 'forward position'. These points seem now to have been taken in some influential circles for early in 1962 the Department of Defense awarded a triservice contract for developing a fighter—officially designated the F-111—to the TFX specification. This represents a blend of Navy and Air Force requirements. It seems that the plane produced will only require a very short take-off run from a bulldozed strip, but will possess a transoceanic ferrying range.

There is little advantage in a plane being able to lift, say, a 4-ton payload into the air after a run of 150 yards, as it is hoped that the NATO MRB-4 battlefield transport will be able to, unless it can do such things from unprepared surfaces. The best way of ensuring this is to fit it with a tricycle undercarriage and

[1] JATO: Jet Assisted Take Off.
[2] See Chapter 6, Section II

to make all wheels as large as possible and mount them in single or tandem pairs. There is a considerable weight and bulk penalty, but it produces the result of a big reduction in footprint pressure. The all-up weight of a fully loaded *Caribou* is 130 per cent that of a *Starfighter*, but the former has a tyre pressure that is only 14 per cent of that of the latter's. In January 1962 an Avro 748 medium transport gave a public demonstration of operation from a deeply rutted ploughed field covered in 2 feet of mud. It took off and landed with a 5½-ton payload on one engine and with a 7-ton load on two engines. It also carried out some complex evolutions whilst taxiing.[1]

The airborne components of the new automatic landing systems being developed weigh about 1 cwt. and are likely to be fitted in various standard bombers and medium transports over the next few years. They will enable these aircraft to land at aerodromes fitted with the corresponding pieces of ground equipment under any weather conditions. The electronic approach aids already in use can enable nearly every type of plane to land in visibilities and cloud bases as low as 500 yards and 300 feet respectively, assuming, of course, the airfield surface is not waterlogged. This means that the weather rarely prevents them using permanent airfields in sheltered or lowland localities even in regions like Monsoon Asia. Some South Vietnam and Laos weather records show this. At Vientiane and Tourane cloud bases below 600 feet are only observed 2 per cent of the time, while at Saigon the frequency is 5 per cent.[2] Visibilities below 550 yards occur on less than 1 per cent of all occasions at all three places. Higher and more exposed districts will, however, have a much poorer climate and operations from emergency airstrips will be more readily curtailed than those from established aerodromes, because the airstrips will tend to be small, have poor surfaces, and lack electronic aids.

If unlimited labour is available, airfields can be constructed with little more than sheer muscular effort. During three months of the last war 100,000 coolies working for the Chinese Nationalists built one with a 2,000-yard runway consisting of a 5-foot layer of stone which was able to accept aircraft of up to

[1] *The Guardian*, January 30, 1962
[2] Investigations Division Climatological Report No. 106, Air Ministry London, 1961

13 tons.[1] Commonwealth and American forces in Burma included aviation engineer units that could be glider-dropped with bulldozers and other light equipment. By covering grass clearings and paddy fields with bituminous hessian, one of them could quickly construct airstrips that could be used by *Dakotas* for several weeks at least during dry weather. Such strips were prepared every fifty miles or so and by the end of their last dry season the 14th Army was having 1,500 tons of supplies air-landed each day, 1,000 tons air-dropped, and 1,000 tons brought in by land transport.

Fifty-five new airfields were built for the United Nations during the Korean War despite considerable difficulties over soil stability.[2] Soil structure was a problem, too, in the Red River delta in North Vietnam and the French found it necessary to employ an average of one ton of crushed rock, which had to be allowed to settle gradually, to make a square yard of runway.[3] As might be expected careful preparation of airfields by these conventional methods takes a long time. Even assuming an 'averagely suitable' site were available, it is reckoned that three heavy engineer construction battalions could not expect to complete in less than three months an air base from which a fighter wing could operate under minimum conditions.[4]

Therefore, in anticipation of a future need to fly the combat planes of an air wing from areas where no ready-made airfields exist, the US Marine Corps has for some years been developing the Small Airfield for Tactical Support system. Its specification states that it shall be capable of being built on a cleared well-drained site by a Naval Mobile Construction Battalion in five days and that when complete it shall be able to maintain an operational combat squadron for a period of a month. A lot of the components have already been developed, including a collapsible and heliportable control tower, a complete range of such portable approach equipment as mirror landing aids, a fuel-dispensing system, and a prefabricated aluminium runway

[1] Lt.-Col. R. A. Harter in *Military Review*, May 1945

[2] J. T. Stewart, *Air Power—The Decisive Force in Korea* (Princeton, Van Nostrand, 1957), Chapter XII

[3] George Tanham, *Communist Revolutionary Warfare* (New York, Praeger, 1961), Chapter V

[4] Field Manual 101–10, Part I, Department of the Army, 1959, p. 427

1,000 feet in length. A portable arrester wire has also been produced that is able to draw to a halt a 20,000-lb. plane travelling at 150 knots. This means that an A4D *Skyhawk* can hook on as soon as it touches down, but that a plane like the *Phantom II* has to taxi in for some distance before it can safely engage. What has yet to be developed is a light, transportable catapult that can be anchored satisfactorily and can provide enough power to get an aircraft off the ground. The best available so far can yield less than a quarter of that produced by the models installed in *Enterprise*. This weakness is made more serious by the fact that SATS installations may often be put down in places dominated by hills or high trees and the planes may at times be required to take off with a following wind.

It is recognized that one of the most useful tasks a SATS unit, or indeed any other kind of airfield construction team, may perform during an emergency will consist of the improvement of existing airfields. Many of these have dimensions adequate for many types of aircraft, yet lack the control and maintenance facilities essential for large-scale activity because their normal peacetime traffic is light. Thus if we examine scheduled flights, which are generally a high proportion of all non-military flights, we find, for example, that of eleven airfields used for civilian purposes in Persia in 1957 only two accepted more than twenty-five planes a week and of these only one more than fifty.[1] Half a dozen of the aerodromes in question were used by the Iranian Air Force and might have handled an average of another fifty landings a week on that account. Examining the situation in Malaya, to take another country with which Britain is allied, we find very much the same picture. Apart from the international airport at Kuala Lumpur seven places are visited during scheduled internal flights and they experience an average of twenty-five landings a week.[2] In this case no air force traffic as yet swells the total. Wartime usage requirements dwarf any of the above figures. An operational wing of seventy-five aircraft may well complete 400 sorties a day. At Myitkyina airfield in Burma in 1945 over two hundred aircraft touched down during one twelve-hour period.

[1] *Oxford Economic Atlas of the Middle East* (Oxford University Press, 1960), pp. 56–57
[2] ABC World Airways Guide, No. 340 (London, 1962)

Insufficient parking space can soon prove a great nuisance, but the most immediate and critical consequence of a marked rise in the rate of use would be, in many instances, a desperate fuel shortage. Unless stockpiling for military purposes has taken place any airfield would have only very modest reserves. They might be equivalent to one or two days' peacetime consumption if it were busy and centrally situated, and perhaps to as much as a fortnight's if it were quiet and remote. Since much of the normal traffic in most cases is very short range, and since a lot of it is carried out by piston-engined machines whose fuel is not very suitable for turbines, pre-existing stocks would soon need to be replenished on a large scale. A fuel-dispensing system does not solve this problem, since it merely distributes the fuel within the airfield. Of course, the larger short-range transports can evade the issue by carrying with them from a main base enough fuel to complete the return journey.

As has already been said, nearly all contemporary fighters look for runways consisting of close on two miles of high stress concrete—the obsolescent *Hunter* is now exceptional in being content with tarmac. If they have to use a weaker surface they soon churn it up and may then very easily suck into their turbines the resulting debris. Since SATS or something like it has yet to be perfected and universally adopted, it has seemed desirable to deliberately improve airfield facilities in various areas considered vulnerable. Thus 220 standard all-weather aerodromes have been created under the NATO infrastructure programme. About twelve of these are in Greece and some of them are connected to a pipeline network about 310 miles long.[1] Something like fifteen are in Turkey. Likewise between 1954 and 1958 a portion of United States economic aid to Thailand went towards rebuilding and re-equipping thirteen civil 'airports' and three military airfields.[2] It seems, however, that most of this money was devoted to turning Bangkok and another airfield 60 miles to the North of it into bases capable of handling considerable numbers of the latest types of machines. Most of the so-called 'airports' in the country remain small and

[1] William Green and John Fricker, *Air Forces of the World* (London, MacDonald & Co., 1958), p. 151
[2] George Modelski (Ed.), *Seato* (Melbourne, F. W. Cheshire, 1962), p. 99

primitive landing strips set chiefly among the remote Northern hills and visited only by DC-3s running 'feeder' services. Only four of them accept more than ten civilian scheduled flights a week. Nevertheless, Thailand remains better served than Laos and South Vietnam, although a recently announced $60,000,000 airfield development programme should improve things in these countries.

It is often assumed that vast expense is involved in constructing a first-class air station but, in terms of the general economics of modern defence, this is not so. The NATO standard airfields referred to have runways at least 8,000 feet in length and, if started from scratch, have generally been built for around $12,000,000 exclusive of barrack accommodation.[1] The cost of one of the new 10,000-feet concrete runways is around $5,000,000.

Much effort is now being directed towards producing fixed-wing battlefield transports and fighters that can land and take off absolutely vertically. As might be expected, some of the former are evolutions from the pure helicopter concept, starting with the stub wings of the Russian *Mi-6* and going on to the Russian *Vintokryl* and the cancelled British *Rotodyne* project with their long fixed wings and horizontal engines, in addition to the power-driven rotor. Other lines of approach being investigated include the fitting of batteries of auxiliary lift engines to the mainplanes of standard transports such as the French *Noratlas*. The United States has recently awarded a triservice development contract for an aircraft that is to be VTOL, but in other respects conform to the NATO MRB-4 specification. Whether VTOL is considered worth going for will depend largely on the terrain in which one is expecting to operate. Where firm flat surfaces abound the weight sacrifice of 5 per cent or 6 per cent involved in a wheeled undercarriage may be worth making in exchange for the considerable extra lift that even a short run provides. Even in Afro-Asia only 2 per cent of the land is more than 100 miles from a landing-strip at least 500 yards long, quite apart from level areas of totally unprepared land that may be suitable. Such a density is sufficient for resupply of brigades or even battalions assuming air-drop-

[1] *New York Times* October 25, 1952

ping is used and assuming that many of the airstrips are not inundated with water at any particular time. It is not, however, enough to give troops adequate air mobility for tactical purposes unless VTOL machines are available to them.

In the case of fighters many of the technical and operational trends of recent years have made VTOL capabilities both more practicable and more desirable but, in spite of this, they have, so far, always involved sacrifices in range and often, too, in speed and reliability. One reason for this is that because vertical and horizontal thrusts are required alternately one has either to tilt the main engines or deflect their thrust or fit auxiliary lift engines with vertical axes or manufacture a plane configured to sit on its tail. The first three methods result in extra bulk and complexity and poor streamlining, whilst the last results in a machine with inferior manoeuvrability. Another difficulty is that the maximum vertical thrust has to exceed the all-up weight of the aeroplane and so it is much greater than the required horizontal thrust. This means that if the same engine is used at both stages it must, while the plane is in flight, run throttled well down and so become expensive on fuel. In a subsonic jet designed for normal take-offs the engine thrust is typically about 30 per cent of the loaded weight and even with Mach 2.0 fighters a characteristic figure is 65 per cent. Therefore, to make VTOL planes it is necessary either to much increase their engine power, which is not to any degree practicable, or to reduce their weight substantially, which usually means slashing their fuel capacity. Furthermore, even when this has been done a weapons system has still not been produced that is entirely independent of fixed ground installations. Apart from anything else those dependent on auxiliary lift engines will probably need concrete launching-pads some tens of yards in diameter to reduce the risk of ingestion of dust particles. Ground erosion is much less of a problem with the tilt-engine or vectored thrust patterns, because of the jets only having to point downward at the instant of take-off.

Despite their inherent limitations, several VTOL supersonic fighters are on the drawing-boards, including some submissions for the NATO NMBR-3 design competition. The NMBR-3 is intended to be supersonic near the ground and to be able to reach twice the speed of sound at high altitude. It will carry approximately 4 tons of fuel and is said to have a planned radius of action of 250 miles when following a predominately high-level flight path at a subsonic cruising speed. This seems too low for many combat requirements and is obviously much too low for long-range deployments. On the other hand, a short run would enable such a machine to lift and carry large external tanks. By adopting this technique it is hoped to provide the Hawker P 1154, which is a contestant in the NATO competition, with a ferrying range of 2,000 miles even without being refuelled in flight.

Appendix A illustrates the fact that those combat aircraft that are dependent on very large airfields would still find it difficult to operate in a dispersed fashion or in large numbers in many countries. On the other hand, the Hawker P 1154 and similar planes should start entering service soon after the middle of this decade, and we can expect to see the first squadrons of the F-111 flying two or three years later. Meanwhile, the United States Air Force is procuring the land version of the F4H *Phantom II*, which is capable of using runways less than 5,000 feet in length.

The design which won the United States triservice V/STOL tactical transport competition was the XC-142A, which is to be jointly produced by Chance Vought, Hilber, and Ryan, who hope to have it in operation by 1965. In its VTOL role it will have an all-up weight of 20 tons, which is about one and a half times that of the *Caribou I*, though only a quarter of that of the C-130 *Hercules*. This and comparable aircraft built in other countries will combine with the increasing variety of STOL transports, which may soon include one model of over 100 tons gross weight in the form of the SC5/31 *Belfast*, to make tactical air movement progressively less dependent on weather, landscape, and terminal facilities.

Meanwhile the number of secondary civilian aerodromes is gradually rising and the scope for rapid improvisation is increasing. These trends, together with developments in aeronautical engineering, suggest that a shortage of airfields will be a less significant inhibition on air movements within potential combat zones than on the long-range reinforcement of such zones.

IV—THE FUTURE OF AIR SUPPORT

For fifteen years after the war strategic airpower continued to
dominate the consideration of total war, as Douhet, Mitchell
and Trenchard had assumed it must. But in recent years the
partial replacement of manned bombers by ballistic missiles
has involved a blurring of the contrast between aircraft and
surface artillery and air forces have begun to lose their monopoly of strategic striking power. In the same way contemporary
trends in the techniques of non-nuclear war may eventually
discredit the classical theories of air warfare.

General Douhet argued that command of the air ensured
victory in the land battle. This thesis was borne out by the
outcome of many of the battles of the last war, but there were
several important ones whose result pointed to an opposite
conclusion. The brilliant armoured victories of Field-Marshal
Erwin Rommel in the summer of 1942 were won beneath
cloudless skies dominated by the Allied Air Forces. Now the
growing power and flexibility of land-based anti-aircraft defences is making it less and less easy to turn command of the
air to decisive advantage. Furthermore the progressive introduction of, and refinement of, V/STOL techniques means that
it is going to become increasingly difficult to get command of
the air which, according to Douhet, means being '. . . in a
position to prevent the enemy from flying while retaining the
ability to fly oneself'. This is because it will not be possible to
achieve air superiority by crippling a limited number of large
airfields. If, as a consequence, a few aircraft from the weaker
side in any conflict remained capable of attacking their opponent's lines, they would automatically deprive him of two
of the most valuable results of unqualified aerial supremacy.
First of all his troop movements would be open to continual
observation. Secondly, the threat of an occasional strike would
inhibit him from packing his supply lines to their optimum
operating density.

The diminution of the strategic combat role of aircraft has
coincided, of course, with the great rise in their importance as a
means of long-range transportation. The Douhet-Mitchell
school of forty years ago were distinctly cool about this prospect,
because they feared the adoption by their beloved air arms of

any roles that seem to relegate them to purely auxiliary positions. Today the strategic transport of ground troops and their equipment is seen as vital and honourable work that enhances the prestige and influence of the air services who carry it out.

Meanwhile, interest is growing in the application of aircraft to the tasks of logistic support and tactical lift within combat zones. There is no doubt that anywhere fighting takes place in which large and modern forces are involved aircraft will serve in such capacities in association with ground vehicles, but which of the two media will predominate will depend upon geography. This is because aircraft only become economically advantageous if operations are being conducted in remote and underdeveloped areas.

A *Chinook* helicopter flying over, say, a 200-mile stage could deliver about 18 tons of mixed stores in a ten-hour day. In doing so it would use 9 tons of aviation spirit and fully employ fifty men. A *Caribou* fixed-wing tactical transport would deliver about 12 tons, consume about $3\frac{1}{2}$ tons of fuel, and employ about the same number of men. The capital cost of the *Chinook* would be approximately $1,500,000 and of the *Caribou* about $500,000. On the other hand, three 5-ton trucks travelling at 30 m.p.h. on straight and direct roads could do as well as the *Chinook*. They would consume about 1 ton of fuel between them and would keep about ten men occupied. Their combined capital cost would be around $20,000.

The balance becomes very different, however, if it is necessary to use 1-ton trucks which require nearly three times as much petrol and nearly five times as much manpower to do as much work as 5-ton ones. The difference is accentuated if circuitous routes double or treble the distances to be driven over and bad surfaces, gradients, or weather conditions reduce speeds to around 10 m.p.h. If no roads exist at the beginning of operations, then the desirability of not wasting time and effort building them provide an unanswerable argument in favour of doing it all by air. In monsoon conditions this preferably means helicopters, not so much because of their greater tolerance of adverse flying conditions, but because of their comparative indifference to the effects which heavy rains have on landing surfaces. There is the additional consideration that

aerial lines of communication are rather less vulnerable than
land ones to interdiction by guerilla parties or long-range
patrol groups.

A recent consequence of the growing recognition of the value
of planes as battlefield transports has been the Howze Report
submitted to the Secretary of Defense by a large *ad hoc* United
States army committee in 1962. It is said to have recommended
the boosting of United States Army expenditure on aircraft in
the five years ending July 1967 from $1,600,000,000 to
$5,450,000,000, so as to increase the planned procurement
from 1,650 to 5,450 machines.[1] A Department of Defense task
force that has listened to Air Force opinions as well as those of
the Howze Board is reported to have made more modest proposals, but these include the provision of three air assault
divisions, three air cavalry combat brigades, two or three air
transport brigades and some supporting units such as air
mobile corps artillery.[2] Each assault division would have 460
aircraft organic compared with 103 in a ROAD division and
forty in a Pentomic one and this would enable it to dispense
with about half its ground vehicles.[3] About 90 per cent of
the machines on the ROAD scale are helicopters, but we can
assume that these new divisions would not have as high a proportion of rotorcraft as that. The air cavalry brigades would
contain 140 aircraft each and, it is thought, would be especially
useful in checking armoured penetrations. The corps artillery
would have some helicopter-launched rockets, but its chief
offensive weapons would be airportable heavy launchers
similar to *Honest John* and *Little John*. The advantage of rocket
launchers in this context is that they can achieve ranges well
in excess of those obtained by guns of comparable weight. The
air transport brigades would chiefly be used in conjunction with
the air assault divisions and would contain 134 aircraft apiece, of
which eighty would be *Caribous*. It has been announced that
one air assault division is about to be formed to try these ideas
out, and the enthusiasm with which United States government

[1] *Army, Navy and Air Force Journal & Register*, September 29, 1962
[2] *Ibid.*, October 6, 1962
[3] The ROAD organisation for a division was introduced into
the United States Army in 1962. The Pentomic one dates from
1956

officials discuss them suggests that they expect them to be fully vindicated by the results of these trials.

What one may call the Howze doctrine is clearly not one that lends support to independent air forces, since its basic tenet is that more and bigger aircraft should become organic to army units. By doing so it helps accelerate a trend which has been firmly established for a decade past, despite the attempt made by Mr. Charles E. Wilson, when United States Secretary of Defense, to place upper limits on the size of army aircraft. His Memorandum of March 1957, which seems to have been a product of United States Air Force pressure, tried to keep the empty weight of army helicopters down to 20,000 lb. and of fixed-wing aircraft to 5,000 lb., but these limits were soon eroded in respect of helicopters and smashed in respect of monoplanes. It is true that Britain's Army Air Corps is still nominally restricted to flying machines with an all-up weight of 4,000 lb., but it has recently created an important precedent by procuring some *Beaver* light transports which weigh just over 5,000 lb. fully loaded. Thus, it seems that the intuitive fears that most of the pioneers of air strategy entertained about the employment of aircraft to carry men and supplies are, to some extent at least, being justified by events.

It is possible, but by no means certain, that the establishment of air assault formations will undermine the position of air forces in another respect. They may prove so strategically immobile that it will be necessary to hold them predominately in theatre reserves rather than airlifted strategic ones. If so, this will be because the sizes and shapes of most of their aircraft will be such as to make them either unsuitable for, or else ineligible for, stowage inside even the biggest cargo planes. The problems created by the alternative solution of flying them over long distances have already been discussed in connection with helicopters, and it must be observed that they are practically as great as far as small and relatively low-powered fixed-wing aircraft like the *Caribou I* are concerned. This is not because their maximum ranges are particularly low, for that of *Caribou I* is as much as 1,400 miles, and it can, it any case, be refuelled in flight by any tanker with a low enough stalling speed. It is more a question of how much the crew can endure at one stretch of flying such slow and uncomfortable machines.

One way of minimizing this difficulty might be to use special crews for ferrying work, so as to leave the regular ones fresh for tactical operations.

The paradox that advances in aeronautical engineering do not necessarily favour independent air arms seems to be brought out again by a consideration of the influence that VTOL methods are starting to have on assault and supply by sea. So far only light and medium helicopters are being employed in these roles, but they may soon be supplemented by the XC-142A fixed-wing aircraft and by the first of the Sikorsky 'flying cranes'. One projected member of this series will be able to lift a 40-ton unit load, and it is reasonable to suppose that, say, six craft of this type would be able to off-load pallet-ized cargo from a logistic ship at something like 1,000 tons an hour—assuming, of course, that the ship was sufficiently auto-mated as to be able to feed pallets to the deck at the same speed and assuming also that its masts, rigging, and superstructure were so positioned as not to impede the work of the heli-copters. Vessels using such a system would be indifferent to the quality of existing ports and beaches and could, in fact, unload across almost any stretch of coastline. Because of the freedom of movement thereby obtained it would not be easy for enemy submarines to concentrate against them or for enemy forces to lay barrier minefields. In any case, 'flying crane' helicopters will be readily adaptable to anti-submarine or minesweeping tasks.

Chapter 8

Ground Forces in Limited War

I—THE NATURE OF THE LAND BATTLE

ANY general estimate of lift requirements must depend partly upon an assessment of the probable pattern of any likely conflict. The key questions are really what strength would be necessary to hold a given sector of front and what offensive strength would be required to overcome it. In the following attempt to provide a few very impressionistic answers it has been assumed throughout that the forces engaged on each side would each be endowed with the latest benefits of technology. Also the old-established convention of talking in terms of divisions has been adhered to in spite of the fact that in several leading armies brigades or 'reinforced battle groups' are regarded as balanced formations capable of sustained independent operations.

At the present time, the NATO forces in Central Europe are equipped to fight with conventional weapons in the first instance. This is not because the authorities predict a large-scale non-nuclear war in that region, but because it is currently felt that fighting may start by accident or through miscalculation and that nuclear firepower would be disastrously inappropriate in such a contingency. Fortunately the equipment and organization required would be roughly similar for each type of war, there being a heavy premium on armoured mobility in both cases. The major equipment difference is obviously that if nuclear weapons were not used combat troops would need a higher proportion of conventional artillery support. Also, a basic structural difference exists at least in the minds of some leading authorities who regard the triangular arrangement of three brigades per division as ideal for traditional frontal war because of the simple command system, and a pentagonal one better for atomic war, since it lends itself to dispersion and all-round defence. On the other hand, there is a powerful school of thought that contends that the 'five finger' structure is the best one to apply to non-nuclear campaigning as well, since it affords more general flexibility. Of course, it might well be that as nuclear weapons become more numerous and variegated the predicted course of a nuclear land battle will alter so much that ideas about the kind of formations required will change considerably. The result might be units that are wholly unsuited to conventional battles. As of the present time, however, it is possible to be ambidextrous.

In the second half of the last war the defence gained a marked ascendancy. The Commonwealth and Allied forces broke through at Alamein only after twelve days of bitter fighting, although they had three times the guns and six times the tanks of their opponents. In Normandy numerical odds of five to one in favour of the attack were generally necessary for the attack to succeed. Furthermore, in these campaigns the Allies had complete air superiority, which is often reckoned in staff calculations to at least double the value of ground troops. Captain B. H. Liddell-Hart believes that this is part of a gradual long-term ascendancy of the defence associated with the fact that improvements in firepower, mobility, and communications have progressively reduced the number of troops required to hold a mile of front in battle.[1] This, he says, was about 20,000 in 1800, 12,000 in 1870, 2,500 in 1917, and less than 1,000 today. He regards the supremacy of the attack in 1940 as an aberration due to the neglect of certain elementary principles by the defending commanders.

However, military history is not a mechanical science and apparent trends like changes in the ratio of troops to space, even if statistically valid, must not be regarded as determinants of the tactical balance but merely as guide lines indicating probable changes in it. At the close of the Middle Ages marked improvements took place in firepower and mobility, and yet these strongly favoured the attack, whilst having little effect on the ratio of troops to space. It would therefore be dangerous to draw conclusions from last-war trends. It would be even more foolish to take it for granted that the situation has stood still during twenty years. We have no recent experience of non-nuclear warfare involving first-class armies on both sides, but despite this we must form some estimate of the tactical

[1] B. H. Liddell-Hart, *Armor*, March to June 1960

significance of current and anticipated advances in technology.

It is usually assumed that communication nets and surveillance systems have much improved in recent years and that this is to the overall advantage of defending forces, since they can determine the general pattern of attack and evoke a balanced response to it in as short a time as possible. Unfortunately, while the conclusion may well follow from the premise, the premise itself is possibly false, owing to the development of all the jamming and deception techniques known collectively as electronic warfare. The attack would certainly benefit from the better prospects for by-passing static fortifications either by exploiting improved ground mobility or by vertical envelopment. The scope for vertical envelopment would be greater now than in 1945, because the advent of the helicopter has more than compensated for the facts that parachutists have become more vulnerable and gliders too vulnerable to use. Meanwhile night operations, which would favour the numerically superior side because they would make possible continuous applications of pressure, are becoming more practicable as infra-red and radar surveillance sets are introduced more widely. However, the hours of darkness would probably still lend themselves more to infiltration or to attacks on thinly held lines rather than to assaults on heavily fortified zones. The attack would also profit from the fact that greater numbers of armoured personnel carriers would now be available to facilitate the passage of men and supplies across fireswept ground or to serve as armoured fighting vehicles to launch guided missiles, mortar bombs, and bullets against their enemies. Body armour is also being widely introduced into the American forces to help protect advancing infantry, though the British authorities are as inert in this matter today as they were half a century back. An overriding consideration is, however, the fact that any conventional war of movement involving the big powers would very likely be short-lived and so the advantage of initial surprise would assume an added importance. Also, the invading forces would stand to gain from a general lack of experience of hitting moving targets under combat conditions and, in some situations, from the lack of time to prepare fixed defences.

On the other hand, certain current trends may tend to

strengthen the defence. One is the much more general employment of the proximity fuses that make high-explosive shells and bombs more effective against troops in the open. Another is the changing quality of tactical air support. I have already suggested that it is becoming increasingly improbable that they who hold command of the skies will be able to turn this to decisive advantage by incessant ground attack and that it will become ever more unlikely that one side in any conflict could achieve absolute control of the air.[1] This trend will in general work to the detriment of attacking forces, because these will tend to be stronger in the skies as on the ground, but, of course, it is possible to think of circumstances in which an aggressor would not have initial aerial superiority. Such would probably be the case, for example, in hostilities involving Communist China.

However, the crux of the matter is the status of the battle tank, about which speculation has been taking place. From the record of the debate it is impossible to avoid the general conclusion that the offensive power of the tank has diminished, though it remains an open question as to how much. The cross-country speed of a modern medium tank is about the same as that of a wartime 'cruiser' and could not be much increased for fear of the extra discomfort caused to the crew. The quality of tank armour is still improving and so the vehicles are becoming less vulnerable to high-velocity projectiles. Also tanks are acquiring the ability to fire reasonably accurately on the move. However, these marginal advantages are being dwarfed by the evolution of the anti-tank guided missile. It is true that these weapons have to be controlled all the way to their targets—a lengthy process which would be difficult amid the noise and confusion of battle—and that the largest of them are slow to load, are potentially vulnerable in the final loading stages, and have a limited arc of traverse. However, the smaller varieties are much easier to site tactically than guns, especially since the operator can lie many yards from the missile. Above all, these weapons have power and accuracy. The British *Vigilant*, which weighs 44 lb. with its container, is able to penetrate any known armour—that is vertical plate up to 250 millimetres thick—at 1,500 yards.[2] The French *SS-11* is of 65 lb. all-up weight and

[1] Chapter 7, Section IV
[2] BAC Report in *Fifteen Nations*, October 1961

can penetrate 600 millimetres of armour at up to 3,000 yards.[1] Both these systems have regularly achieved 80–90 per cent accuracy in range tests against fixed and moving targets. The results of field tests have been less spectacular, but, of course, penetration of its armour does not inevitably stop a tank either moving or firing. Also sloping plate will present a greater relative thickness along the lines of flight than its width as measured and spaced armour is much better at resisting a missile's shaped charge than solid plate is. A development of this latter technique with, perhaps, very wide spacing might be a partial antidote to this new challenge. Tanks may still stand a chance, especially at night, of saturating the defences in a narrow sector of a front and so burst through to the rear area and all its easy targets. But the inherent growth potentialities of guided missiles are far greater than those of battle tanks. The next generation of them, for example, may proceed at much higher velocities under beam guidance. Arguments about stress and morale tend to be double-edged. Tanks are cumbersome, very uncomfortable, largely deaf, and partially blind, and their occupants need the assurance that they are not readily penetrable. Moreover, the *Vigilant* costs only £500 and what little user training is required for it can be done largely with a simulator: a battle tank costs £60,000. Of course, if the statement is true that tanks are becoming more destructible than heretofore the potential consequences for land warfare are profound. Tanks are the only weapons that can give instantaneous high-explosive fire support to advancing infantry.

Writing several years ago Captain B. H. Liddell-Hart assumed that the numerical superiority which he considered had been necessary to overcome qualitatively equal forces during campaigns in the temperate climate of Western Europe in the second half of the last world war still held good.[2] The ratios he named were five or more to one on the principal axes of advance which, he said, created a requirement for an overall majority of three to one along the whole front. It may well be true that the point of balance remained about the same in the decade after 1945 largely because technology was then chang-

[1] *Interavia*, 1/1959.
[2] B. H. Liddell-Hart, *Deterrent or Defence* (London, Stevens & Son, 1960), Chapter 16

ing only slowly, but since then innovation has been rapid and the result seems to have been another shift in favour of the defence. However, to arrive at an exact conclusion one would need to do a most thorough piece of operational research that would have to be repeated at least every couple of years to bring the findings up to date. In any case, it is unreal to postulate qualitative parity. Qualitative differences in men and equipment are getting increasingly difficult to estimate but they undoubtedly exist even between the first-class powers and might prove decisive in the event of hostilities. Furthermore, the skills and temperaments of the opposing commanders and other accidental factors must continue to count for a considerable amount. In view of all these imponderables and variables it is probably best to stick to the three-to-one ratio when assessing general force level and lift requirements.

The few authoritative statements that have appeared about temperate lowland environment should be able to hold an eight-to-twelve-mile sector against forces several times its strength. A highly mobile division would probably be able to screen twenty-five miles, but the odds it would be able to accept would be less. This is because its success would depend on the frequent launching of counter-attacks at points of penetration and this would entail sacrificing the advantage of resting on the tactical defensive.

The supporting weapons most required in mountain areas are pack howitzers. Small groups of tanks were widely used in Italy and Korea in direct support of infantry, but they would find it difficult on mountain slopes to maintain the rapid and semi-concealed movement necessary to keep down losses when confronted with an opposition equipped with guided missiles. Mules have traditionally been the means of off-road transport, but aircraft are now better. The numerous peaks and ridge crests are often tactically defensible, though the impediments they present to mobility often result in divisional frontages being reduced. However, the influence of topography depends very much on the direction and nature of its grain, and extensive longitudinal valleys may, especially in the absence of equally good lateral routes to permit the transference of reserves, facilitate offensive action.

Hot desert topography naturally varies with the geological

structure and climatic history of the area in question. However, despite characteristically steep scarps and areas of shifting sand, the landscape has often in the past proved ideal for armoured thrusts supported by tactical airpower. In any future hostilities, on the other hand, armoured fighting vehicles and tactical aircraft would have to depend for such immunity as they enjoyed on concealment and surprise respectively to a greater extent than heretofore. Both these advantages would be difficult to obtain over open landscapes with wide horizons. Another new perspective on desert warfare that has emerged from recent American and Canadian engineering research is that, contrary to traditional beliefs, wheeled vehicles negotiate sandy surfaces better than tracked ones.[1]

The mud of jungle lands favours tracked vehicles, but their weights normally have to be kept well down. Thus tanks of 35 tons or above are generally considered too large. Otherwise equipment requirements are broadly similar to those of mountain régimes, except that the tremendous opportunities for infiltrating and interrupting fixed supply lines result in an even heavier premium being placed on air movement, particularly in this case by helicopter. Frontal assaults have often proved extremely costly, but, on the other hand, restricted visibilities and fields of fire and the necessity for all-round defence have usually resulted in divisional defended sectors being very narrow. This fact, together with the need to spread armies thinly because of the poor communications, has generally resulted in large gaps between major units. At the height of the Burma campaign, the Allies generally had eighteen divisions spread over 700 miles. Such campaigns have normally degenerated in a series of fierce, though often long drawn out, contests for vital communication links, and this would probably be true again. In such operations the forces on the strategic defensive could not rely on being able to repulse attackers of similar calibre as much as three times their number.

It is impossible to design balanced formations of brigade or divisional size which are suited to operating for prolonged periods in any one of a variety of campaign conditions. Different regions create different needs, in both quantitative and qualitative terms, for tanks, armoured personnel carriers, lorries, wire-

[1] R. M. Ogorkiewicz in *The Army Quarterly*, January 1962

less sets, and many other important items. If a composite force of several thousand men were sent into an environment for which it was badly adapted, it would at the best be inefficient and at the worst less than useless. The new American ROAD divisional organization is a conscious attempt to anticipate these dangers. Each ROAD division consists of a headquarters unit and between five and fifteen battalions which can be variously armoured, armoured infantry, infantry, or airborne according to the task anticipated. In theory a division could be built up from an appropriate assortment of these battalion units with great rapidity, but, in practice, this could only produce an organic war machine if the battalions had trained together for a long time. One objection to the British 'regimental system' is that postings take place on a whole regiment or battalion rather than an individual basis. This means that at frequent intervals the fund of common experience within brigade groups is completely dissipated. It is not possible to rotate brigade groups around the globe, for the simple reason that under present peacetime conditions some brigade groups, designed for European service, have a substantial proportion of tracked armour, whilst the others do not. Also in several places infantry battalions form independent overseas garrisons.

The effectiveness of strategically mobile forces is normally discussed in terms of the time they would probably take to deploy in certain strengths over certain distances. However, the time scale only becomes significant if we can make reasonable assumptions about the prospects of strategic warning and if we can also predict the average rate at which an aggressor would be likely to be able to advance before the local balance of power was restored. The British 'Bladeforce' in North Africa in 1942 and Malinowsky's armoured spearheads in Manchuria in 1945 sustained average speeds of over 100 miles a day for several days on end. However, these were exploitation movements conducted against negligible resistance, and so the columns rolled forward almost as fast as if they were executing a routine march order. The standard planning factors used by the United States Army postulate that an armoured division proceeding in convoy is capable of covering 100 miles a day and a motorized infantry division 150. The upper limit for non-motorized formations can be taken to be about twentyfive, which may, of course, mean less than ten, measured as the crow flies. Mechanized units fighting forward against even weak defensive screens maintain much lower net speeds. The Germans in Greece in 1941, the allies during the breakout after the Battle of Normandy in 1944, and the North Koreans in the first few weeks of their 1950 offensive averaged fifteen miles a day. Sustained advances of over forty miles have been exceptional in the recent past, even in favourable terrain, and, given the potentialities of the modern defence, are likely to remain so in the future. In jungle country rates are much slower. Pursuing a broken Japanese army through the Burmese summer monsoon in the months following the battle of Imphal, the British and Commonwealth troops under Field-Marshal Slim managed to average only two miles a day despite the large-scale air support for transport and strike purposes. During the last week or two of the pursuit to Rangoon the following spring the rate rose to ten miles.

II—LOGISTICS[1]

The most modern and comprehensive tables of organization available for any Western army are those published in respect of the United States Pentomic divisions. They must inevitably be different from those that will have been worked out for typical ROAD divisions which will incorporate many new changes, including more tactical aircraft and more field artillery guns. Likewise they will be different from those of the French and British armies, despite the attempts at standardization that are being made within NATO. However, we are concerned here mainly with acquiring a general sense of what is involved in moving around major formations from the leading Western armies and in keeping them supplied. For that purpose the Pentomic tables are adequate.

Each Pentomic infantry division contains five battle groups of 1,427 men, who are predominantly infantrymen. Together they hold half of its individual and half of its crew-served

[1] Except where stated to the contrary, the data presented in this section is drawn from Field Manual 101–10, Part I, US Department of the Army, 1959

weapons, and each has two 76-millimetre gun tanks, four 90-millimetre self-propelled guns, and two armoured personnel carriers. There are in each case 120 trucks, nearly all general-purpose models, which are able to carry between them a payload of up to 140 tons, and about 100 trailers able to carry another 80 tons. The tracked vehicles weigh 110 tons altogether and the wheeled ones 330 tons. The total unit weight is calculated on the assumption that it will have with it enough food (Class I supplies) for three days' sustenance, enough petrol, oil, and lubricant (Class III or POL) to move 300 miles, and a basic load of ammunition (Class V). A basic load is a prescribed allowance authorized and required to be in possession of a unit. It is intended to correspond to the amount that will normally sustain the formation in battle until resupply can be effected. The quantity in the case of a battle group is 120 tons and this, together with 40 tons of food and POL and some miscellaneous equipment, brings the overall battle group weight to around 780 tons.

In addition to its battle groups and to various headquarters detachments the infantry division contains one specialist battalion for engineering, signalling, ordnance, medical services, and transportation respectively. There are two artillery battalions, a tank battalion, and a cavalry squadron. The armoured unit weighs approximately 7,600 tons and the divisional artillery about 3,000 tons. The signal battalion weighs 2,300 tons, the transport and ordnance ones about 2,000 tons each, the engineer battalion 1,000 tons, and the medical one around 400 tons. The aggregate total of 22,300 tons can alternatively be broken down on a basis of physical characteristics. Thus the tracked vehicles weigh 6,800 tons empty and the wheeled ones 9,900 tons. Non-self-propelled, crew-served weapons are equivalent to another 300 tons. Divisional food supplies amount to 150 tons, fuel to 1,050, and ammunition to 1,400 tons. About 1,600 tons should be allowed for personnel and nearly 1,500 for miscellaneous items. What emerges from the breakdown of these tables is the great weight of the vehicles, and of the tracked and armoured ones in particular, as compared with all the other elements. Taken together with the facts that all these vehicles have low densities, and that many of them have awkward shapes, these calculations bring out clearly the conflict between strategic and tactical mobility in mechanized warfare. Another point of interest is that at 3,000 tons the cargo-carrying capacity of the motorized transport is a little above that of the sum of the standard loads for the different classes of supplies.

A Pentomic armoured division on full establishment is much heavier than an infantry one, largely because it contains four tank battalions and because its four armoured infantry battalions have organic to them enough tracked armoured personnel carriers to move practically all their riflemen at once. There are over 30,000 tons of tracked vehicles and about 10,000 tons of wheeled. Therefore, on the standard assumption that the division takes with it 5,400 tons of supplies, its overall mass is about 48,000 tons.

Of course, the maintenance of a division on active duty involves a large number of men, including many combat troops, outside the division itself. Thus a corps or army may have infantry battle groups or armoured cavalry regiments under independent command. These echelons will also normally contain all the *Corporal*, *Honest John*, and anti-aircraft batteries and many support and maintenance groups either similar to or more specialized than their counterparts at divisional level. The United States Army standard planning factor gives the overall divisional slice as being 63,250. This is made up of 14,000 in the division, 18,500 corps and army troops, 10,750 in the communications zone in the rear of the theatre of operations, and 20,000 in the 'zone of the interior', i.e. the continental United States. Naturally actual slice strengths will vary substantially from these standards in certain campaign conditions. Thus the average theatre divisional slice in the Far East in August 1945 was 96,000.

To calculate the tonnages involved in achieving a given build-up within a theatre it is necessary to estimate the minimum stocks of supplies required. This is usually worked out in terms of days of consumption under 'average' combat conditions. Analysis of various Second World War campaigns and the Korean War suggests that the average man in a combat zone (that is under division, corps, or army command) in European latitudes consumes 0.64 tons a month, of which 0.18 tons is POL and 0.20 tons ammunition. In the jungle the total of 0.52 tons includes 0.11 tons of the former and 0.13 of the latter. To this should be added 0.10 ton of food, as well as spare parts, replacement vehicles, weapons, and constructional materials. Within the communications zone the latter are less important and of a global mean monthly expenditure estimated at 1.14 tons as much as 0.62 consists of petrol, oil, and lubricants. However, the depth and nature of communications zones vary greatly and no statistical norms mean very much in practical terms. In this respect there is a big difference between communications zones and combat zones, for within the latter geography is not as dominant an influence on logistic requirements as might be expected. What really controls the volume and kind of supplies needed by the men in the battle area is the intensity and course of the actual fighting. Munitions consumption is particularly erratic and it is, in fact, postulated that on the first day of a heavy enemy offensive a divisional slice will probably fire off a 1,000 or so tons, whereas in pursuit it will use a mere 100 tons. In each case 60–70 per cent of the total material expenditure takes place within a division. It must be remembered, of course, that these estimates are themselves averages and so to quite an extent conceal the full range of experience.

In view of all these variables it may fairly be asked whether the concept of what a typical division-slice will consume on the average day is anything more than a Platonic Idea. However, even if not it still gives some impression of the magnitude both of the problem of resupply and that of accumulating reserve stocks, and so the standard planning values are worth recording. They indicate that 370 tons per day, including 50 of fuel and 190 of ammunition, will be used in the division area. In corps and army areas 310 tons will be used, including 180 of fuel and 8 of ammunition. For the communications zone, the figures are 400 aggregate, of which 220 consist of petrol, oil, and lubricants.

The reserve supplies, measured in consumption days, considered necessary at each level varies with the circumstances and the prevalent military doctrine. NATO planners ask for ninety-day stock levels within the theatre, but this figure is to be interpreted in the light of the fact that they assume any major European war will be nuclear. On this basis very low consumption rates are allowed for during the last sixty days.[1] The British Expeditionary Force in France in 1939 had seven days' reserves within twelve miles of its forward positions on the Belgian frontier, ten days' at field depots, and thirty days' at base. Later on Middle East Command kept ninety to 120 days' reserves of which about ten days' were normally at the railhead or beyond.[2] In 1945 the United States Army regarded sixty days' equivalent within the theatre as a minimum safety level and this value was adopted, at least for ordnance, by planners in Korea.[3] On the other hand, even in the 1943 to 1945 era certain airlifted and maintained operations in the South West Pacific were being conducted with a target theatre level of fourteen days' supplies and actual levels ranging between one and seven.[4] At least one recent United States Army exercise has been carried out with an eleven-day build-up in the combat theatre, including two within the division.[5] However, it seems that current American doctrine favours fifteen days' reserves of most consumables being kept in the combat zone. Thus in the case of petrol, oil, and lubricants there would typically be eight days' at army level, four at corps, and two within a division. Holdings of munitions are rather greater, because consumption is more erratic. They would usually include six within the army, four in the corps echelon, and eight in the divisional one. Naturally the optimum requirement would not be fifteen days' stocks in absolutely every situation. The amounts considered desirable would depend on the expected duration and intensity of conflict and on the length and vulnerability to interdiction of lines of resupply.

In calculating standard planning factors, it is assumed that each division will be supported by two air combat wings, each of which will contain seventy-five interceptor and strike aircraft and be located wholly within the communications zone. It is taken as including 7,000 men of whom 2,500 belong to the wing itself, 3,500 are other Air Force personnel, and 1,000 are

[1] F. W. Mulley, *The Politics of Western Defence* (London, Thames and Hudson, 1962), p. 197

[2] Sir Wilfred Lindsell in *The Army Quarterly*, October 1947

[3] P. H. Slaughter in *Military Review*, August 1950 and J. A. Houston in *Military Review*, February 1957

[4] A. Green in *Australian Army Journal*, June 1957

[5] H. E. Nelson in *Army*, February 1960

Army troops. The long-term average rate of consumption of stores is taken as being 570 tons a day, of which 350 tons are POL and 75 tons ordnance. Some idea of the mass of ground equipment involved can be got from corresponding United States Marine Corps tables. Thus the ground equipment organic to a first-line interceptor squadron of 235 men and twenty planes typically weighs some 230 tons, about 86 per cent of which is made up of the twenty self-propelled vehicles and twenty trailers.

Far too much notice had been taken of the effect that varying levels of troop welfare have on the logistic requirements of different national forces. Figures given above demonstrate that the overwhelmingly dominant items are munitions and petrol and not food, mail, or washing powder. If any two divisions differ in consumption rates, the one making less demands will almost certainly be doing so because it is inferior in one or more of the following respects—firepower, mechanized movement, and combat strength. Comparative statistics are not available, but the myth cherished in certain European countries, to the effect that units of their armies need far less of everything than similar American ones, has almost certainly lost any substance it ever had. Likewise it would be naïve to assume that the mechanized Soviet soldiers of today need little more administrative backing than did their largely horse-drawn counterparts of 1944. It is true that one of the fully motorized Russian divisions in Eastern Germany, although it contains over 200 battle tanks and two regiments of artillery, is included in an overall theatre slice of 20,000, whereas a 14,000-man Pentomic division is part of a 43,000-strong standard theatre slice.[1] However, one cannot find an adequate explanation in the better American field kitchens or in their more civilized arrangements for burying the dead. What is more important is that the Pentomic structure allows for 3,000 more men within the division—all of them infantrymen. Also the Americans would normally have several thousand combatants under command in corps and army echelons. Furthermore United States battle tanks are heavier, divisional electronic equipment for fire-control and surveillance superior, and the division's aggregate firepower substantially greater. The Soviet Army's famous

[1] A. R. Fitch in *Canadian Army Journal*, Vol. XVI, No. 1

artillery barrages are still largely provided by special support divisions that have not been considered in the above calculations. Another consideration is that the Soviet Army is designed to operate at very modest distances from its supply bases. It is probably true that a Pentomic divisional slice consumes rather over twice the supplies per day that a Soviet motorized one does in similar situations, but, conversely, it can be said to have something approaching twice the combat power.

Communist armies in the Far East do enjoy one special advantage and that is that their staple diet rice swells to three times its previous bulk when cooked in water. Therefore a thousand men need only about 1 ton of solid food a day and so the Vietminh standard planning factors were able to stipulate that a coolie carrying 55 lb. of rice and vegetables could march about 400 miles across a plain or about 250 miles through mountains before he exhausted those supplies. This Vietminh army was very simply organized and equipped. It had few bazookas and heavy mortars and very little field artillery. Even in 1954 it only had about 1,000 trucks to serve 300,000 regular troops and a 10,000-man division would often have 40,000 regular and auxiliary troops as porters.[1]

Apart from its spearhead of 100 T-34 tanks the North Korean army in 1950 was similarly on very light scales, as were the co-belligerent Chinese forces. It has been said, for example, that a North Korean division could sometimes suffice on 50 tons a day.[2] Likewise the average Chinese theatre divisional slice was 12,500, which is remarkably low, even allowing for the widespread impressment of civilian labour and for the fact that some divisions were well below establishment.[2] However the concomitant of such traits was, as usual, low firepower and inadequate mechanized mobility. Inadequate firepower is clearly a major reason why the Communists sustained four times the battle casualties the United Nations did in the course of that war. Since Korea the establishment of a Chinese division has increased from 11,000 to 14,000, while the overall average divisional slice (including those of training divisions) is about

---

[1] George Tanham, *Communist Revolutionary Warfare; the Vietminh in Indo-China* (New York, Praeger, 1961), Chapter III

[2] James T. Stewart (Ed.), *Air Power in Korea* (Princeton, Van Nostrand, 1957), p. 283

20,000. Firepower has considerably improved, but the motor transport is very inadequate for long-distance strategic movement by road or for mobile warfare in open country. Unless she is willing and able to become heavily dependent on Soviet supplies the mechanization of China's armed forces may be greatly impeded by a chronic fuel shortage. The American tables show that on active duty a motorized division theatre slice together with its air wing will probably get through 300,000 tons of oil a year, whereas the Chinese petroleum production in 1959 is estimated to have totalled less than 2,000,000 tons. Furthermore geological conditions give little reason for expecting dramatic improvements in output, and it will be some time before China will be able to exploit the rather sophisticated and very costly techniques of hydrogenation from coal.

III—SUPPLY NETWORKS

Geographers are, *qua* geographers, disappointed men. They tried to make their subject a branch of natural science only to find the subjects they had hoped to embrace, such as meteorology and geology, were becoming so specialized that they could not be satisfactorily integrated into a general theory of geography. They then tried to demonstrate the organic unity of knowledge by proving that man was a creature of his natural environment. Unfortunately ever since it was first canvassed, this hypothesis has become less and less tenable.

It is, therefore, all the more paradoxical that they have neglected the one great field of intellectual endeavour to which they could still make a major contribution, namely military studies. Soldiers at war are much more directly and completely influenced by their geographical environment than are the citizens of any but the most primitive society at peace. They live more frugally and engage in struggles in which slight variations in relative performance may prove immediately decisive. Furthermore they are often operating in environments into which they have been plunged at short notice and which have had little or nothing in the way of preparation to receive them. In such circumstances details like the height of a mountain or the state of a road can be critically important. Yet military historians and analysts have frequently failed to emphasize the influence of topography and vegetation, underrated the effect of climate and weather, and ignored the limitations imposed by existing roads and railways. Deprived of much of the possible source material, military commentators have neglected these factors, and geographers have failed to fill the vacuum.

These sins of omission can be partly explained by the fact that the variables are hard to quantify and to compare one with another. This is a difficulty, but not a complete inhibition. Many times throughout history generals and their staffs have had to decide what forces are necessary for a given task, or what forces can be sustained over given supply lines. All that is required is that the kinds of considerations that they have had to bear in mind should be defined and described more systematically than heretofore, and that they should be introduced more freely into scholarly analyses of past campaigns and into public debates on current policy.

There is no reason to doubt the basic premise that in any theatre of operations, and particularly in ones lying outside Western Europe, physical and human geography would set definite limits to the numbers of troops that could be committed, however simple their scales of equipment.

What the ceiling is predicted to be for a certain sector at a certain time will depend to a considerable degree on the circumstances in which it is thought fighting could begin. Even if the correct assumptions are made, there is still plenty of scope for miscalculating any ceiling, since many of the variables involved do not lend themselves to refined quantitative analysis. In any case all such ceilings alter as technology evolves and as economic development takes place within the areas in question. Nevertheless the proposition that maximum force levels do exist for each and every conceivable limited war situation remains valid. It is also generally true that the tonnage of war materials that invaders could move across a given frontier line is less than that which the defenders could move up to it. This is because topography, economics and politics combine to ensure that national boundaries—except in the Middle East and Africa—are almost always communication barriers.

Roads and tracks are obviously the supply and movement

channels of most significance to a soldier. For planning purposes typical load-carrying capacities have been worked out,
and are reproduced in Table IV for various kinds of two-lane
routeways carrying mechanized transport. If these figures are

TABLE IV

Highway type	Daily tonnage of supplies		Reductions applicable under various conditions		
	Communications zone	Combat zone	Rolling terrain	Mountains	Seasonal bad weather
Bituminous	36,000	8,400	10%	60%	30%
Gravel	6,000	3,400	20%	70%	60%
Earthen	4,900	1,600	25%	80%	90%

Notes: In applying any appropriate reductions the relevant factors are multiplied together to assess the cumulative effect. If only one lane is open
to traffic the overall estimate is reduced by 25 per cent. The differentials
between the communication and the combat zone derive from the
need for wide spacing between vehicles in the latter because of the
interdiction threat

Source: Field Manual 101-10, Part I, Section 7 : 15
US Department of the Army, 1959

exceeded for more than a short period of time a rapid deterioration of the road surface will ensue. It will occur, in any case,
if tanks proceed over it regularly, unless the maintenance is on
such a scale as to amount to continual reconstruction. Bridges
are very often obstacles to the smooth movement of vehicles,
especially those that are armoured. Therefore, the presence of
weak and narrow bridges may reduce actual capacities to levels
far below those suggested in Table IV unless a high proportion
of the vehicles are amphibious. Other factors which may
hamper the use of motor transport are previous demolitions,
streams of refugees, maintenance gangs at work, and interdiction by aircraft or guerillas. All in all it is not surprising that
soldiers feel that any Western division in the front line needs, in
order to ensure an adequate flow of supplies, at least one two-
way axial earth road forward of its rear boundary and that a
full corps needs, within the corps' area, two double lane improved roads perpendicular to the front and a series of lateral

roads. Troops in well-prepared static defensive positions may
well be able to stockpile enough material to see them through
a month or more, but this solution is, by definition, ruled out for
advancing forces. Initial forward movement, for mechanized
forces, is likely to be even more of a problem than subsequent
resupply. Though a Pentomic infantry division normally includes over 2,200 self-propelled vehicles and 1,300 trailers, it
has to accept another 400 trucks and the same number of
trailers in order to become fully motorized.

Of course, air assault divisions created in the United States
Army along the lines suggested by the Howze Board will have
a much shorter division train on the ground, and their dependence on the road network within the divisional area will be
substantially reduced. On the other hand the amounts of aviation spirit consumed in the rear divisional echelons and at corps
level will be several times greater than a division depending on
road transport would require. We may find that the same is
true in respect of ammunition, because by employing rockets
as their principal form of field artillery, they will be exploiting
a technique that involves the use of relatively light launching
systems, but relatively heavy projectiles. Similar conflicts between the advantage of being thoroughly mobile on and around
the field of battle, and that of keeping down logistic requirements, can frequently be observed in formations with a more
orthodox structure. Thus, although many standard lorries now
coming into use have five gears, six-wheel drives, and fully-
articulated chassis, which enable them to travel away from the
roads when gradients and vegetation permit, they usually only
do so by travelling more slowly, consuming more fuel and
carrying a reduced payload. Conversely ground vehicles designed expressly for off-the-road mobility inevitably have an
unimpressive on-the-road performance. Tracked vehicles generally manage about half the mileage per gallon on roads that
comparable wheeled ones do. They are often slower, need
several times more maintenance, and are a great deal noisier.
Likewise with their large-diameter wheels and low-pressure
tyres the GOER vehicles show a trend exactly opposite from
that exhibited in standard designs—and so are clearly sacrificing on-the-road efficiency. In the United States an army contract has just been awarded to investigate the value of walking

vehicles for negotiating rough country. If such a principle of locomotion was of value on level, firm, low-friction surfaces, the bicycle would never have been invented.

It is estimated that engineer construction battalions building a single lane unsurfaced road on flat grassland take an average of 2,500 man hours a mile. This compares with 27,000 across very rocky mountains. To make a two-way lane of such length typically requires 3,500 and 70,000 man hours respectively. For a double lane to be surfaced with asphalt requires 14,000 more hours of work a mile in a grassland environment and 33,000 in an intensely mountainous one.[1] But no tables could reflect the enormity of the construction and maintenance problem in places like North West Burma. Here complex and geologically recent folding has produced an immature mountain structure whose profiles are characteristically steep and irregular. The climate has produced wide surfaces of deep and unstable mud covered in primary jungle, whose trunks and foliage succumb to bulldozers, but in so doing create piles of debris, for which there are no dumping-grounds. Monsoon rains and snow-melt cause main rivers to rise perhaps 60 feet in the first weeks of summer, while throughout the wet season heavy thundery showers flood the innumerable stream courses to produce landslides and washouts. Those military historians who think that supply operations are too mundane to discuss should investigate the record of the lorry drivers during the Burma campaign. They sweated along mud tracks that in some places were supported solely by great curtains of bituminous hessian pegged into the hillside and which were gradually sliding down the whole time. For all this perilous improvisation, the earthen surface of the main Assam line of communication was carrying 9,000 tons a day by early 1945. One danger unfortunately inherent in any such programme of highway construction or improvement is that it provides the enemy with corridors of advance, and one of the few advantages of terrain such as that just described is the scope it offers for defensive demolition. In other sorts of country fewer opportunities exist for creating bottlenecks during a withdrawal, but even a metalled road running across, say, a flat open prairie can be made unusable

---

[1] F.M. 101–10, Part I, *op. cit.*, Section 8 : 5

by churning the asphalt up with 'router' vehicles and sowing the detritus with mines.

The single-track railway from Pusan to Seoul was used during the Korean War, despite an acute initial shortage of engines, rolling stock and local labour, resulting from the rapid Communist capture of Seoul in the course of their initial offensive.[1] The reason why that railroad proved so valuable was that the campaign in question was a prolonged but very generally static one during which the road system behind the United Nations forces became seriously overburdened and during which, too, the United Nations retained absolute control of its own airspace. Any future limited-war emergencies will very probably have markedly different characteristics, and they will most likely emphasize the weaknesses of rail supply from the soldiers' standpoint.

Railways are vulnerable to air interdiction. Another drawback is the time and effort generally involved in rendering lines fully operational, even assuming enemy action is not impeding the process. Specialist railway battalions are needed to augment or replace local civilians. Also much extra rolling stock normally has to be shipped in and, since many locomotives weigh over 100 tons, this can be a formidable task. Grading requirements make new construction through rugged country very tough and slow going, and, even where the going is good, it takes nearly as long to lay a mile of standard gauge single track as it does to lay a two-lane macadamized road: even if well furnished the track could probably not cope with more than ten forward trains of 400 tons capacity each a day. If it were a double track it might handle thirty such trains under ideal conditions.[2]

All large mechanized formations drink inordinate quantities of fuel and, as suggested above, the embarrassment is likely to increase a good deal as air mobility develops. Among the more elementary solutions are those of carrying lorryloads of 5-gallon cans or 50-gallon drums, towing 1,000-gallon roller conveyors, or using tanker lorries which, with a tanker trailer apiece, can carry between 500 and 8,000 gallons per unit. A much more economical approach is that of using a network of pipelines radiating from tank farms. In NATO Europe extensive civil

[1] Crump Garvin in *Military Review*, April 1962
[2] F.M. 101–10, Part I, *op. cit.*, Section 9 : 5

networks are available and they have now been supplemented by over 5,000 miles of pipeline and 160,000 tons of storage capacity that have been built under the infrastructure programme. In most other places the network would have to be constructed after a crisis had broken. Tank farms intended for use in campaign theatres are normally made up of, perhaps, a dozen steel tanks able to hold up to 1,500 tons each, which feed pipelines varying between 4 and 12 inches in internal diameter. A 4-inch steel or aluminium line complete with pumping stations can be laid by an engineering troop or company at the rate of five or six miles per day and it can normally manage a daily throughput of close to 1,000 tons a day. One of 12-inch bore takes more than twice the effort to lay, but can do about twenty times the work.[1] Within the last two or three years collapsible and portable 'pillow' tanks made of fabric have been brought into use to take the place of the ones made of bolted steel in cases where quick installation is necessary. Pillow tanks of over 100 tons capacity are now being designed, and, when empty, four such containers together with their manifolds can be packed on one 10-ton lorry. When full they can feed 4-inch flexible hose, but one of the problems being encountered is that the liquid cargo leaches the inner linings so badly that the hose cannot be used over a cumulative distance of more than ten miles. This matter is, however, the subject of extensive, and encouraging, research.

IV—THE LIMITS ON TACTICAL MOBILITY

Too much stress has been laid over the last ten to fifteen years on the size of the armies of Russia and China as reflected in their order of battle. The extent to which divisions vary in manpower, firepower, and mobility has often been overlooked, as has the extent to which the last two can compensate for deficiencies in the first at least in regular warfare. The firepower that counts is not, however, only or even primarily that of light automatic weapons firing solid bullets. It is predominantly that which is provided by high-explosive warheads. In Korea, as in, for example, Italy during the last war, 85 per cent of Allied

[1] *Ibid.*, 7 : 16 & 8 : 10

casualties were caused by shells or bombs. Even in the tropical rain forests, where it might be thought the opportunities for concealment and dispersion would make a field gun a mere encumbrance, artillery has often played a key role. Time and time again during the Burma and Pacific campaigns artillery was responsible for breaking up infantry attacks. The weight penalty has to be paid, both in the form of heavy equipment and in the form of the continual need for petrol and ammunition, but it is worth paying. It is now also becoming apparent that the best way of ensuring tactical mobility, even in under-developed areas, is through heavy investment in modern equipment. Whether lorries or aircraft are used, heavy extra expenditure on petrol and on the general maintenance of specialist supply troops is again incurred, but the net advantage remains strongly in favour of those with the most internal-combustion engines.

The remarkable compactness of his principal source of food does give an Oriental soldier a certain logistic advantage, but it does not make him independent of supply lines. The history of the Japanese army after the battle of Imphal affords a graphic demonstration of this. It had based its hopes of continued advance and, indeed, survival on being able to capture the main British supply dumps at an early stage in the campaign. Having failed to capture them at all, it fell back into a chaotic retreat in the course of which it suffered agonies from malnutrition and disease. Neither should the record of the wars in Korea, North Vietnam, and the Sino-Indian conflict of 1962 be taken as proof that Asiatic soldiers have the ability to deploy in vast numbers over the most impossible country. The success of the Chinese in infiltrating through the United Nations during their initial offensive across the Yalu in 1950 was not due to the latter being overmechanized. It was partly the result of their lines being overextended and their tactical reserves being too few, both of which errors reflected a political miscalculation about the preparedness of the Chinese to enter the war. The fact that the United Nations was roadbound should not be regarded as a product of mechanization, but rather the consequence of having the wrong kind of vehicles. One or two air assault divisions would have made a marked difference to the situation.

In North Vietnam the French tanks, jeep-mounted recoilless rifles, bulldozers, and tactical aircraft did fail and the failure cannot in this case be explained by the fact that their equipment was not built to the right specification. The point about that campaign was that it was an anti-guerilla one, and so the enemy's base, to use the phraseology of Mao Tse Tung, was the population itself: a base of that kind is not open to isolation or bombardment. Dien Bien Phu was the only major episode in the war that took the form of a regular contest between armies. The Vietminh won this because they managed to obtain a modest number of medium support weapons from China, and because they managed to concentrate these, together with five out of their seventeen infantry divisions, in the battle area. By virtue of these achievements they captured the town after months of effort and after incurring casualties several times higher than those they inflicted on the defenders.[1] By the same token, the fighting in the Himalayas in 1962 should not be taken as a demonstration that the Chinese find themselves able to ignore geography. Less than one soldier out of every two hundred in the Chinese army took part in the storming of Tawang.

A primitive army consisting predominantly of foot soldiers can make its initial deployments with far less strain on the communications system than can a motorized one. Similarly porters are almost entirely independent of prepared routes and so have certain advantages as the media of supply in or near the scenes of fighting. The economics of porterage do, however, become progressively less favourable as the range over which it is used increases and for hauls much in excess of 100 miles a heavy dependence on wheeled vehicles is practically inevitable. Since the hitting power of any army is closely controlled by the weight of supplies it can bring forward, this means that there are finite limits to the amount of strength that can be deployed offensively across any particular sector. Conversely the width of the front that a modern division can be expected to hold is rarely less than ten miles and is often considerably more.

When the current preponderance of the defence over the offence is fed into the equation, the conventional superiority of the Communist armies appears far less awesome than it has generally been thought to be. This cannot, of course, be taken

[1] Tanham, *op. cit.*, p. 97

as a justification for complacency, for, quite apart from anything else, all the relevant factors are in a constant state of flux.
But it does constitute an argument against regarding the ideal
of non-nuclear deterrence as one that is impossible to realize.
Before passing final judgement, however, it is desirable to look
at the various sectors of the Iron Curtain and assess what kind
of strength the Communists could bring to bear in each case
and what the prospects would be of conducting a successful
defence.

Chapter 9

The Potential Battlefields

I—THE FLANKS OF NATO

THE view has been put forward that to reinforce the NATO forces in Germany during times of high tension is not a symbol of determination but of weakness. This is said to be because such movements could never be militarily effective and would only betoken our fear of employing strategic nuclear weapons.[1] However, the Soviet Union and her allies are persuaded that large armies are relevant to all kinds of wars, and so long as this holds true they are capable of being deterred by improvements in the dispositions of other people's armies. Furthermore, if the hostage theory is valid at all it must apply particularly to the Central Front, where an effective reply to any full-scale offensive would almost certainly result in general war. Nevertheless the hazards of a war in Germany are common to both sides and if the Soviet Union felt sufficiently bold and malevolent to attack any NATO territory she would almost certainly choose some on either the northern or southern flank.

Arctic Norway is always regarded as being one of the places which it would be extremely difficult to defend. This is partly because of the marked imbalance between the local Norwegian brigade and the several Russian divisions maintained around Murmansk. It is also because the several NATO standard airfields within the area could be dominated by the tactical air power the Soviets could bring to bear. Some years ago a Norwegian estimate put the number of airfields and airstrips in the Kandalaksha–Murmansk sector at fifty, of which five, including some large ones, were within fifty kilometres of the border.[2]

Another reason why it would not be easy to mount a successful relief expedition is that climate and latitude combine to produce conditions that take a lot of getting used to. North and central Norway have a mean temperature below 50°F

[1] H. A. Kissinger in *Foreign Affairs*, July 1962
[2] *New York Times*, January 29, 1953

even during their four warmest months. In consequence the subsoil is permanently frozen, vegetation is sparse, and, during the summer, low-lying surfaces are very marshy. Hence, the winter offers better scope for offensive action, but, in a winter war in such a régime, seasonal features like prolonged darkness, snow cover, low temperatures, and strong winds combine with permanent ones like mountain topography and recurrent magnetic storms to render life uncommonly difficult for men who are not experienced and equipped for such surroundings.

In any case if the Soviets launched a blitzkrieg offensive it is hard to imagine that any outside assistance based on conventional firepower could arrive in time to prevent them from occupying Finmark and most of Tromsö. Several divisions driving down or parallel to the coastal road from Kirkenes, supported by extensive seaborne landings and by many tactical and transport aircraft, would be capable of quickly overwhelming a brigade and seriously impeding, if not crippling, attempts at aerial reinforcement.

It was these considerations that led General Norstad to say at one time that an attack on Northern Norway could only be defeated by means of tactical nuclear weapons.[1] At first sight this seems a viable solution, since the area is detached and sparsely peopled, but against it must be set the closeness of Russian territory and the remoteness of SHAPE headquarters in Paris. Long-distance wireless links that work smoothly in peacetime might get damaged at the start of a war. Furthermore decisions would have to be based on intelligence fed in from local units, whose high-frequency wireless might be badly affected by enemy action, hills, or magnetic disturbances, and whose surveillance abilities might be reduced by topography, weather, or the winter night. The temptation to delegate nuclear authority to commanders on the spot and so invite escalation would be considerable. The best hope of defending the region lies in the fact that a Soviet attack is unlikely except after a spell of general world tension lasting several days at least. Therefore there would almost certainly be a period of grace during which allied conventional reinforcements could be moved in by air or sea.

The strategic weakness of Macedonia and Thrace lies in their

[1] *The Guardian*, April 13, 1960

lack of depth as witness the fact that it is only forty miles from the Bulgarian frontier to the coast at Kavalla. One consequence of this is that the road and rail network not only lies across the 'enemy' front but is slender and inferior. A four-lane macadamized National Road running along the coast from Athens to Salonika was completed in 1962, and beyond it two recently improved National Roads form a loop to Kavalla, but from Kavalla to the Turkish frontier roads are generally only suitable for two-lane traffic in dry weather. They are paralleled by the single-track railway which winds over and tunnels through steep gradients between Salonika and Istanbul. It is similar in capacity and characteristics to the track to Florina that constituted the main supply line for half the 200,000 troops on the Albanian front in March 1941.[1]

The common frontier between Greece and Bulgaria extends through some 200 miles of upland forest terrain. At its western extremity lies the Struma valley, whose river and marshes afford good natural protection to what would be the forward operating base at Salonika, whilst the border itself is strengthened by the man-made fortifications of the Metaxas line. The traditional policy of not improving communication links across the border is being maintained, and apart from the two-lane road from Sofia through Rupel gorge to Serrai and three narrow and poor-quality roads over the mountains there is nothing except sheep tracks. Even assuming the narrow gorges were not blocked by snow or demolitions, it is difficult to imagine more than twelve semi-motorized divisions being brought to bear in any offensive. This was, in fact, the number the Germans deployed from Bulgaria in 1941.

The Greek Army could quickly bring ten divisions to war establishment and concentrate them in Macedonia and Thrace. The difficulties it would then face would derive from shallowness of the defended territory. It would not be easy to maintain what the generals call a 'balanced posture'—that is one able to counter a series of attacks from a variety of different angles. After a time resupply would become necessary, but would be hard to arrange if the few land routes were under heavy attack. To compensate for the lack of land room for manoeuvre and logistic support, it would be desirable to make use of air- and

[1] Brigadier C. S. Brunskill in *The Army Quarterly*, October 1947

sealift. This would create a need for transport aircraft, assault and amphibious shipping, and mobile anti-aircraft defences.

The consequence of any Turkish involvement in a Greco-Bulgarian war would be to present the Bulgarians with opposition far too solid for them to take on single-handed, particularly since any army invading North Greece would be gravely embarrassed by the threat of a turning movement up the Maritsa valley. The Maritsa valley is usually soft and marshy, but it does contain one good trunk road. A high proportion of the Turkish Army has traditionally been stationed in Europe and Istanbul is an important logistics base.

Eastern Turkey had good natural defences which man has further strengthened. Although Kars fell to a surprise Russian attack against denuded defences in February 1916, the climate is such as to render summer campaigning much more practicable. Most years snow lies for four months at Kars and Erzurum and the surrounding passes are usually blocked for six or eight months. Even in the summertime the winning of any substantial amounts of territory, from about ten Turkish regular divisions in excellent static positions, would be a slow and costly business. Apart from the metalled road and the railway following the valleys from Leninakan through Kars none of the axes of advance is good. Even allowing for the administrative support that invading troops could get from the clusters of airfields in Georgia and Azerbaijan and, perhaps, from sea transport, the Soviets would find it hard to deploy effectively more than ten divisions on any one axis or more than twenty-five along the whole front. These limitations might be reduced in significance by the prospect of catching the defenders off balance, for lateral movements would be difficult for Turkish forces anywhere east of the Sivas–Malatya line, partly because of the grain of the topography and partly because the Soviet Union would probably enjoy initial air superiority over the forward areas. All the same, there is no reason to suppose that such dour defensive fighters as the Turks could be outfought within the borders of their own homeland, and, in fact, the real strain would come if heavy fighting continued for two or three weeks and their combat supplies began to run low. As the crow flies it is over 500 miles from the Russian border to the nearest Mediterranean ports, and the slender road and rail communications would make

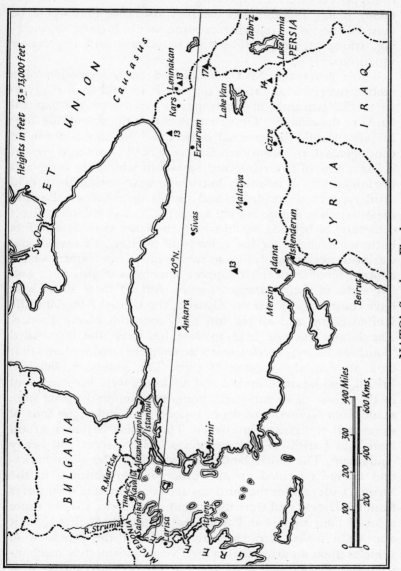

NATO's Southern Flanks

re-supply very difficult especially if widespread interdiction was taking place. The forms of external assistance that would be most efficacious in relieving pressure would include engineering, transport, and anti-aircraft battalions, and interceptor squadrons.

Three years ago NATO embarked on the creation of a mobile reserve whose special purpose is to hold itself ready to go to the assistance of the countries located on the exposed flanks of the alliance. The intention is that the size of this 'fire-brigade' should be gradually increased by the addition of contingents drawn from each and every NATO state. At present it has a core of five reinforced battalions which are composed predominantly of infantry, but which have within them field artillery, armour, engineer, and signals detachments. Each of these battalion groups is from a different country. Under direct command of brigade headquarters there are some *Honest John* batteries intended for the delivery of nuclear or conventional warheads over ranges of up to twelve miles. Six countries have allotted some tactical air support squadrons to this force and five some of their transport planes. Among those states who have contributed so far are Canada, the United Kingdom, the United States and all the full EEC countries except France. The largest exercise held to date has been the one called 'Southern Express', which was a deployment to Macedonia that took place in the autumn of 1962. The American, Belgian, British, and German armies and air forces were involved, and in the course of seventy-eight hours two hundred flights were made from Germany to deposit 4,000 men and 1,500 tons of stores and equipment in Greece. The British battalion group landed at Larissa to pick up prestocked transport and heavy equipment. The others landed at Salonika. After disembarkation all units formed up and proceeded to positions in the Struma valley. After the third day they drew most of their stores from the Greeks and were dependent upon them, too, for quite a lot of their signals and rear-area transport. At first sight it appears a foolish arrangement to rely for the provision of vehicles upon an army that is itself very inadequately mechanized, but, in fact, it is quite sensible. Greece, in common with several other countries has a detailed and frequently tested scheme for the impressment of vehicles in time of emergency and many of her 30,000 lorries and buses would be very suitable for supply and movement work down to brigade level.

It is by no means certain that the policy of seeking contributions to the NATO mobile reserve from as many member countries as possible is the most appropriate one. A better way of reflecting, consolidating, and exploiting the solidarity of the alliance might be to have an international mobile reserve command and planning staff, but to seek contributions of actual forces from, say, two or three countries chosen because they seemed well placed to provide whatever is required. At the moment the excellent Bersaglieri mountain troops of the Italian Army are being wasted guarding Alpine passes that no one proposes to attack. If they were earmarked as a whole or in large part to form the infantry striking force of the reserve the strength of the alliance would be increased. The acceptance of the principle thereby implied would also make it easier to obtain highly technical formations. As I have suggested, it is these that would be in greatest demand, at least on the Mediterranean flank, in the event of a limited war.

II—THE INDIAN OCEAN

Her geography makes Persia the most vulnerable of all the non-Communist countries fringing the Iron Curtain. At no time in the foreseeable future would the Turkish Army find it easy to deploy into Persian Azerbaijan. This is because large lakes and high mountains would inhibit tactical deployment and because the only conceivable routes are vulnerable. The metalled highway from Erzurum to Tabriz and the CENTO railway that is now being built to connect Tabriz with Erzurum and Van lies parallel to and close to the frontier, whilst the CENTO road that is to run south of Lake Urmia to link Cizre with Zenjon will have to cross the 8,000-foot Kazim Pass. The best hope would be for one or two Anglo-American beachheads to be established on the shores of the Gulf that would control an important bargaining counter in the form of oilfields and that would involve such a commitment of forces that any Soviet attempt to evict them would invite nuclear escalation. Whether such a remedy was practicable would depend largely on how long it would take Soviet forces to cover the 600-odd miles from the Caucasus to the Gulf, for that, except in winter, would be the main corridor of advance. They would have to advance over a road network that is still very poor despite the £130,000,000 development scheme initiated in 1956. There are fewer than 20,000 miles in the whole country that are motorable under any conditions and of those only about a quarter have even the roughest metalling. Captain Liddell-Hart estimated in 1958 that the maximum number of divisions that the Soviet Union could employ in a sustained advance of the Gulf was fifteen. Today the figure is probably somewhat less, because the new Soviet divisions need more logistic support.

The American Military Aid Advisory Group in Teheran has dissuaded the Persian government from a projected increase in their army and this may herald the beginning of a greater emphasis on functional efficiency as opposed to a paper order of battle. The poorly equipped and indifferently organized army that Persia possesses today, much of which is crouching immobile on the Caucasian frontier, could be overwhelmed with pathetic ease. A reduced force could be expected to have better leadership through the process of elimination and to have more firepower and mobility as a result of a more concentrated use of foreign aid. Such an army might become capable of conducting a fighting withdrawal, coupled with a scientific demolition programme, into an Anglo-American beachhead. In doing so, it might gain for the West a breathing space of two or three weeks in which to feed in the three to five divisions that would probably be required to make a beachhead viable.

The conflicts in the Himalayas at the close of 1962 illustrated clearly the controlling influence of transport links. The Indians deployed about one division and this formation received a lot of its supplies through the Chusul airstrip by means of C-119 *Packets* and helicopters flying in from Srinagar and Chandigarh. The Chinese troops, whose equipment included, surprisingly enough, a few light tanks, advanced over the existing frontier along the two or three routes fit for only the sturdiest kinds of motorized transport and reached the limits of their boundary claims. They failed, however, in an apparent attempt to push on farther and take Chusul. As of the time of writing there has been no renewal of the fighting in the area, but China has instead launched a strong, and so far very successful, diplomatic courtship of Pakistan aimed at exploiting the tradition of good relationships between Kashmir and China. India has every reason to feel apprehensive about the possibility of this Chinese initiative leading to the formation of a Peking-Rawalpindi axis. Not the least menacing consequence might be a rising, at some singularly inconvenient moment, of the many fanatically Islamic tribesmen, some thousands of whom are already armed, who are just biding their time inside the Indian-held portion of Kashmir.[1]

The other battle area lay over 1,000 miles away, on the fringes of the North East Frontier Agency in which two or three Indian divisions were concentrated; they were supplied by means of the good road, the railway, and the chain of airstrips running up the Brahmaputra valley. Nominally this army had a 400-mile front to cover, but along it there were few places through which their opponents could attack in strength. Moreover, the overall scale of any Chinese effort along the Himalayan border in general or against the NEFA in particular was limited by the total size of the forces they could maintain in Tibet itself, and by the extent to which they were preoccupied with protecting themselves against the thousands of guerillas still at large in a country that, with all its forests and precipitous valleys, lends itself to raids by small parties armed with rifles and dynamite.

Official Western sources estimated in 1960 that there were then six Chinese divisions in Tibet.[2] Mr. Patterson has put the 1961 figure for South Eastern Tibet at 200,000. While the fighting was raging last autumn Mr. Nehru gave it as his informed opinion that there were 300,000 Chinese soldiers in South and East Tibet.[1] It would be unwise to place too much reliance on any of the above figures, and they are all, in any case, approximate, but the gradual build-up they imply has, very likely, occurred. One thing that has made it possible has been a big expansion of food production through the use of forced labour, collectivization, and the importation of many Chinese farm workers.

[1] George Patterson in *Royal United Service Institution Journal*, May 1963
[2] *New York Times*, October 27, 1962

Communications with other areas controlled by China remain poor. Since 1957 an unmetalled motor road has run from Sinkiang through Ladakh to Gartok and on to Lhasa and is now being used by many jeeps and six-wheel lorries. On a round trip even a large truck must consume a weight of petrol roughly equivalent to the useful load it carries and it is safe to say that while one vehicle is completing the round trip many more are engaged in the weary task of replacing the fuel it is drawing from supply dumps *en route*. It is clearly, therefore, a singularly inconvenient and expensive supply line to employ, but despite this it is much more fully utilized than the only alternative road that now exists. This converges on Chamdo from two points of origin and then threads its way as a single track through very difficult country to Lhasa. Attempts were made to drive a road and a railway straight across the Tibetan plateau from the Tsaidam area but these were abandoned on account of the damage caused by alternating frost and thaw and by the guerillas. There are also some airfields in Tibet and one recent report speaks of there being one jet and two non-jet aerodromes, together with numerous landing strips within fifty or sixty miles of the McMahon Line. So far they have just been used for tactical troop movements and a certain amount of logistic support. One of the features of the 1962 conflict was that neither side escalated the conflict to include air interdiction. At first sight it seems as if the Indians would have put themselves at an advantage by so doing, but it is doubtful whether this would actually have proved to be the case. The Chinese main supply road through Gartok ran chiefly across a flat plateau and so had for all practical purposes an infinite width. The one from Chamdo was so well concealed by forest that it would have been hard to hit or even see. It is, moreover, not readily apparent what immediate effect such interdiction would have had on the situation at the front. The Indian government quite naturally felt that it was not worth extending the war for such uncertain benefits and incurring the risk of Chinese reprisals against Indian cities. The Chinese would not have been able to inflict significant damage on the settlements in the Ganges valley, but a mass panic like the one the Japanese induced by a few tip-and-run raids on Calcutta in 1942 would have been greatly to their benefit, in a struggle the chief purpose

of which was to heap humiliation on New Delhi. The announcement that nationwide civil defence planning has begun is a
measure of the attention the Indian authorities are paying to
this latent peril.[1]

In another respect the Indian rear areas were, like those of
the Chinese, not entirely secure. In a wide area around Kohi-
ma, which was the centre of one of the greatest battles of the
Burma campaign, the Naga tribesmen had been in revolt for
some time and the Chinese had established a liaison with them.
The New Delhi authorities say that this internal security
operation has been tying down 40,000 of their troops, but
the Nagas claim the involvement has been substantially
greater.

The main Chinese assault came down through Tawang to
Bomdilla. The former small town fell to some 10,000 attackers
five days after an artillery and 120-millimetre mortar bombardment had heralded the crossing of the McMahon Line sixteen
miles due north. The heavily outnumbered Indian troops had
relied on a jeep road to supply Tawang. This road wound over
a 200-mile route to cover the forty-five miles from the main base
at Tezpur and it had kept thousands of maintenance men
constantly at work. Beyond Tawang supplies had been carried
by porters along narrow paths and, in places, up rope ladders.
After Tawang fell the Chinese waited for three weeks whilst
large gangs of coolies drove a road to Tawang. The offensive
was then reopened by a division outflanking the Indian forces
dug in with twenty-five-pounder artillery guns astride the jeep
road from Tezpur and Bomdilla at the 14,000-foot Sela Pass.
The Indians accordingly withdrew in some disorder and Bomdilla fell to forces estimated in Tezpur to be over 50,000 strong.[2]
The Chinese pressed forward for a while and then halted in
positions on the edge of foothills and well south of the McMahon
Line. By dint of hard marching they had covered about fifty
miles, measured in a direct line, in the course of a week.

The buffer states between Ladakh and NEFA have traditionally placed their trust in the security of obscurity and so
have used poor communications with the outside world to

[1] *The Guardian,* January 10, 1963
[2] *Daily Telegraph,* November 11, 1962

buttress their natural isolation. Once upon a time any motor-cars that were to be seen in the streets of Katmandu had been assembled there after all the necessary bits and pieces had been carried in over narrow mountain tracks from India. Today this is no longer the case, for there are several motor roads running across the boundary. There are at present 500 miles of motor-able roads inside Nepal and another 900 are to be added to them with Indian and American help. Meanwhile, the country is being used by several thousand armed Tibetan refugees as a base for sorties into their homeland.[1]

A quite good road now leads straight through Sikkim, follow-ing the old caravan trail from Lhasa to Darjeeling. For some years past this road has been used to maintain a concentration of up to 80,000 Chinese troops on the Eastern frontier of this small state. Their strategic significance derives from the fact that immediately South of Sikkim the territory of the Republic of India becomes a slender neck, which at one point is only twenty-three miles wide, between Nepal and Sikkim on the one hand and East Pakistan on the other. Within Sikkim there are today some 300 miles of roads and tracks fit for jeeps to use in good weather. The building of several of the stretches has been paid for, with obvious strategic intent, by the Indians.

The easternmost of the 'buffer states' is Bhutan, and this, too, is being affected by the winds of change. India is financing a scheme of road development scheduled to cost nearly £10,000,000 which has already produced the first road run-ning into the state from North Bengal. Until its completion the only road across the frontiers of Bhutan was the one into Sikkim.

When buffer states have lain between a pair of great powers who are reluctant to come to blows, they have been useful by way of giving a measure of reassurance to both of them. Siam and Afghanistan fulfilled this function in the late nineteenth century. When they have been interposed between two states, one or both of which has subsequently become expansionist, they have been unsuccessful. Sometimes they have lulled a defensively minded power into a false sense of security, as witness the French in the 1930s, who, believing that history

[1] George Patterson in *Royal United Service Institution Journal*, May 1963

does not repeat itself, persuaded themselves that the German armies would not swing through Belgium. On other occasions they have provided opportunities either for the fomenting of diplomatic crises or for piecemeal military aggression. If China is now seriously expansionist in her aims, then the Himalayan buffer states add considerably to the general instability of the Indian Ocean basin. Many factors combine to produce this instability, but not the least among them is the continuing weakness of most of the indigenous forces and their lack of the means for long-range mobility.

Against this general background the thin spread of western forces between Suez and Singapore appears all the more alarming. The only army theatre reserve of any size in the whole area whose movements are not liable to be handicapped by political considerations is the 24th Infantry Brigade, which is at present in Kenya but which will soon go to Aden. The 28th Commonwealth Brigade in Malaya is, under the 1957 Agreement, only to be used to defend the Commonwealth and to preserve peace in South East Asia. It could not go to somewhere like the Persian Gulf. When the Federation of Malaysia is formed this limitation will be imposed, also, on the Far East Fleet, assuming it is still based exclusively on Singapore. This could mean that the amphibious task force with a one-brigade lift that Britain will soon have operating from Aden could easily find itself without any support or protection.

With the paucity of theatre reserves must be coupled the inherent difficulties of strategic reinforcement. The whole of the MATS military airlift would probably take two weeks to move an airportable division, complete with its equipment and a minimum of war stores, from California to the Arabian Sea area, even assuming it encountered no trouble about negotiating the best route. This interval may well have been slashed by half by the time the *Starlifter* procurement is complete in 1969, but even then it will still be excessive. Britain has brigade group stockpiles at Aden and Singapore, but she bases her contingency plans on the expectation that the men who may use them will arrive via one or the other of the increasingly fragile air corridors that cross the Middle East.

What is needed is a task force of at least two brigade groups with enough amphibious ships attached to lift all their combat

elements simultaneously and with a squadron of warships in
attendance for escort and support duties. This combat fleet
should have adequate and secure bases and arrangements
should exist to ensure that the fleet can be doubled and the
ground forces more than doubled at short notice.

Though the United States would be the country best able to
provide the bulk of any strategic reinforcements called for, she
would not be well qualified to provide the theatre reserve. A
permanent United States naval presence in the Indian Ocean
would lend credence to the capitalist encirclement theory and
so strengthen the hand of residual Stalinist elements within the
Communist world. Furthermore divisive strains already exist
within the Atlantic alliance, on both sides of the ocean, on
account of the disproportionate share of the total deterrent that
the United States is providing and this does, in fact, produce
an imbalance that is even more marked outside the NATO area

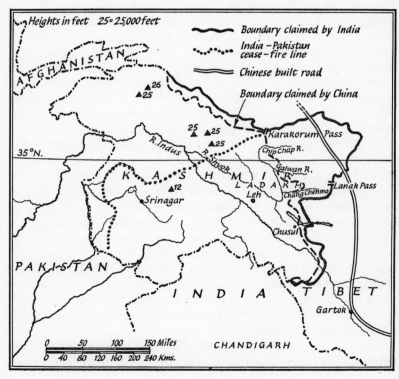

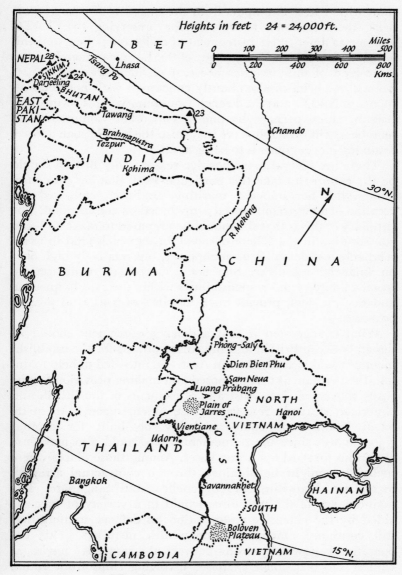

Heights in feet   24 = 24,000 ft.

The Eastern Himalayas and Laos

Opposite: The Ladakh Front

than within it. Quite apart from the question of relative burdens, there is much to be said for preserving the SEATO alliance as an effective instrument of collective policy, and this is only conceivable as long as one of the European members has some kind of military presence east of Suez. In recent years France has been predominantly concerned with her commitments to NATO and the French Community. This means that Britain, aided perhaps by one or two other Commonwealth members, will probably have to furnish the bulk of such a force, assuming it ever comes into being at all.

There are several more positive reasons why Britain should be the country to take this particular lead. She has, in consonance with her imperial maritime tradition, eschewed the creation of a large continental army based on conscription. The corollary of this is that she should be prepared to make a special contribution in the sphere of naval forces which tend to make relatively low demands on manpower, but relatively high ones on financial resources. She does, moreover, retain certain specific interests and responsibilities within the area in question and does, in fact, provide such mobile forces as it at present possesses.

What is suggested is that a defence agreement should be signed between Britain and the Anzus powers for the establishment of naval base facilities in Australia intended to help maintain the permanent task proposed and making provision for the ready movement into Australia of elements of the British and American strategic reserve in case of emergency. Adequate naval installations could probably be built for around £50,000,000, since the permanent force would also make use of various forward operating bases. Among those places where such bases might be obtained through contractual arrangements are Mauritius, the Seychelles, and Singapore. The maintenance of the task force would in a variety of ways be aided by the extensive co-operation on defence matters that still continues among Commonwealth members. This co-operation is especially strong between the respective navies, as witness the occasional exercises involving ships from India, Pakistan, and Britain. If it were deemed advisable to keep the 28th Commonwealth Brigade in Malaya as a token of commitment to Malaysian defence, the second infantry brigade might be obtained by combining the contingents that currently are scattered around the Mediterranean. Through such measures quite a lot could be done to fill what is today a major gap in the structure of deterrence.

III—THE FAR EAST

The policy of the United States in Laos is geared to the proposition that if any more collapses of the Royal Laotian army occur she will be able to move in forces sufficiently fast to hold both the line of the Mekong River and a series of enclaves on its eastern side around Luang Prabang, Vientiane, Savannakhet, and Paksane. The aim would be not only to sustain the morale of the Thai government but to keep control of such built-up areas as Laos possesses, thereby establishing a stalemate and so obliging neutralist and Left-wing forces to negotiate. Once already operations have been carried out that represented the initial stages of such a manoeuvre. This was in May 1962, when a regimental combat team of Marines, an army battle group, and a F-100 squadron were sent into Thailand to reinforce combat aircraft, Marine Corps ground troops and a military aid mission already there. At the peak period 11,000 American servicemen were committed and they were supported by token contingents of the Royal Air Force and the Royal Australian Air Force. The combined strength was reduced to 3,000 men in the course of the year as the numbers of Vietminh estimated to be still in Laos diminished.

The mountain backbone of Laos is wet and clad in heavy jungle, and its tortuous topography includes many almost vertical slopes. The Mekong valley is flatter, drier, and covered with more open woodland, and so means of transportation are more developed although they remain anything but good. The most important road is the one from Vientiane to Luang Prabang, which is one lane wide and almost unusable during the monsoons that last from May to November. There are about another 3,000 miles of seasonal track-ways in the country, of which all but a few hundred have some kind of rough surface. The Chinese are now building a road that leads fifty miles across the border to Phong Saly, where it will meet another one the North Vietnamese are driving in from Dien Bien Phu.

Another road is being built across the Laos-Vietnam frontier to Sam Neau.[1] Two more possible channels of military movement lie along the very inferior roads that wind through high passes to Luang Prabang and Savannakhet respectively. The latter route is the one employed to deliver supplies to the Viet Cong in South Vietnam.

In addition to several airstrips there is the former French airfield at Seno that can handle some varieties of four-engined transport aircraft and the one at Vientiane which has a 6,000-foot metal runway that at different times in recent years has been used by many DC-3s and IL-14s. Good air-dropping zones exist in the Plain of Jarres and on the Boloven Plateau. The Communist powers have a series of aerodromes in North Vietnam and Yunnan Province which are within flying distance of all parts of Laos.

In most of Thailand the network of communications is considerably stronger than in Laos, but the strategically important north-eastern province is still badly provided for. It is served by two roads branching out from Bangkok, one of which parallels a single-track narrow-guage railway to Udorn and Vientiane. The airfield at Udorn was made the location for the Marine combat team and A4D *Skyhawk* squadrons in the summer of 1962.

A great deal of the current £600,000,000 economic development programme will be carried out in the north-east and much of it will be devoted to road improvement. Meanwhile a new stretch of arterial road is being built to the immediate north-east of Bangkok. This work has been undertaken by an American army construction battalion from Okinawa because the existing routeway crosses a whole series of weak timber bridges and, in addition, very easily becomes flooded.

The exact strength the Chinese and the Vietminh could deploy in any offensive against Laos would depend upon the weather, the level of food stocks within Laos at the particular season in question, and the amount of prestocking and road improvement they had managed to do beforehand. In the spring of 1962 the left-wing and neutralist forces within the country were stated by their leaders to include some 40,000

[1] *New York Herald Tribune*, January 10, 1962

regular soldiers in addition to many local defence militia. The Vietminh invasion that temporarily overran most of Northern Laos early in 1953 was undertaken by three divisions, each of which had a war establishment of 10,000 men and had a large group of coolies in support. This army seems to have represented the maximum strength the Vietminh were logistically capable of projecting into that particular district at that particular time. The same can probably be said of the four divisions and several artillery battalions the Vietminh used to invest Dien Bien Phu. They were backed by some 40,000 coolies and the operations were preceded by several months of laying roads and accumulating stores. At that time approximately 1,000 motor vehicles were in service with the Vietminh.[1]

South Vietnam is unlikely to be the zone of frontal warfare unless the *status quo* collapses in Laos and Cambodia. Nevertheless, it is a country worth examining, because the anti-guerilla campaign currently in progress is providing plenty of practical examples of the effort required to keep tactically mobile in monsoon lands. The Mekong Delta is half covered in water during the rainy season and so great interest is being shown in the application of light waterborne transport. Meanwhile, the jungle uplands are being penetrated by military roads despite formidable natural obstacles and fierce opposition by guerilllas. A preliminary survey has been done of a proposed road between Saigon and the Laotian border and it has been found that although it will cover a linear distance of less than 300 miles it will require the construction of hundreds of bridges.[2]

No one considers Hong Kong defensible in tactical terms if only because of the acute embarrassment that would result from the presence of 3,000,000 civilians living in desperately overcrowded conditions and dependent on the mainland for much of their water supply. The Chinese Nationalist islands of Quemoy and Matsu are tougher obstacles. Their garrison of 70,000 men gives them a density of troops on the ground ten times as great

[1] George Tanham, *Communist Revolutionary Warfare; the Vietminh in Indo-China* (London, Praeger, 1961), Chapter III

[2] Department of Defense Appropriations, 1963. Hearings before Subcommittee of House of Representatives Committee on Appropriations (Washington, US Government Printing Office, 1962), Part 2, p. 199

as that which the defenders of Okinawa enjoyed at the commencement of the 1945 invasion. Furthermore the fortifications have been gradually extended over many years and now include numerous dug-in heavy artillery emplacements and massive subterranean stores containing many weeks' supplies. The most serious foreseeable difficulty is the one that might arise if, when large-scale replenishment at last became necessary, the Communists were not (as in 1958) deterred from using planes and guns to interfere with it by the mere presence of United States forces. Even if they did interdict, however, it is difficult to believe that they could force resupply rates below critical limits without establishing local aerial superiority, and this they are not likely to find possible for some years to come. Nevertheless, as long as it is deemed sound policy to retain these off-shore islands a need is liable to arise to air drop quantities of supplies on to either or both of them to supplement or replace the more vulnerable 'over the beach' methods.

The Republic of Korea is currently defended by nineteen South Korean and two United States divisions. They would have to hold a front extending just over 100 miles through very defensible country. By the middle of 1951, the Chinese and North Korean armies south of the Yalu numbered 1,000,000 men, two-thirds of whom were formed into the sixty or so divisions stationed within the battle area. These divisions were predominantly infantry ones, with an average strength of 7,000 to 10,000 men and they were equipped with small arms, recoilless rifles, mortars, and about a dozen field guns each. The remainder were independent artillery divisions with some 120 guns apiece and it was from these units that a great deal of the heavy firepower came. They, like the United Nations forces, were largely dependent for the transit of supplies and reinforcements on the two reasonably good roads and half-dozen earth tracks that threaded their way across the battle area. The two main roads were the ones running from Sinuijin through Seoul to Pusan and from Chongjin to Seoul and Mokpu. Both sides used the thin network of railways as much as possible, but those north of the front had their traffic decimated by air attack. Since 1953 communications have been rebuilt and improved, except in the demilitarized zone now established between the two states, and the North Koreans have also undertaken a great deal of airfield construction. The new airfields could be used for the deployment of the Chinese air force and so the Communist powers would be able to contest the command of the Korean skies in any future conflict much more effectively than they did during the recent war. The allied interdiction campaign then never succeeded in crippling their supply system, but it was almost certainly the chief factor responsible for keeping down the size of the army they concentrated in the forward areas.

All the same, it remains unlikely that sufficient strength could be amassed to make much headway in frontal assault against the armies entrenched in South Korea. The real problem of defending that peninsula would lie in its dependence on a few very tenuous and fragile lines of communication leading from the ports of Inchon and Pusan. Between 1950 and 1953 Pusan just managed to fulfil its role as the main supply base, but at that time it was never troubled with air or sea attack. If it were, it is difficult to see how it could work to anything like capacity, even if heavy anti-aircraft protection was moved in. Of course, proximity to the front line makes the potential exposure of Inchon to interdiction greater even that that of Pusan. Despite that, it has been made the main United States Army sea terminal in Korea. Perhaps this is because the Far East Command wishes to demonstrate as ostentatiously as possible a complete disinterest in the military security of its rear communications. If this is the case, the purpose must be to imply that any attempt by an aggressor to take advantage of the vulnerability of the supply system would compel the defenders in their turn to escalate the hostilities considerably, both in terms of geography and in terms of the kinds of weapons employed.

IV—THE USE OF STRATEGICALLY MOBILE FORCES

The first-line ground forces in the continental United States which are strategically mobile consist of the six regular divisions in Strike Command and two of the Marine Corps divisions. Behind them will stand, as soon as the current reorganization is complete, the Marine reservist division and, at two months' readiness, nine Army Reserve and National Guard divisions.

The remaining twenty-three reservist divisions will have under 10,000 men, including a proportion of corps troops, and so will be incapable of becoming battle-worthy without undergoing many weeks of recruiting, training, and equipping. Likewise, hardly any brigades from the British Territorial Army would be fit for deployment until some months had elapsed, and there are still, in any case, legal restrictions on its employment. For all practical purposes Britain's strategically mobile ground forces are made up of the three infantry brigades that have been accorded this role and the two Royal Marine commandos that are stationed in England. France will hold her light division and some marine battalions ready for overseas service and two of the brigades in Canada have been earmarked for NATO Europe. The total for the three countries, taking into account only those units that could be on active service within two months, correspond to approximately twenty divisions.

The contingencies that they might have to meet fall into three main categories. There is, first, the deterrence or defeat of localized aggression on the part of one of the Communist powers. The North of Norway would require a reinforcement of approximately divisional strength which could come from the NATO mobile reserve, the British strategic reserve, the regular armoured infantry brigade in South Norway, or the five reservist armoured infantry brigades the Norwegians hold ready. The parachute brigade of the British strategic reserve could be air dropped. An increase of several divisions in the force level in Germany might be desirable to match a comparable Soviet build-up and ensure that any probing action could be blocked. On the south-east flank the chief requirement would be for specialist formations. An invasion of Persia could only be checked by the dispatch of several divisions which would have to come almost entirely from outside the theatre. The ground forces that would be required to conduct any deterrence or defensive operation against any effort on the part of the Chinese to expand in the Far East could, however, be provided by the indigenous armies and by the mobile forces that the Commonwealth and United States maintain within that theatre. These are equal to about three divisions.

It is conceivable that a large-scale deployment of ground forces into Western Europe might have to take place as part of a programme of deterring general war. Soviet strategists still think that large armies would play a very important part in general war, through the occupation of enemy territory during the interval between the big nuclear exchanges and the commencement of peace talks, and they stress that the relatively limited depth of Western Europe makes it comparatively easy to overrun. They also believe, in common with everybody else, that a general war will be, by any historical standards, of very short duration. The logic of this is that in certain circumstances the Soviets and their allies might move many divisions into Eastern Germany and Czechoslovakia to improve the chances of the Warsaw Pact nations winning such a conflict. The total number of divisions they could amass in these two countries would be rather more than 100, but it would take them at least a couple of months to achieve this. Some years ago the official Western estimate of the maximum rate of reinforcement the existing roads and railways could sustain at forty a month and the capacity of the transport network has not changed much since. Such a concentration would also be retarded by the fact that it would depend also on the mobilization and retraining of reservists. If, in the meantime, the West brought in, say, ten extra divisions, to reinforce the fifty or so regular and reservist ones there will be in Western Europe from 1965 onwards, it would probably have done enough to restore the balance, bearing in mind that it is generally believed that even in nuclear war the attacking forces would need a certain numerical superiority in order to overcome the opposition. Although it is very hard to accept the thesis of the Soviet delegation to the Eighteen Nation Disarmament Conference that the West could reinforce their forces in Europe faster than the Soviet Union, there is not much doubt about its ability to affect an increment of ten divisions in two months.[1] The MATS military airlift could deliver an airportable division and all its equipment from the United States to Germany every four days and, in any case, there is already in Germany enough equipment for the first two divisions which would arrive. Soon the various military airlifts would be supplemented by amphibious shipping and by a great deal of civilian air and sea transport. The ten

[1] e.g. Mr. Kuznetsov, Speech in plenary session, August 4, 1962

army and marine divisions which the United States holds in a state of ready reserve could be especially useful in this particular situation.

Any examination of the prospects of making an adequate non-nuclear response to an actual or threatened non-nuclear attack along each segment of the Iron and Bamboo Curtains is basic to the whole discussion of graduated deterrence. Nevertheless, if present trends are maintained any fighting involving Western mobile forces in the foreseeable future will take place away from the periphery of the Communist world. The several crises of recent years give us a good indication of the size of the armies that might have to be committed. About four divisions were assembled for Suez and six alerted for a possible invasion of Cuba. The equivalent of rather less than one was landed by the United States in the Lebanon: the United Nations deployed in comparable numerical strength in the Congo: approximately one brigade group was moved into Kuwait.

Our assessment of whether the mobile ground forces the West has now created are adequate to cope with any emergency must be governed by how much risk we feel there is of local wars starting in widely separated places almost simultaneously. In the event of a retrogression to the crudest form of power politics outbreaks of hostilities might occur at points far distant from each other. On the other hand, assuming international conduct does not reach those depths of barbarity, large reinforcements will probably never be needed simultaneously or almost simultaneously in more than one theatre. It is true that the bombardment of Quemoy and Matsu was begun in 1958 whilst the Lebanon landings were in progress, and it is also true that five Soviet divisions started to move into Hungary just before the Suez operation began, and that the Chinese attacks along the Himalayan border in 1962 coincided with the Soviet attempt to establish missile bases in Cuba. But during the Korean War, which remains the one violent collision between great powers that has taken place in the nuclear age, the Communists took great care to avoid a direct confrontation elsewhere. Likewise no serious evidence exists to support the contention that Soviet pressure on West Berlin has been modulated in accordance with changing situations in Laos, the Congo or other areas of East West rivalry. The danger of heavy and prolonged fighting continuing on more than one front seems remote.

This suggests that the balance between the size of the theatre and strategic reserves and the demands that might be made on them has become favourable. If this is true, however, it is subject to certain qualifications and provisos.

For political and economic reasons, the indigenous forces of some allied or Commonwealth countries may be cut down over the next few years, and if this happens they will become, potentially, more dependent on external support. This tendency may be increased by an acceleration in the rate of technological innovation which will widen the qualitative gap between first-class and second-class armies. These judgements are, moreover, based on the assumption that reinforcements are always in position by the time any fighting starts. If not, and if as a result they have to set about recapturing extensive tracts of land, then all the arguments about the supremacy of the defence have to be reversed. Again divisions or brigades may get so badly damaged in the course of heavy fighting that they have to be withdrawn and re-formed. It must be remembered also that even a successful blocking action may be a purely negative achievement. The Korean War dragged on for two more miserable years after the front had become essentially static, even though the United Nations was still able to employ a great weight of airpower as a means of inducing the Chinese and North Koreans to sign an armistice.

Stress has already been laid on the fact that most of the secondary friendly and alliance powers are short of specialist army units, and it can be noted that in this connection the independent specialist battalions being incorporated in the new American reserve structure assume a special importance; even though they would probably not be available for immediate dispatch themselves, they might be used to replace regular formations detached from Strike Command. It has also been emphasized that the smaller powers are particularly short of anti-aircraft artillery, and that the possible consequences of this are aggravated by the limited depths of airspace over most of the countries concerned, and also by the critical part that a very few ports and airfields would still play as points of entry for mobile forces. An important rider must be added which is that they are just as short of interceptor and strike aircraft. Thus, the American standard planning factors postulate that an army normally has seventy-five tactical aircraft per division slice and, indeed, the division slices that comprise Allied Forces Central Europe have 140 each.[1] On the other hand, the Persian and South Korean armed services have about twelve per division and those of Taiwan and Turkey twenty. Some of the planes involved are comparatively modern but the tactical wing of the Iranian Air Force is still equipped in part with F-47D *Thunderbolts* which are nearly twenty years old. The one hundred or more divisions of the Chinese Peoples Army are matched by just over twenty aircraft apiece, but, since most of the army and much of the air force would be held back for home defence in the event of a local war, it is difficult to guess what the ratio might be within an expeditionary force. The most modern aircraft in the Chinese Air Force are still those of the MIG-19 type such as entered service with the Soviet Air Force nine years ago.[1]

In the light of these statistics the fleet carriers of the Western nations can be seen to be an important element in the spectrum of deterrence, since they can put to sea with over 1,000 combat aircraft on board. The land-based airpower of the United States and Britain is also capable of making important contributions outside the NATO area. The most important strategically mobile American component is, of course, Tactical Air Command, with 900 modern aircraft in regular squadrons, that can be drawn upon to provide, at any one time, two CASFs of up to 300 planes apiece, and with about the same number of older aircraft in the reservist squadrons. To recognize the continuing importance of these units in the year 1963 is not, however, to deny the arguments advanced earlier for expecting a gradual decline in the deterrent influence which tactical airpower can be expected to exert.

[1] *The Military Balance 1962–3* (London, Institute for Strategic Studies, 1962)

Chapter 10

Conclusions

EVER since the Cold War began Western governments and their peoples have been concerned with the existence of the large Sino-Soviet standing armies as potential instruments of local aggression. The fear of a mighty Chinese army is relatively new, but the fear of a mighty Russian one is not. It was widespread in nineteenth-century Britain. Many British statesmen and diplomats during that period became obsessed by what they pictured as vast Czarist forces that could use their interior lines for a massive, swift and secret concentration at any selected focus of aggression. This fear induced errors like trying to preserve the Turkish Empire in Europe at all costs, or endeavouring to keep the new Balkan states as small as possible, on the assumption that they would fall under Russian control immediately after independence. Another consequence was a recurrent nervousness about the Russian threat to India which, as Lord Salisbury remarked in 1878, would not stand the test of large-scale maps.

The preoccupation with the awesome might of Russia was formulated into a doctrine by Sir Halford Mackinder, whose Heartland theory, enunciated in 1904, stated that those lands that drained into inland seas or the polar ocean were immune to maritime incursions and predicted that they would rule the world once their latent advantages in industrial production and transportation had been exploited. This thesis asserted without proof that river drainage patterns basically determined whether sea-power could exert itself over land areas. It flouted all the historical evidence about the superiority of the sea for bulk commercial transport and equated economic with strategic power. Above all, it took for granted that geographical factors rigidly control historical trends. It is hard to avoid the conclusion that it attracted the attention it did because it sustained a myth.

This is not to deny that Czarist Russia often displayed

ambition or to suggest that she was incapable of giving it military backing. She invaded the Turkish Empire several times, and in 1849 brutally suppressed a Hungarian rising on behalf of the incumbent régime. The record does show, nonetheless, that, when tested, her army always turned out to be far less strategically mobile than had been expected in Britain. Its performance was poor during the Crimean and Russo-Japanese Wars and in the First World War: in each case part of the explanation lay in logistic inadequacy. Today logistic problems little inhibit the movement of the Soviet Army within its own territory, but the same is not true for the Chinese Army or those of Eastern Europe; at the same time the scale on which any Communist army could deploy in an offensive anywhere on the margins of the Sino-Soviet Bloc is kept well down by the width and nature of the border zone in question. It would, moreover, be extremely dangerous in this nuclear age for the Communists to launch simultaneous attacks at widely separated points.

Seen in this context, the relationship between the strength and dispositions of the British and American theatre and strategic reserves, and the tasks they may be called upon to execute, appears, on the whole, satisfactory. West Berlin and Hong Kong are tiny enclaves set too deep in the Communist strategic orbit to be defensible against any large and overt assault without recourse to nuclear weapons. The Indian Ocean is still too sparsely covered by mobile forces and this deficiency is aggravated by its distance from the Atlantic area. Otherwise it seems that the West is already in a position to move in enough non-nuclear support to deter or help to repulse any attack by either a Communist or non-Communist state as long as it was preceded by a reasonable period of strategic warning.

On the evidence of the last decade or so crises are always preceded by some weeks or months during which the political situation becomes such as could cause hostilities. Usually this is either because events have occurred that have intensified long-standing grievances, or else because a change in the political status of some territory has been projected. Then when the crisis breaks it does so at such a speed as to require decisive action after about five to ten days. The Ruler of Kuwait did not feel obliged to ask for protection until five days after Kassem had made his speech and eight days after the sheikdom had become independent. The Chinese bombardment of Quemoy and Matsu began suddenly and violently, but it had been preceded by a strong fighter sweep through the Formosan Straits the previous week. United Nations help was sought by the Congo eleven days after independence and seven after the mutiny of the *Force Publique*. The introduction of ballistic missiles into Cuba began on October 14th, American troop movements on the 17th, and the naval blockade on the 24th. In the spring of that year the situation in Laos became unstable at the end of a rather casual twelve-day battle that resulted in the capture by the Pathet Lao of Nam Tha.

What is likely to cause the greatest pressure on time is not the suddenness with which a crisis breaks but the reluctance of those governments who are in jeopardy to seek assistance, and similar inhibitions on the part of the Western powers, about granting it if, as it probably will be, the local situation is very uncertain or complex. The governments of the Lebanon, the Congo and Kuwait all delayed asking for help until their overthrow seemed imminent. The start of the Geneva Conference on Indo-China was made the occasion of the final mass assault on Dien Bien Phu so as to make sure that any United States intervention that did take place was postponed until well into the eleventh hour. If intervention is so delayed, this puts a great premium on moving with both weight and speed at the last moment. In the opposed landings at Suez this premium was increased by straight tactical considerations.

The characteristic way in which crises have developed in the nuclear age confirms the view that reserve forces that can be made operational within a time span of one or two months are worth having. There is also, apparently, a great deal to be said for getting a fractional increment to the forces in being by holding some reserve combat and transport elements ready for active duty at one or two days' notice.

To see the significance of this analysis in terms of the desirable division of labour between air and sea transport, it is necessary to do some very elementary cost accounting. To carry an infantry division in a single lift, ten Landing Ships Dock would be needed and they would cost £80,000,000 to build. If they allowed one frigate each for escort purposes, the figure becomes £110,000,000. The task force would then have to be manned by 5,000 sailors and there would be a similar number supporting them ashore. A medium air transport fleet of comparable capacity would, on the other hand, cost £800,000,000 to £1,000,000,000 to procure, and would constitute an investment that would depreciate rapidly by virtue of its rates of obsolescence and physical decay. The air and ground crews which would be fully occupied keeping such an armada flying would total well over 100,000 men. The larger and longer-range transports tend to benefit from certain economies of large scale, but still are more expensive than ships for single journeys. The great compensating advantage of air transport is that it is ten to twenty times as fast. This makes aircraft best adapted to two kinds of operation. The first is rapid movement of part of a strategic reserve to some trouble spot which is beyond the immediate range of any theatre reserve that may exist. The second is the gradual concentration within a given theatre of a large part of a strategic reserve. Such movements can involve repeated journeys, which means that the airlift forces kept permanently in being for such contingencies do not have to be too large. They can also be facilitated by the stockpiling of equipment and supplies near the termini. This will ease the pressure on the load-carrying capacities of the aircraft concerned and will enable the troops being brought in to avail themselves of items, such as battle tanks, that are not airportable. The equipment used by a British infantry division costs about £25,000,000 and ten days' War Maintenance reserves for it rather less.[1] The equipment of an armoured division costs about £50,000,000.

The converse of the above is that when forces have to be deployed within a theatre assault shipping is often the best form of transport for the purpose. The ability to hover at varying distances offshore means that a task force can close on a particular spot as soon as trouble starts to loom up without committing itself or its country. What is more, the large numbers of men and amounts of material that it can carry in one journey means that it can put large combat elements ashore *en masse*, either in a tactical posture or else ready to adopt one soon afterwards. Assault shipping is, moreover, less dependent upon good

[1] Based on figures provided by W. F. K. Thompson in the *Daily Telegraph*, June 29, 1960

terminal facilities than aircraft and the terminals they use are not quite so easily incapacitated. Sometimes, of course, circumstances will favour the use of aircraft rather than ships as the predominant means of effecting a movement within a theatre. Nevertheless, in general the balance of factors seems to favour the ships.

Various long-term technical trends show promise of improving both the speed and flexibility of amphibious forces. The largest of the Sikorsky 'flying cranes' now on the drawing-boards is intended to have a lift capacity of 40 tons. This may mean that by the time it is in service it will be able to carry a battle tank, since this is a type of vehicle that is liable to decrease in size or weight. Together with other VTOL machines the 'flying cranes' should be able to make their parent ships almost indifferent to the form of any coastline across which they have to off-load, as well as to the nature of the hinterland immediately beyond. A corollary is that it ought to become possible to build assault ships much larger and sleeker than those in service today. Such vessels would be able to exploit to the full the extra power that is to be obtained from nuclear reactors and so task forces with sustained speeds of 30 knots would become practicable. A well-balanced task force would also require some small ships and hovercraft and it would be necessary to ensure that they could keep station. This might be done by having some large nuclear-powered fleet tankers in company with the force. The dimensions of most ocean basins and the characteristic time scales of crises are such that the difference between a sustained speed of 30 knots and one of 20 would enhance the deterrent influence a task force could exert and, in addition, confer upon it considerable immunity from submarine attack.

Aviation will continue to be dogged by its own inordinate fuel consumption and this means that it can only be expected to make modest advances as a method of deploying troops over distances of thousands of miles. The heavy fuel reserves that long distance aircraft have to carry, and the fact that in all cases their horizontal thrusts are likely to be less than a third of their loaded weights, will almost certainly mean that no vertical take-off and landing strategic transports will enter service for at least another ten years. On the other hand, a whole range of techniques will be more and more widely applied to every class of aircraft to enable them to use shorter runways and to improve the choice of terminal facilities open to them. Likewise the variable-sweep-wing fighters and very large strategic transports are going to be able to make long transoceanic flights without having to stop *en route*. Nevertheless when air bases or staging posts are available they will be of advantage. The shorter each stage length is the more it is permissible to increase payloads at the expense of fuel reserves. Furthermore an air base that is held on contract or through sovereign right enables a great power to effect a concentration of troops without undertaking an irrevocable commitment. It can be said that they bestow on airlifted reinforcements something analogous to hovering capability of ships. The prospective decrease in the number of air bases under British and American control is therefore bound to work to the detriment of airpower as a means of long-range reinforcement. The same is true with regard to the tendency for over-flight permission to be granted more sparingly.

Because their operations are likely to be little affected by adverse political changes and because they alone are able to exploit the possibilities latent in nuclear power, it appears that the relative merits of ships as against aircraft as the means of delivery of mobile forces are likely to increase. Their relationship will remain an essentially complementary one, however, as both become progressively more able to apply weight with speed and flexibility. Meanwhile, as the strategic stalemate deepens, the parties to any dispute will become ever more anxious to give a full account of themselves before resorting to violence, and so the chances of warning signals of any threat to the peace being received well in advance are growing stronger the whole time. Between them these technical and political trends will enable non-nuclear mobile forces to become increasingly effective instruments of deterrence.

APPENDIX A

Large civil airfields in various countries outside Europe

	Airfields with a main runway between 6,000 and 9,000 feet long	Airfields with a main runway over 9,000 feet long
Bechuanaland	3	0
Israel	1	0
Ivory Coast	1	0
Kenya	3	2
Libya	3	0
Union of South Africa	6	2

Source: ABC Directory of Aviation, 1961

APPENDIX B
Military Transport Aircraft

	All-up weight (1,000s lb.)	Date in service	Cruising speed (in statute mph)	Maximum operational range (statute miles)	Payload maximum range (1,000s lb.)	Range maximum payload (statute miles)	Maximum payload (1,000s lb.)	Loaded take-off run (ft.)
C-141 Starlifter	316	1965	558	6,265	33	3,000	94	5,300
Vickers VC-10	310	1964	538	6,450	24	5,527	38	6,000
C-135A Stratolifter	275	1961	530	4,265	45	—	88	8,850
SC.5/10 Belfast	200	1964	381	4,500	23	1,000	81	7,050
C-124 Globemaster II	185	1950	272	—	—	1,232	56	—
Britannia C.1	185	1959	355	5,300	26	4,170	37	8,000
C-130E Hercules	155	1962	365	4,850	20	3,650	33	4,250
Beverley	135	1955	175	3,690	10	200	44	1,340
Argosy	97	1962	269	1,094	20	345	29	4,000
C-47 Dakota	26	1936	207	1,510	—	—	8	—

Source: *Jane's All the World's Aircraft*